Hunter Davies was at the heart of London culture in the Swinging Sixties, becoming close friends with The Beatles, especially Sir Paul McCartney. He has been writing bestselling books and widely read columns for over fifty years. He lives in London. This is the third book in Hunter Davies' much-loved memoir series, following on from *The Co-Op's Got Bananas* and *A Life in the Day*.

HAPPY OLD ME

How to Live Long and Really, Really Enjoy It

HUNTER DAVIES

**SIMON &
SCHUSTER**

London · New York · Sydney · Toronto · New Delhi

A CBS COMPANY

First published in Great Britain by Simon & Schuster UK Ltd, 2019
This edition published in Great Britain by Simon & Schuster UK Ltd, 2020
A CBS COMPANY

1 3 5 7 9 10 8 6 4 2

Simon & Schuster UK Ltd
1st Floor
222 Gray's Inn Road
London WC1X 8HB

www.simonandschuster.co.uk
www.simonandschuster.com.au
www.simonandschuster.co.in

Simon & Schuster Australia, Sydney
Simon & Schuster India, New Delhi

Pages i and 292: 1958 Valentine card from Hunter's then girlfriend,
Margaret Forster, listing 100 reasons she loved him.

A CIP catalogue record for this book is available from the British Library

Paperback ISBN: 978-1-4711-7363-9
eBook ISBN: 978-1-4711-7362-2

Typeset in Palatino by M Rules
Printed and bound by CPI Group (UK) Ltd, Croydon, CR0 4YY

MIX
Paper from
responsible sources
FSC
www.fsc.org   FSC® C020471

Contents

CONTENTS

INTRODUCTION

I have an old book on my shelves called *How To Be Happy Though Married*, published in 1886. It was written anonymously, by 'a graduate in the University of Matrimony', who turned out to be a minor cleric, born in Ireland and educated at Trinity College Dublin, the Revd Edward John Hardy.

It was a serious handbook for people about to get married, full of sensible advice with chapters on the choice of wife, choice of husband, honeymooning, money, servants, health and rows or, as the author puts it, if 'they had a few words'. It was witty and clever with good anecdotes.

He tells a story about a young girl wanting to marry a young man. 'My dear,' says her father, 'I intend that you should be married but you should not throw yourself away on a wild worthless boy. You must marry a man of sober and mature age. What do you think of a fine intelligent husband of fifty?'

'I think two of twenty-five would be better, Papa,' replies his daughter.

Good joke, and one that seems very modern. I hope I can manage to be as modern and informative and amusing on the subject of being eighty.

But the aim is not just to appeal to those about to be eighty, but to everyone everywhere who feels they are getting on, that oldness is creeping up on them – goodness, whatever happened to the years? – which can strike you at twenty-nine and not just seventy-nine. With a bit of luck and the wind behind you, you could all make it to eighty. This is what it is like, more or less, so be prepared. Don't dread it. Embrace it.

Unlike the Revd Hardy, I intend to make my offering totally personal, as it is also a memoir. It is my report on being me, reaching the age of eighty.

The first volume of my memoirs, *The Co-Op's Got Bananas*, covered my long and exciting and wonderful life from my birth in 1936 to 1960, the year I got married – a period of some twenty-four years. Volume two, *A Life in the Day*, went from 1960 to the death of my wife in 2016, covering some fifty-six years.

This present memoir should in theory therefore cover an even longer period, let's say sixty years, which will take me up to the age of 140. Can't wait to read it. And even more so to live it. Meanwhile, this book will be solely concerned with the past two years of my life, since I turned eighty.

We all do live longer these days. Being eighty is not at all out of the ordinary – in fact it is commonplace. There are 1.4 million of us over-eighties in the UK cluttering up the hospital waiting rooms and the decks on cruise ships, sitting on expensive properties, with money in the bank. The Bank of Grandma and Grandpa is far better funded these days than the Bank of Mum and Dad. Some of us of course are impoverished and ill, with no home and no savings. Some of us are lonely, having ended up on our own, for a variety of reasons. We come in all shapes and conditions, we elderly folk.

My main concern is personal: to record and ruminate on what it has been like for me to be eighty – what are the pleasures and pains, the joys and ignominies, and perhaps to pass on a few wisdoms, learned as well as stolen. One of the joys of being eighty is that we have been young, while the young have not been old. We know what it is like. They don't. So we are the winners. Listen up.

Reaching eighty, I found a strange thing happening to me – I started boasting about being eighty. For most of the early part of my life I was rather embarrassed by looking and acting and being taken for someone much younger. Going to interview famous people for the *Sunday Times* in the 1960s, I was often shown to the tradesmen's entrance while they waited at the front for the real and grown-up journalist to arrive. It was one reason I grew a moustache, to make myself appear older.

Until very recently, while still in my seventies, I did not generally reveal or mention my age, though I was always pleased when I was taken for younger. It would not have affected my career or social contacts, having my age known – unlike a footballer or dancer or actor, who, over a certain stage, about say twenty-five, never want their age mentioned. I have spent a lifetime writing books and journalism, an occupation where no one cares how old you are, how smelly, how unfit, how haggard, how drunk, just as long as you can turn in the words on time and in some sort of readable order.

But once I reached eighty – on 7 January 2016 – I found myself constantly bringing it into the conversation: 'I was talking first – don't you know how old I am? Certainly I will have another bottle of Beaujolais – don't you know old I am? 'Scuse me, I was at the top of this bus queue – don't you realise how old I am?'

I will be unbearable if I ever reach ninety.

Reaching eighty coincided with my wife dying, after

fifty-five years of marriage. I suddenly had to cope with being a widower, a single person, something I had never been in my adult life, living on my own, trying to manage all the domestic stuff I had never bothered to learn. I had to get to grips with being old and on my own, an elderly person, no doubt about to fall to pieces, with all the aches and pains that age brings.

So many decisions I had to make, once my wife died – boring stuff like funerals, probate, wills, and then stuff that was personal and peculiar to me and Margaret. We had, for example, a country home at Loweswater in the Lake District, where for thirty years we had lived half of each year. What was I going to do with that? Could I possibly live there for any length of time on my own?

And my London home – the three-storey Victorian house that we had lived in since 1963 and where our three children were born and grew up. It seemed obscene and gross to contemplate living in this large house full-time all on my own. Yet how could I bear to sell it and move somewhere smaller?

Just as unthinkable – could I possibly tolerate someone else living here with me? A lodger, a stranger, entering through my front door, striding through my house?

And then chums, a companion. What was I going to do without someone to talk to, confide in, shout at, argue with, have meals with, go on holidays with, just be with, at least now and again? Obviously I was thinking that a female companion would be most pleasurable, but would I feel guilty, ashamed, embarrassed? And anyway, how would I go about it, at my great age, after fifty-five years of marriage to the same person? And what would it feel like?

My wife Margaret enjoyed being on her own. She was self-sufficient, never liked parties or social occasions, happy with her own company, along with a good book and of course visits from our children and grandchildren. She could have managed on her own. But my image of me, my character and personality, was of a jolly social animal, who loved people and parties and action, so I had always imagined I could never cope on my own. It was the thing I most dreaded. God forbid, I used to think, I hope I will never have to live on my own, just with myself, stuck all day with me. Oh no, save us from that.

So those were the problems and challenges I faced, and the decisions I had to make, serious and trivial, passing and permanent, personal and yet universal, for there are people in similar situations all over the country, all over the world, going through roughly the same things. Always have been. Always will be. This is how I personally solved them. More or less.

London, July 2018
(My eighty-third year. Thanks for the presents.)

1

MEMORIALS FOR LOVED ONES

Margaret died from cancer on 8 February 2016, in the Marie Curie Hospice in Hampstead. She had been there for four weeks, which on the whole she declared to be 'pleasant'. She was aged seventy-seven and we had had three children, Caitlin, Jake and Flora.

My first reaction had been 'straight to the crem', which was what her father Arthur, who died at ninety-six, used to say all the time from about the age of eighty onwards. He didn't want any fuss or delays, just to get it over with. I felt the same. Margaret herself would have been against any event or memorial, wake or celebration, but on the other hand she had always said that the dead should have no say in such matters. They were not here any more. It was up to the living, those left behind, to do whatever they wanted to do, whatever they thought would please them – and others – and also be suitable and seemly.

When we got married in 1960, we had only two people there, apart from us – two of our best friends, who acted as witnesses. It was a register office wedding in Oxford – can't remember what the licence cost. There was no reception, but I did splash

1

out and take all four of us to lunch at the Bear at Woodstock. What a spendthrift I was in those days.

The day before the wedding I had failed my driving test. Oh the shame, especially as I had just bought my first car, a 1947 2.5 Riley, which cost £100. I had to get Mike, one of our witnesses, to come on the first stage of our honeymoon, driving me in my own car to London.

We had managed okay with only four at our wedding, so I thought an equally humble funeral – a maximum of four people, me and my three children – would have pleased Margaret fine. So for the first few days after she died, I said to the children that we would stick to what I felt sure she would have wanted – the minimum of fuss, and definitely no wake.

But then I thought about after the cremation: what would happen? What should we do? Perhaps we should have some sort of simple ceremony in the chapel at Golders Green, invite relations, close friends, publishing colleagues of Margaret's who had worked with her over the years on her books.

I decided against having any sort of cleric to lead our simple event in the chapel, a stranger who had no idea who Margaret was and had never met her. I thought, *I can do it*. Jake and Flora agreed to speak. Caitlin, our oldest and tallest, and with the nicest speaking voice, could not face it. But her daughter Ruby, aged sixteen at the time, gave a most touching address. All three spoke beautifully and without notes. I wished Margaret had been there. She would have been so proud of them.

All the guests were then invited back to our house for tea and buns, and they all came, and it was very jolly and noisy and afterwards I was glad I had done it, that we had marked Margaret's passing in some way, for our sake if not for hers.

Afterwards, when they had all left the house, the silence was frightening. I was suddenly left all alone, wondering what to do, what I would do with myself from now on, with whatever was left of my own life.

I knew I was lucky – with a house, income, family, friends, reasonable health – unlike so many people to whom this happens. But losing a lifelong partner is a shattering blow for anyone, at any stage.

Over the next few weeks, various friends and relations, in London and in Loweswater, asked if there would be a memorial service, some sort of non-religious public gathering where they could pay their respects and listen to friends and admirers of Margaret giving their own memories of her.

These memorial events are very popular these days, and enjoyed by all. There is usually a reasonable gap after the person has died, so the weeping is over. It is more a celebration, an entertainment; show business rather than something solemn and funereal. It is a social occasion with amusing speeches and music. People love memorials.

I have been invited to loads, but never been to any. I hate funerals, even the fun ones, the memorial entertainments.

Friends up in Loweswater, where we have had a house for thirty years, were most disappointed when I said there'd be no memorial. The tea and buns after Margaret's cremation had been short and sweet, hastily arranged. Only my brother and his wife had come down from Cumbria. None of our Loweswater friends were there. Margaret was a true Cumbrian, born in Carlisle, and proud of her Cumbrian heritage. She had written so many books with a Cumbrian connection, non-fiction and fiction. Her last novel, published posthumously (*How to Measure a Cow*), is set mainly in West Cumbria. I think her friends and fans up there felt a bit cheated.

Then I woke up one day and thought, really, I should do something in Cumbria to mark her passing, acknowledge her Cumbrian life and heritage, and especially her love for Loweswater.

Neither of us was religious, despite each of us being brought up in God-fearing households and having to go to church every Sunday. But in Loweswater, the local parish church is a focal point, and the excellent parish mag, *The Link*, serves the whole community.

I had gone over the years to many local weddings, christenings, funerals and countless tatie pot suppers in the village hall. I saw them as community events. As the years had gone on I'd come to know almost everyone who attended them. Rural churches these days, if they are anything, and if they are thriving, reach out to everyone, religious or not, binding everyone together. I had got to know personally all the vicars who had come and gone since 1986 when we bought the house. I don't think we ever talked about religion. There was one vicar, the Revd Margaret Jenkinson, who was a mad-keen football fan. During World Cups and Euro Nations cups she always sported an England flag on her little car, like a football hooligan, rather to the disproval of some of the older, more conservative parishioners.

Next door to us at Loweswater when we first arrived lived a retired vicar of Loweswater, the Revd Geoffrey White. Our house had been owned by his wife's family. During our first summer up there I was cutting the grass when two low-flying jets suddenly shattered my ear drums, flying up the valley so low you could almost see the pilot's eyebrows. I stood and shook my fist, effing and blinding.

I hadn't realised that Geoffrey was over the fence in his

4

garden, in his baggy khaki shorts. He was standing to attention, saluting the jets as they flew over. That was when I first discovered he had been an RAF chaplain during the war and had been a prisoner of war. He explained he was saluting the jets because he said the RAF was still making our lives safe and secure.

I would often glimpse him through his study window. At first I assumed he was working on a sermon, but then I realised he had his phone in one hand, a fag in the other, the sporting pages marked in front of him, and was putting on some bets. Geoffrey loved a drink, a smoke and the horses.

Our connection with Loweswater church, the clerics and the churchyard had been long and enjoyable. So I thought, *Why not have a gravestone to Margaret, erected in the churchyard?*

The local church in Loweswater had regularly featured in Margaret's life. Most days on her afternoon walks she had begun or ended by sitting in the graveyard, looking out towards Crummock Water and the high fells such as Grasmoor and Melbreak. She knew all the names on the gravestones, the past and the present, people and families, farmers and friends we had known. She loved spotting all the local surnames, going back centuries. She knew the local gossip about a certain farmer whose only stipulation in his will was that his grave be as far away as possible from the grave of his wife. He had had enough of her in his lifetime.

If, however, I had asked Margaret in her own lifetime if she would like to be buried here, she would have said certainly not. Just as she would have said certainly not to a funeral. But she had gone. Hard cheese. She had given up her right to a veto.

These days you don't have to be religious to be buried or

have your ashes scattered in a churchyard, or be religious to get married in church, but a vicar, for various reasons, can refuse you. I didn't know at first if I would be allowed to have a gravestone for Margaret. But it turned out she was acceptable, as a local resident for thirty years, and a Cumbrian. There would be no objections, as long as I obeyed the rules about the size and shape and contents on the gravestone.

I soon learned that you don't technically 'scatter' ashes in churchyards – you have to intern ashes in a hole, in an agreed spot, about half a spade deep. The rules about gravestones are quite complicated, running to several pages at Loweswater.

On the gravestone, you can't use nicknames, photographs or garish colours. In council-owned cemeteries, you can put almost anything you like on a council gravestone, but rural churches are very traditional.

I decided to use a local firm of monumental masons, Walker Brothers, who had been going since the 1870s. I used to buy wood and materials from their yard in Cockermouth when we first moved up there. I rang them up and made an appointment. It was only later that I found to my horror that they were no longer in their old and atmospheric premises off Main Street in Cockermouth, near Wordsworth's house. They had moved to an industrial estate near Workington. I hate industrial estates. I always get lost. I once had to go to this one a few years ago to visit the Eddie Stobart depot, when I was doing a biography of Eddie Stobart, and gave up, unable to find it.

I got proper directions, taking them down carefully, and eventually found the new depot and showroom for Walker Brothers. I looked at all the possible gravestones lined up, waiting for deaths, like a high-class but very solemn supermarket. Should I get granite or slate? I assumed they must both be local stone, but Andrew Walker, third generation in the firm, said that these days 80 per cent of the granite in gravestones comes from either China or South Africa. You can get local slate, but that is about 50 per cent more expensive than the imported granite, despite not having come halfway round the world. Isn't economics weird? I went for granite.

I was then faced with a choice of about 100 different fonts and sizes and styles for the lettering. I decided to splash out on an image to go at the top of the gravestone – which of course had to be ever so tasteful and agreed upon by the church. I picked a nice old-fashioned quill pen and ink bottle.

Margaret wrote all her books by hand, never used a type-writer or computer, so the quill pen and ink would be a private joke, which would amuse those who knew her. For the words themselves, I stuck to conventional sentiments and wording. I did think of a few smart remarks, but thought the rural dean might not be amused.

I was rather surprised when the total price of the gravestone came to £1,546, including VAT. I had vaguely been thinking, *Well, lump of old granite, can't be expensive, can it?*

Before it was finally erected, they sent me a scan of the finished gravestone. It looked lovely, till I noticed a misspelling. The name of our daughter Caitlin had come out as 'Caitline'. Oh lord, how could that have happened? I went through my old emails and proofs and it was not my mistake. It was their fault.

Spelling mistakes on gravestones do occur, if rarely, but how ironic that it should happen to a writer who was a brilliant speller. Unlike me. I can't spell for toffeee. Fortunately, I have people on my staff who can spell.

When I told Caitlin that her name had been misspelled, she just laughed and said leave it, it's funny. I said don't be daft, we can't have a spelling mistake on a gravestone. I do have standards.

Walker Brothers apologised, and agreed to have it redone. The stone had to be refaced, a few millimetres shaved off the whole front of the gravestone, and all the words redone. Chipping the 'e' off Caitline could not be done without being obvious and ruining the look of it.

When I was a boy journalist, many decades ago, and we worked with metal type, you could chop out an offending word, or a comma, quite easily. Not that journalists dared do it. The compositor did that. Touch the metal or the stone and it was All Out.

I had been dealing with our rural dean, Revd Canon Wendy Sanders, as our actual vicar was ill at the time. She had guided me through the rules and regulations and procedures for scattering ashes – sorry, interring them.

On the day it finally happened, I rather stampeded her into doing it there and then. I think she had just come to the house to have a general chat, not do the actual deed. But I persuaded her, explained I had the spade ready and Margaret's ashes in a discreet little green box supplied by Leverton, the Kentish Town undertakers.

So off we went to the church, just a few minutes' drive away. We stood alone in an empty churchyard, me and Wendy. I dug the little hole, put half of Margaret's ashes inside, then carefully placed the divot back over the hole. Wendy spoke rather movingly about Margaret – whom she had never met – about her life as a mother and a writer, then she gave a short prayer and a blessing. Meanwhile, I closed my eyes and looked suitably solemn. I was in fact quite moved by the simpleness and speed of it all.

Then we left the churchyard and went next door to the

Kirkstile Inn, my favourite inn in the whole of Lakeland, and had lunch. I had tatie pot, as I always do. Wendy had some stuffed mushrooms.

Over lunch, I asked her about her life as a vicar. Like so many clerics these days, especially women, she had come to it late, having worked as a secretary for a local joiner and undertaker in Halifax. She moved up to Cumbria about thirty years ago and had been a curate and then a vicar in several Cumbrian parishes. As rural dean, she was looking after eight benefices containing thirty-two churches.

Most rural parishes these days are in little clusters, coming together for economic reasons, with one vicar looking after several churches and parishes. The vicar of Loweswater these days looks after three churches – in Buttermere and Lorton, as well as Loweswater. In the old days, not so long ago, they each had their own vicar and vicarage.

In all, Dean Wendy was looking after thirteen full-time clerics. I asked how many were women, expecting her to say the majority. The answer was nine male priests and four women. I was rather surprised, having made a general assumption, based on recent years at Loweswater, that women must now be taking over the Church of England.

In Loweswater, our last two vicars had been female. I have this fantasy that the daughter of my dear old Cumbrian friend Melvyn Bragg, the Revd Marie Elsa Bragg, will one day become the Loweswater vicar. I recently asked her to apply next time there's a vacancy. Her eyes lit up and she said yes, she fancied it – but one day, not now.

After lunch, Wendy jumped into her car to drive back home to Cockermouth. I noticed she had a personalised number plate – as I have, despite being teased about it by my friends.

Wendy's began with 'RV', which you could mistake for 'REV', ending with 'WES', her initials. A bit flash for a rural dean? Wendy said it was handy when tootling round the country lanes in rural Cumbria, as everyone now recognised it. It was a surprise present from her daughters four years ago for her sixtieth birthday. She was now officially retired as a priest, just helping out for the moment as rural dean. Retired at sixty-four? A mere child.

It always astounds me when I discover that people of that age, and younger, have retired. Several of my contemporaries who were at Durham with me back in the 1950s retired as young as fifty-five. They were teaching in schools or colleges which were amalgamating or closing and were offered generous redundancy payments and pensions to pack it in, so had jumped at it.

How could they? I think I would die if I ever had to retire. When I have met them since they go on about being ever so busy, never a spare moment, travelling the world, or on the internet booking off-peak, cheap flights and special deals.

My main ambition in life now is never to retire. I can't imagine life without work of some sort. I count my blessings that I fell into the career I did. Until the age of twenty I assumed I would end up as a teacher, to please my mother, and because I could not think of what else I might do. Then by chance I wrote a so-called funny column for my student newspaper, when they happened to have a hole in the page one day. And that was it. I had stumbled on something I could do. Still at it, after sixty-two years.

* * *

Only half of Margaret's ashes ended up in Loweswater church-yard. I like to think it might become a little pilgrimage place, where I and my children and their children might visit, and also our Cumbrian friends and relations, perhaps even some of her loyal readers. I have been up there several times in the past year and have been delighted to find that local friends have added flowers, heather or wild plants at the foot of her gravestone.

You can't miss it. On the right as you go into the churchyard through the little iron gate from the Kirkstile. Look out for the quill pen and ink bottle. The shading and line work, all done by hand, is awfully artistic. Overall it is discreet and modest. Just like my dear wife.

The other half of Margaret's ashes are here, in London.

During Margaret's last few months at home, when she was on heavy-duty drugs and then morphine, she spent most of her days resting on the day bed downstairs, when she was not violently vomiting. The thing about modern cancer drugs is that the worse you get, the worse the drugs they make you take, which mainly make you feel worse. The side effects are appalling – not just hair loss, but weight loss, loss of pleasure, loss of any energy, loss of interest, loss of will to live, loss of anything, except pain.

She had long given up her daily two-hour walks round Hampstead Heath, and for the previous three months had had to be content with hobbling round our back garden, taking ages, resting against the wall every few yards.

One day I had a brilliant idea – a summer house. Let's put one at the bottom of the garden where nothing ever seemed to grow. The whole bottom of the garden had been a dead area when we had first seen it in the snow and ice of the winter of 1962. I didn't know what was there. It was not till the spring that we realised the funny-looking mound covered

11

with weeds was an old Anderson air raid shelter, left over from the war.

I eventually replaced it with a shed, then a proper garage, when parking became hellish in our street. I always wished I had kept the air raid shelter. It would have been Exhibit A when my children and then grandchildren were studying the Second World War at school. I could have organised guided tours.

But the area to the right of the garage had remained empty, overgrown with weeds. I suggested to Margaret that it would be a perfect place to erect a summer house. It would use the wasted space and make a focal point for her walks, or at least her staggerings, round the garden. It would be something to aim for, where she could sit down and rest, look back at the garden and the house, and contemplate the long and happy life we had lived there. One of her most successful books had after all been called *My Life In Houses*.

'Over my dead body,' she said. 'I don't want any more work done in this house, ever.'

The previous year I had talked her into having the wooden decking torn up outside our back door. It had been all the rage when we had had it installed ten years earlier, as seen on TV, as described in all the gardening mags, as raved about by the gardening experts. What a mistake.

It had looked good at first, then it went brown and mossy, became slippery, a death trap in wet weather, especially when Margaret got ill and could only stagger, scared all the time she would fall. Even worse, it became an adventure playground for rats. They bred like ... well, rats, underneath the decking. I got the council in twice but all they did was put poison down, which killed them off for a while and created the most appalling stink. The next year they came back. In the end we gave up, ripped it all up and put down York stone. It was one of the best things I have ever done at the house. Even Margaret agreed. It gave her such pleasure in her last few months at home, just looking at the York stone paving from her day bed. In different weathers, in sun or rain or wind, the colours and the textures of the stone changed all the time. It felt like getting back to nature, as if we were part of a Lakeland landscape. Decking always looks man-made and artificial, which of course it is. Decking is cheating. York stone is real.

But a summer house would have been a step too far. While she was alive, I knew she could never have stood the noise and the mess and the work. When she was informed she only had three months to live, she wanted her last days to be totally quiet and peaceful.

She died in the February and when spring started springing that year I remembered my suggestion, thinking it a really good idea. It would brighten the bottom of the garden, be a focal point, a place where the grandchildren can play, where adults can have drinks. It would also come in handy for me in the future – when I am old and staggering round the garden.

You do see some amazing summer houses for sale these days – architect-designed, little palaces, twee country cottages. And at amazing prices. I went online and ordered a cheapo, off-the-peg summer house from Wickes at £479. What a bargain. It came in two enormous flat packs, which were dumped on our front pavement. I could not open, far less carry, them. I asked the delivery man, a bright young Lithuanian man called Sven, if he knew anybody who might erect it. He offered himself. He would come down from the Midlands on his day off and do it for £200. He spent a day putting it all together, and painting it.

I was so pleased and proud when it was finished that I decided to throw a garden party, an opening of the summer house party, for the neighbours and children. Flora, my younger daughter, made curtains for it and her husband installed electricity. I put in some furniture and books and wall hangings.

On the official day, the neighbours all sat in rows in front of the summer house, its doors closed and curtains drawn, having drinks and little snacks. Then, suddenly, when I gave the sign, some awful pop music blared out, the doors of the summer house burst open, and my two youngest grandchildren, Amarisse and Sienna, then aged nine and eight, along with two little friends, all in strange costumes, emerged and did a show. They danced and did handstands in front of the summer house, then chased each other round the garden, shouting and roaring, pretending they were running after some jewellery robbers, some complicated plot they had made up that no one could follow. I laughed so much at their antics I almost choked. The audience clapped and cheered when finally they had finished, lying exhausted on the lawn.

I then made a little speech, telling the story of how Margaret had said over her dead body had she wanted a summer house. I then officially opened it – and revealed that half her ashes had been scattered underneath.

So it all came true. Over her dead body, she did end up with a summer house.

WISDOMS

- You cannot love someone who is dead as you did when they were alive.
- Your love kept evolving when they were alive – death is just one more change, which does not ruin the true love you had.
- The best we can all hope for is that we will be remembered by our children – and possibly by their children, if they were old enough to remember us. After that almost all of us will have gone from sight, and gone from living memory.
- But a physical memorial is nice, such as a gravestone, a bench or seat, something modest, erected in honour of the dearly departed.
- Fortunate are those who have created something in their lifetime – a song, a painting, a play, a book, an invention, an idea – which might live on through the generations.
- But we can all leave our own scribbles, letters or diaries, proof that we were here. So get writing now, or talk into a tape recorder. You are only here once.

ANECDOTES

- Samuel Johnson was reading the glowing epitaph on a gravestone of a man who had not conducted his life in exactly the right and proper manner. 'In inscriptions, a man is not upon his oath.'

- Charles Lamb, when a little boy, was being taken round a graveyard by his older sister, Mary. He noticed how all the tombstones commemorated people who had been virtuous, pious, charitable, beloved. 'Mary, where are all the naughty people buried?'

MOST POPULAR FUNERAL SONGS

1. Monty Python's 'Always Look on the Bright Side of Life'
2. 'The Lord is My Shepherd'
3. 'Abide with Me'
4. *Match of the Day* theme
5. 'My Way'
6. 'All Things Bright and Beautiful'
7. Elgar's 'Enigma Variations'
8. 'You'll Never Walk Alone'

2

LEGAL POSITIONS

Thank goodness my wife died before me. I don't mean that selfishly – that I stayed alive and she did not, that she went through awful pain and I have not (so far). What I mean is I wouldn't have wished upon her all the financial and legal faffing and flaying and fiddling around that happens when anyone dies, anywhere, at any time. That was supposed to be my field, money matters. After all, she did practically everything else.

But we can't choose when we will die or, for that matter, how or where we are going to die. In the end, Margaret knew she had only three months left to live, but until then, we lived in hope and expectation that we would both live to a grand old age, have grey hair and rosy cheeks, though not much chance in my case. I have always had a wrinkled phizog, just like my mother.

It would save so much time and money if we all knew well ahead when our time was due to be up. I will be really, really furious if I pop it just after having had the windows cleaned, or buying twenty-four bottles of Beaujolais, or renewing my BT broadband contract or my subscription to the *Oldie* mag. All that money, wasted.

I also don't want to die before getting round to cashing in my National Savings Certs. I have saved them over a lifetime, my plot being to live on them when I was old, cash them in, bit by bit. And as they are all tax-free and need not be declared, I would never need to have an accountant, ever again. If I go without cashing them in and without spending all the money on my own selfish pleasures, tax will have to be paid on them as they will go into my estate. Oh help.

As for all my collections, my endless shelves and drawers and files full of rubbish (I mean treasures), I would like to give away certain choice items before I go and then sell the rest, if just to see how stupid I had been, buying a load of rubbish, now worthless. My wife had no interest in any of my treasures – did not know what they were or what they were worth, and considered them all just dust-gatherers. Margaret always said that if I went first, then it would be straight to the skip. She didn't mean giving my body to the bin men – at least I hope she didn't – but that the first thing she would do would be to clear all my junk out of my room, the best room in the house, so it happens, which she always wanted to recapture. She would hire a skip or make the kids take all my stuff, at once, now, to the council dump. That did used to scare me, making me determined to hang on as long as possible and not be the first to go.

Once left alone, with no one else here to moan about the dust, I realised I could take over the whole house with my treasures, should I want to. But I discovered I had so much other stuff to do.

What I had not bargained for was the massive amount of paperwork and decisions, meetings and arrangements, digging and searching that death throws up, trying to think and remember back, trying to find stuff about the life we had led.

In theory, and in practice, all financial and legal matters had been totally my domain. I just used to tell Margaret to sign here, and she did, with no idea what she was signing. I could well have been off to South America in the morning with all her money.

There was a period, in the 1990s, when for a few years she earned more than me, having a string of non-fiction books (*Hidden Lives*, *Precious Lives*, *Good Wives*) for which she got large advances. I was very proud, thrilled she had done so well. One of the things about having a wife/husband/partner in the same field, in our case writing, is that people think you must be jealous of each other. In fact it doubles the pleasures, doubles the interest. There are twice as many possibilities of good or half-decent news and excitements when there are two of you working down the same mine. We each got just as much pleasure, often more, out of each other's triumphs, however piddling.

The first thing everyone has to face after a death is the death certificate, proof of death. In the UK, you have to have a doctor sign the death form before an undertaker can do anything. It took for ever when Margaret died as the doctor on duty at the hospice that morning had not personally seen her in the last week. We had to wait till a doctor who knew her came on duty.

The undertaker needs the death form, otherwise the body can't be taken away. You need proof that someone has medically died.

Then you need a death certificate, an official government form, for which you have to pay. Best to pay for lots of extra copies, as you will need them. I sent one of my children to fill in the details and get lots of certificates, but we missed one vital element – the bit that you tick so that they pass on notification of the death to all the other various government departments, such as pensions, tax and so on. That saves such a lot of time. Most bereaved people are new to death, unaware of what needs to be done, of all the officials who will have to be informed. The sooner you do it the better, before the paperwork and problems mount up.

A few weeks later, I received something called a Bereavement Payment of £2,000 from some government department I had never heard of. I did not know such payments existed and had not applied. So that was a good example of bureaucracy at work.

Then came the biggest, most bureaucratic jungle and official madness and nightmare problem of all – probate. I used to think the most annoying, irritating, scary, awful, nasty word in the English language was vat. Or should it be VAT, as it is an acronym for Value Added Tax? Either road up, VAT has hung over me since it all began in 1973, when it was 10 per cent. Every year I get in a lather trying to find all the bits and pieces of paper.

I have to charge people when I provide a service, then hand it over to the government. Why don't they do it themselves? What a nonsense. I suppose it does keep tens of thousands of accountants, bookkeepers and VAT inspectors off the streets.

For four months, I struggled to answer all the probate questions Fig was throwing at me. No, Fig is not another acronym, just a nickname for my solicitor who was handling it all. I have known Fig since she was a little girl, as she went to primary and secondary school with my eldest daughter. She lived in the street opposite and at the time was known as Fiona Legg, which I suppose is where her pet name came from.

She went to Edinburgh, got a first and became a solicitor twenty years ago, got married, becoming Fiona Mullane, and settled in Scarborough. I did have a West End firm of solicitors when we bought this house in 1963, just because one of the partners lived in our street. I stayed with them till a couple of years ago, though not giving them much work.

When I realised that Fig, in the practice where she works in Scarborough, specialised in probate, I thought I would give her the job. I do like to help northerners. It must be so awful for them. (Very old Victoria Wood joke.)

I asked how she came to specialise in probate. Was it because no one else in the practice wanted to do it? She said it was because she had always enjoyed filling in forms. The world is full of strange people. Also she likes the one-to-one relationship with clients.

Apart from her fees being cheaper than London solicitors, so I hoped, I thought I would be able to boss her around, having known her since she was eight, at children's parties in our house. She came down for my wife's funeral, as a family friend. I still call her Fig, which I am sure none of her clients in Scarborough do. But for four months she was bossing me around. I simply did not know how much I didn't know.

The point of probate – from the Latin *probare*, to test or prove – is to give proof of all the assets and liabilities of a person who has just died, the main and ultimate object being to charge inheritance tax of 40 per cent, if and when the total value comes to more than £325,000. I think that's right. At least it was in 2016, when we were in the midst of this probate nightmare.

My wife had no idea how much money she had, or what we had, as we only ever had a joint account. My mother, who had no money, and never had a bank account, was appalled when we were first married to discover that Margaret did not have her own bank account: 'Oh, Margaret, have ye nae got your ayne money, pet? Oh you should have your ayne money, pair wee thing, so you are. What will happen if you want to run away?'

Throughout our married life, as soon as we started making any money from books and films, I put the money into National Savings or building societies, the same amount for each of us.

The teenage scribblers on the Money sections of the newspapers always say this is daft – you should put it in stocks and shares, investments funds, and of course always use a financial advisor. They pointed out that interest rates in National Savings, as with Premium Bonds, were rubbish, always have been. Shares were the thing to have. My thinking was that National Savings returns might be modest, but they were tax-free. Also I hate all financial advisors – or advisors of any sort, really. If they are so clever, why are they not living in Barbados? I like to control my own money, know where it is, know no one is creaming stuff off the top, just for giving so-called advice. So over the decades I always went for every new National Savings issue, either fixed or index-linked – Peps, Tessas, ISAs and all the other girls' names I have now forgotten.

When Fig asked me how many certs my wife had, in order to fill in her probate forms, and also their current value, I simply had no idea. Over the decades, when they matured, I just put them back into the next issue. Their numbers and names changed, which makes it hellish to work out when exactly they were first bought.

I also had quite a lot of building society bonds, mainly five years, fixed-rate, going back decades, in things like Northern Rock. Yes, I know they don't exist, having become Virgin, but I exist, with my same name, and intend to call them Northern Rock for ever.

Fig told me that not only had I got to find all these certificates, names and details, but that I had to work out what they were worth on the particular day that Margaret died, 8 February 2016. Dear God, how could I possibly do that with joint investments, in our joint names? I also had to state how much interest she had earned and the tax paid during that tax year, up to when she died. As if *I* knew. Even more complicated, I had to declare, also for tax purposes, what she had earned *after* she had died, during the rest of that current tax year. If only she had died on 6 April, it would have been so much easier. So thoughtless of her.

I went to bed each night with my head throbbing. All my own fault of course. I really should have kept neater records. I do have them all, somewhere. The problem was finding them, then understanding them, then bringing them up to date to the day she died.

You have to do all this, have probate completed, with all the various stuff owned by the deceased or due to the deceased neatly tabulated and listed and submitted to the government for them to check and approve. That is the law. Until probate is proved, you can't transfer National Savings from your spouse's name to your name, even though she has left everything to you in her will. Premium Bonds are different. Ownership cannot be transferred. They have to be cashed in. Don't ask me why. One of their many mad rules.

All her pension annuities, which she had been receiving in recent years, came to an end the moment she died. The insurance companies then kept the lot, whatever was left of the monies in her pension pots built up over the decades. Well done, Equitable Life, you were on a winner. Or at least the Pru, who took over the pension funds we had with the Equitable.

At long last, I managed to gather all the relevant figures

together. Fig was able to fill in the dreaded IHT400 form – for the inheritance tax accounts. It came to about fifty pages, including all schedules. Fig's fee for all this stout work came eventually to around £2,500 – worth it for the aggravation she took off my shoulders.

Perhaps the worst and most depressing element about the whole probate exercise, which drove me mad for so long, was that it was totally pointless.

Pointless in the sense that, having painfully worked out what Margaret was worth on her death, no inheritance tax was taken anyway. It did not matter either way, if she had left little or a lot. She had died before me.

The rules are that there is no inheritance tax to pay when the first of a married couple dies. I assume the very sensible reason for this is that millions of widows or widowers would be homeless, out on the streets, if 40 per cent had to be suddenly found when the first spouse died.

But, ah-ha, the government of course gets all the due tax in the end. When the second one dies, then your estate has to pay up all of it. Not stupid.

It's my children I now feel sorry for. How on earth will they cope when I pop it? Like my wife, they have no idea of my investments, and no real interest. The only solution I can think of is not to die. So that's my plan, from now on.

There were two other legal situations I had to face that first year after Margaret died, one slightly aggravating and one that amused me greatly.

Margaret and I had made wills several years ago, identical wills leaving everything to each other and appointing our children as executors.

Once I got probate sorted out, and managed to transfer

whatever I could that she had owned into my name, I then carried on as I had always done, the income going into our joint account, which was now just in my name.

During this first year I was receiving, as usual, money from Margaret's royalties from her books and various rights, such as her posthumous novel, *How To Measure a Cow*.

I then realised, at the end of the first year, that her income from her books and rights was going on top of my income, and being treated as my income, rather than remaining in her name, with her own tax return, allowances and expenses, as in the past. I was paying tax on her earnings at the very top rate, 45 per cent. Yet I didn't actually want her money, or to own her copyright.

Then someone pointed out that there was something known as a deed of variation. For two years after a person has died, you can change some of the details of their will, altering who owns what in their estate. She was working up to the end, still earning money, which meant her income was seen by the tax people as a business income, which apparently could be transferred to another member of the family.

In the future, our three children will own Margaret's estate anyway, and when I die, mine as well. They will have to make decisions about book rights, say yes or no when in years to come someone wants to make a film or musical or ice show or animation out of some long-forgotten novel. Dafter things have happened.

So the sooner I passed Margaret's literary estate on to them, the better. Not just to save me paying tax on her income now, but to save paperwork and decision-making in the future. We were not talking about a lot of money. In the first year after she died her literary income came to about £20,000. It will be likely to go down, year by year, as her books get forgotten and go out of print.

A deed of variation sounded a pretty easy thing to do. A sentence should cover it – something like, 'I hereby pass on all my wife's literary estate, which she left to me, to my dear children.'

I asked a local high street solicitor to do it, as he said he could. But after some weeks it transpired he had gone to a barrister for help, complications and questions came flooding in, and I could see the bills mounting. I do have a son who is a barrister, but not that type, and anyway he could not deal with a document from which he was going to gain.

The official deed, when it finally emerged, covered only one page of legal prose – yet the bill came to £1,600. I was furious – all that money for such a simple thing, from which I personally was not going to get anything.

I remember many years ago having lunch with Auberon Waugh, the son of Evelyn Waugh. His personal share of his father's literary estate that year had been £20,000 – a huge amount at the time, due to film and TV rights still flooding in. He was one of a large family, so the total from the estate must have been pretty massive.

I expect that my children, and their children in due course, will inherit a piddling and increasingly dwindling return from our royalties, so lucky them. Anyone who has written books or songs or created such things in their lifetime is able to pass on the copyright of their creations to their estate, though it does not last for ever. Copyright on books runs out seventy years after the death of the author.

Margaret owned the copyright to all her works – not that it bothered her or occurred to her or was of any concern to her. When offers came in, she always told her agent the same thing – fine, just accept; on no account try to get them to pay more.

When I was doing the first volume of my memoirs, *The Co-op's Got Bananas*, which covers our courtship, I described how we met, how we fell in love, how we argued, how she said she was never getting married and never having children. I would reply by saying, 'Who's asking you, pet?' And then of course we did get married and lived happily ever after, tra la la.

We never did soppy things, or made soppy remarks to each other, such as 'love you', 'love you more', 'love you most', which young couples seem to say to each other all the time these days, even if they are just parting for ten minutes to walk round the block.

When I was writing that book, I happened to find a Valentine's card which Margaret had made for me in 1958, the first year after we were going out together. It was a home-made card, on a sheet of white paper, done in the shape of a heart, in which she had listed, on the front and back, 'One hundred reasons I love you'. I don't think she ever sent me another Valentine again. I sent her one, now and again, when I remembered, usually an ancient First World War silk, as they are called, the beautifully embroidered cards that soldiers sent home to their loved ones from the Front.

I always sent Valentines to my two daughters when they were young, and in turn I still send a Valentine to each of my four granddaughters – just jokes, pretending they are anonymous, as if they can't guess they are from me. It amuses me to try to be funny. When they were younger, and comparing notes at school with other girls, I always knew they were getting at least one Valentine.

When I told Margaret that I had found her home-made

Valentine to me from 1958, when she was nineteen and I was twenty-one, she was furious. She said she never knew I had kept it. She assumed I had lost it or destroyed it, which she would certainly have done if she had come across it.

'Didn't you know it was all a joke?' she said. 'I was being ironic. Surely you realised?'

I did not, I said, neither then nor now. It is one of my treasured possessions, I explained, so I am going to use it in my memoirs. It will be a lovely illustration from our courting days, all those decades ago in Carlisle.

'Oh no, you are not,' she said. 'It is *my* copyright and I am not going to allow you to publish it in your stupid book.'

She was right of course. Legally, the piece of paper itself, under the copyright law, belonged to me, as she had given it to me. I could sell it, give it to the children, give it away, do anything I liked with the actual piece of paper. But, ah-ha, the contents, the actual words she had written, were her copyright and would remain her copyright. So that was it. She forbade me to publish it.

Now I look at it, some of her reasons are deliberately soppy: 'You have eyes so bright they light me up.' Some are funny: 'You eat pies at the wrong time.' Some are true: 'You have a shambling walk.' Some are contradictory: 'You are conceited', followed by 'You are humble.' Some get a bit repetitious. After all, she had set herself the task of thinking up 100 reasons and squeezing them onto a single piece of A4 paper, so by number 100 she was running out of topics.

I have just noticed she misnumbered her list. She jumps from thirty to thirty-nine, thus missing out eight reasons. What a cheapskate. Perhaps by that stage she was running out of ideas or out of space and was regretting having started.

WISDOMS

- Always write your will.
- Always write down where you have left your will.
- Always write down a list of what and where your investments, treasures and collections are. Even if it is just milk-bottle tops.
- If you have anything you really love but think your family won't appreciate, sell or give it away, NOW.
- You can't take it with you. Even milk-bottle tops. You can try of course, but they won't be appreciated by the undertaker or the crematorium.

ANECDOTES

- Ninon de Lenclos (1620–1705) was a French courtesan whose behaviour led her to be sent to a monastery where, so she wrote in her diary, she was seduced by 439 monks. In her will she left only a few francs to pay for her funeral, but she did instruct her lawyer that his son should receive 1,000 francs from her will to pay for his books, as he appeared very clever. The lawyer's son grew up to be Voltaire.
- The composer Carlo Menotti named all the people in his will who had been nice to him, leaving them either a little object or a little money. His lawyer said to him, 'Sr Menotti, this is not a will. It is a jumble sale.'

- Cecil Rhodes left much of his vast fortune to fund Rhodes scholars, still going to this day, which rather upset some of his family. 'It seems to me', said his brother Arthur, 'that to get any money I will have to win a scholarship.'
- The playwright Richard Brinsley Sheridan had fallen out with his son Tom and told him he had cut him out of his will. 'I am sorry to hear that, sir,' said the son. 'You don't happen to have a shilling about you now, do you?'
- The German poet Heinrich Heine left his entire fortune to his wife, but with one catch: she had to remarry, 'because then there will be at least one man to regret my death'.
- Robert Louis Stevenson, in his will, left his birthday to the daughter of an American friend in Samoa who had been born on Christmas Day, which R. L. S. thought was a most unfortunate day for a birthday. R. L. S., who was a qualified attorney, added a legal clause in which, if the daughter did not claim the birthday, the rights reverted to the President of the USA, which remains the case to this day.

QUOTES

- 'The only difference between doctors and lawyers is that lawyers merely rob you, whereas doctors rob you and kill you, too.' Anton Chekhov

- 'The only way you can beat the lawyers is to die with nothing.' Will Rogers
- 'If there were no bad people, there would be no good lawyers.' Charles Dickens

3

INHERITANCES – WHAT MARGARET ALSO LEFT

I did vaguely think that Margaret might have left me a letter. If I had been aware, as she was, that I had just three months to live, and was mentally all there, I would have written a letter to her and our children to be read after my death, just to amuse them, amuse myself, sum up what it was all about. I would have died smiling in anticipation. So I fondly imagine.

But that is me. That was not her. Our children agreed she would never have done anything so soppy or self-indulgent or self-reflecting. I said what about that Valentine's card, all those decades ago? That was pretty soppy. Yes, but that was her joke, they replied. And it was a long time ago.

So I never got round to looking for any letter to me, or anything else, and did not manage to clear her room till months later, when it was almost Christmas. It wasn't through grieving or sentimentality, superstition or morbidity, fear or loathing. I was just so frightfully busy.

Some people I know have cleared away every sign of their dearly departed almost as soon as they have departed, desperate to move on. Far more put it off and put it off, not wanting to remove all the traces that he or she existed, feeling almost that it would be a betrayal to wipe away their belongings, along with the memories.

I did tell my two daughters, after Margaret died, to chuck out all her clothes, just empty her drawers and wardrobe, straight to the charity shops, but leave all the papers and books and notes and stuff in her office and in her desk. In due course I would go through all of that properly.

One of the things they chucked out was a pair of Biba boots – a fab pair which I so loved, purple canvas, laced to the knees, ooh. I had totally forgotten about them. Some lucky person got a bargain from Oxfam in Kentish Town High Road. Must be a collector's item by now.

When I did get round to clearing up her room, I started on her desk, first of all examining the stuff she had left on the top. I noticed her fountain pen, lying there at the ready. All her books, almost forty of them, had been written in pen and ink. Beside it was a pile of A4 pages, sixty in all, in her immaculate handwriting. The top page was entitled '27'. It took me a while to realise what this meant – it would have been her twenty-seventh novel. Because I had foolishly put off clearing her room for so long, it had been lying there all summer, the sun beating down on it, and the top pages had all faded.

I knew roughly what it was about. About a year or so earlier, she had told me about a novel she had in mind, which was unusual for her. Usually she kept everything about the novel she was working on secret, never talking about it, never admitting she was even working on a novel. With non-fiction books it was different. She talked about them all the time. But novels were private.

She said how she had become fascinated by all the refugees flooding into England and the various detention centres that had been set up where the refugees were being checked and interrogated. She saw a reference to women translators who were doing work in one of the camps, interviewing women and children. She began wondering about the lives of the interviewers – were any of them mothers? Did they have children?

It was typical of how several of her books had begun – imagining herself into a woman's life, into her situation, about which she knew nothing. She would put her mind into the mind of the woman, and weave a story round her.

Inside a folder I found some torn-out newspaper cuttings about these refugee detention centres. It wasn't like Margaret to do any sort of research before beginning a book. Her normal working method was to make it all up. Only afterwards would she check, say, if her heroine was a psychologist, how one became a psychologist.

I put the unfinished manuscript carefully in the folder and started opening each of her drawers in her big pine desk in front of the main window of her office. It was at the very top of the house, overlooking the back gardens, where she could see but not be seen by any neighbours. I often thought when she was sitting there that she was like a captain on the prow of his ship, looking out at the sea of trees and gardens stretching into the distance towards Hampstead Heath.

Alas, I found no letter addressed to me or to the children. But I carried on clearing her desk and room because the British Library had by now become interested in acquiring her archives.

In old paper carrier bags I was surprised to find she had kept many personal bits and pieces. I always thought I was the squirrel in the family, having created twenty different collections and kept almost everything from my life. I found swimming certificates won at Carlisle Baths in 1948, her baptismal card from St Barnabas Church, cuttings from the *Cumberland News*, speech day programmes from the Carlisle and County High School for Girls.

I was mainly looking for the original handwritten manuscripts of her twenty-six published novels and her ten biographies and non-fiction books, which were mainly what the British Library wanted.

All of her books – novels and non-fiction – had been written in her immaculate handwriting, with no crossings out, no corrections. It all just flowed, seamlessly.

When working on a novel she would sit at her desk for an hour and a half each morning. She would start on a blank sheet every morning, never bothering to read what she had written the day before. Nor did she make any notes. This is most unusual. Almost every novelist I have ever met makes copious notes long before they begin and almost always start the day by reading what they did the day before.

Margaret would not read what she had written till she had finished, usually about 300 pages later. Then at last she would number the pages, read quickly through to check that during the book the heroine had not changed her name or the colour of her hair, then send it off to the typist. She had had the same one for many years who lived out in the country.

I would scream at her for posting off the only copy of her manuscript. What if it got lost in the post? She said hard luck. She had had the fun of writing the book, now wanted to forget it, usually adding that it had not worked out the way she had hoped it would. But that was it. It was now over.

In her fifty years of writing, none of her manuscripts did get lost in the post, but often they were delayed, went to the wrong house, leading me to have a heart attack on her behalf. I think she did it to wind me up.

I found a lot of her manuscripts in her room, in drawers, stashed on the floor behind her desk, but not the very early manuscripts from the 1960s and 1970s. They were not in her room, even hidden in corners, so I decided to look up in the loft.

In our fifty-five years of marriage, with each of us writing endless books, we had bunged old material, research notes, first drafts, manuscripts and proofs in the loft. Climbing up on the ladder at the end of every year, we had opened the hatch and just chucked stuff in. What a mess. What a dump.

The most surprising find, stuffed in an old, mouse-eaten Habitat carrier bag, was the manuscript of *Green Dusk for Dreams*. She swore she had torn this up. I believed her, for that would have been typical of her.

After we got married, on 11 June 1960, the day after she finished her final university exam, we moved into a flat in the Vale of Health on Hampstead Heath, for a rent of six guineas a week. I went to work as a journalist and she stayed at home, writing a novel. As a little girl, she had originally wanted to be a missionary, then an MP, but now, at twenty-one, she wanted to be a writer.

She spent three months writing it in pen and ink, then another three months laboriously typing it out on my portable with one finger. She had been told that no London literary agent would accept handwriting. Not that she had ever met or known any literary agents – you didn't meet such creatures on her council estate in Carlisle in the 1950s. Nor today, come to that.

She sent it off to a young new agent whose name she had been given, Michael Sissons. After a few weeks, he wrote back. He had some criticisms, but he was interested and asked whether she could come in and talk to him.

She never did. She took this as the bum's rush and immediately gave up all thoughts of writing a novel. Instead, she took a job as a supply teacher in a girls' secondary modern school near Pentonville Prison.

She always said she had torn the novel up. I knew roughly what it had been about. Before going up to Oxford, she had been an au pair in Bordeaux for a few months. France was a huge experience for her, never having been out of Carlisle before. On her return, she had got it into her head that she would write a Balzacian novel based on her life with this strange family in Bordeaux – about which of course she knew very little. It sounded pretty pretentious to me, the bits I had read, though what do I know? The soppy title gave it away.

After two years teaching, she decided to try another novel, this time basing it on something she did know about, and wrote a light-hearted romp about a working-class girl at Oxford entitled *Dames' Delight*. Tom Maschler at Jonathan Cape accepted it, and it did well. Then she did *Georgy Girl*, which did even better.

For the rest of her life she hated both those early books, and would never talk about them. She never included *Dames' Delight* in any list of her works and it has not been in print since 1964, as she refused to let any publisher reprint it. *Georgy Girl* became a very successful film, so it was hard for her to deny she wrote it, but she still didn't like talking about it. Neither was the sort of book she really wanted to write.

Some years later I got to know Michael Sissons. I asked him if he remembered this young girl writing to him with a novel set in France. He did, and had always wondered why she had never contacted him. I told him she was so upset by his letter that she tore up the manuscript. He was horrified. At the time, he had just been starting out, and considered it one of his best, most encouraging letters. He later changed his ways.

Margaret could be a terrible fibber, but I had always believed it when she told me she had torn up that first novel. With it, to my surprise, she had also kept the letter from Michael Sissons. It was dated 13 December 1960, from A. D. Peters, where Michael was working at the time. The wording was as I had always remembered it. He had 'some rather strong criticisms to make but could you come to the office for a talk?' I wondered whether I should give the British Library this early, unpublished manuscript, along with the originals of her published work. Would she be furious that I had come across it now, all these decades later, when she had wiped it from her mind and her records, insisting she had destroyed it?

I also found a stage play I had forgotten about. Unlike that first novel, it had a good title, *The Last Stand of Billie Shift*. Margaret wrote it in 1970 and it was bought by the West End producer Harold Fielding. He got Shelley Winters lined up to play the lead, and things were tailored to suit her. We had lots of amusing meals with her, then she changed her mind and went back to the USA. Margaret then dumped the play, shoved it in the loft.

But the biggest find was one million words I never knew existed – written in her diaries.

We knew in the family that she kept an occasional diary, for she mentioned it to me and the children, but she always maintained it was purely domestic jottings – what the children were doing, their funny little ways, when they first walked and read and rode a bike. It sounded very boring and none of us was interested.

Every fifth year for a whole year, before she started on her morning's writing, she had completed a page a day in a large-format hardback diary. Each day she did about 300 words, hence each of her eleven diaries is almost 100,000 words.

Very slowly, I started reading through the diaries. It is true they are heavily domestic, but she had lied when she said they were not personal. She wrote about her own writing, how her novel was going, or her latest biography. In real life, she would never talk about her novel, dismiss it as playing, would drop everything if the children came into her room. Until they were late teenagers I don't think they properly realised she had a writing career.

There was a period, in the 1970s and 1980s, when she did join in the London literary world, going on radio and TV arts programmes, reviewing books, serving as a Booker judge, being on the Arts Council and even, amazing though it seems to the family now, attending literary parties. But in the last twenty years of her life she did not go anywhere, refused to do signing sessions or go to book festivals, and had it in her agreement with Chatto, her publisher, that she did not have to do any of these things.

It wasn't just because of her cancer – she had had a double mastectomy back in the 1970s – that she wanted to conserve her energies. She decided she did not like that part of herself that performed, shooting her mouth off, having instant opinions, being fluent and glib, the perfect Oxbridge interviewee. But in her diaries, she did talk to herself, about her struggles with various novels, the threat of the cancer returning, and also about the world at large – at least the literary part of it – with some sharp and rather disobliging but amusing remarks about well-known literary figures of the day.

Hidden among these large-format adult diaries I found three schoolgirl diaries, which I'd had literally no idea existed. In the earliest diary she is aged ten at primary school, in another aged fourteen at the Carlisle and County High School for Girls, and again aged sixteen and sitting her O levels.

I told her publisher, Becky Hardie at Chatto & Windus, about my discovery of all these diaries, adult and schoolgirl ones. She was so amused and delighted by the sixteen-year-old-schoolgirl diary that they decided to rush it for Christmas. *Diary of an Ordinary Schoolgirl* was published in December 2017, to excellent reviews.

I was surprised. I had assumed the publisher would prefer to publish the adult diaries, as they are more easily understandable and would surely have a wider readership and be of more general interest.

The 1954 diary, which they published word for word, is a mixture of current events, based on what was in that day's *Daily Express*, her father's paper, mixed up with schoolfriends, her schoolwork, swimming galas and loads of reading. It is remarkable how many books she read, considering there were no books in her council house, and no one in her family home ever encouraged her. Her father went off each day in his boiler suit to the Metal Box factory where he tended to the machines.

Her 1952 diary, when she was aged fourteen, reveals she read 136 books that year, with critical comments in her diary about each one. In 1954, aged sixteen and with exams coming up, she read sixty-six. She also listed and commented on all the plays she had either heard on the radio or seen at the local rep theatre in Carlisle.

She saw nineteen films that year and gave them all a rating, finally announcing the best was *Odette*; the funniest *Doctor in the House*; and the most interesting *The Ascent of Everest*. The best film actress she saw in 1954, in her unhumble opinion, was Jean Simmons. Best film actor was Stewart Granger.

She also listed all the plays during the year, but it is not often clear how or where she saw or heard them. Then I realised that as the year progressed she was going to the theatre, Her Majesty's Theatre, of blessed memory, for the summer season of the Salisbury Rep who came to Carlisle every year.

In the winter months she was clearly listening to a play on the radio, usually *Saturday Night Theatre*. So often she never heard the end of an exciting play, thanks to her dad Arthur coming back from the pub, the Horse and Farrier in Raffles.

In those days a household had only one radio set, often connected to the overhead light socket. He was not a drunk – it was his only beer of the week – but he didn't like that tripe on the radio when he came back from the pub for his supper and always made her turn it off.

The fact that the diaries are all set in Carlisle, a remote town in the far north of England, with references to local cinemas and shops now mostly gone, is in a sense irrelevant. It could be anywhere in the UK at that time. We all listened to the same radio programmes, watched the same films. Big events of the day are mixed up with a super gym lesson, a wizard history essay and contempt for girls who were swanking.

And a lot of her expressions are of the period, influenced by girls' stories and Enid Blyton, even though at sixteen she had given up such children books, and now loved Dennis Wheatley.

It could also be a young girl any time, growing up anywhere, desperate and eager to learn and to progress. And they still exist – *oh* yes. So we all hope.

By the end of her sixteenth year, you can clearly see her strong, opinionated character developing. She seems unaware that some of her fellow pupils and even some of her teachers are growing in awe of her, though she dismisses her fans in the lower years as soppy.

After the publication of her sixteen-year-old-schoolgirl diary, which I edited and did an introduction for, I was left with a slight moral dilemma. What if Chatto decided they would like to go on and publish her more modern adult diaries, containing personal confessions, medical history and also unflattering remarks about people still living? Should we, the family, as the copyright owners, allow it?

I have just finished reading all the diaries. It's taken me a whole year, and I have made notes on the contents. Chatto have not read them yet, but I hope they might be interested in publishing some of them.

I am sure Margaret would have said no to publication in her lifetime, would have hated the very idea. But she is no longer here to say no. I don't honestly think she would have any objections if she knew that people might be reading her diaries after her death. She always said, when we discussed funerals and memorials, that it was the people left who had to make decisions. Not the dead.

I came across an interesting remark in her 1998 diary, on 12 January, in which she is musing about why she is writing these diaries:

Why am I keeping this diary? I have to have a reason. It can't any more be to record the children's lives. They are grown up. They can record their own or simply remember what they want. So that's not a reason. Nor is it posterity – definitely not, that is absurd. So the only reason is for myself – and why would I want to do that? Well sometimes it's true I have looked back at old diaries and liked the way I've been transported back – but not often. Or am I keeping it for an unknown future person who, like me, likes to read of past lives? Isn't that posterity? Not in the way I mean it. Ordinary folks don't think about posterity. They just want to make their marks to themselves. Oh for God's sake, I've started now, so quit fussing ...

And so she carried on, right up to 2013, writing her massive five-year diaries. Sometime she did an extra one, such as in the year 2000, to celebrate and record the millennium in her and our lives.

It is clear to me from that quoted paragraph, and from other references, that she was aware that she could be writing social history, that she was conscious that one day other people might well be reading her diaries.

I naturally would like to see them all published, word for word, apart of course from any libellous or hurtful remarks about people still living. She did often make some rather tart and critical and disobliging remarks about people, including dear friends, neighbours and close relations, as we all do behind their backs.

However, my three children are uneasy and do not quite agree with me that the diaries should be published. They found it unsettling during the first year after her death that I constantly seemed to be writing about her in my various columns and books. I also did a BBC Radio 4 programme on the first anniversary of her death, 'Losing Margaret'.

During that first year after her death, writing so much about her and how I felt about losing a wife, I probably did tend to forget that the three of them had lost a mother. They had rights and sensitivities as well, which perhaps at times I was not aware of, or ignored.

They still feel that Margaret would not have been pleased to know her diaries were being published, as she was a very private person. All very true. But she is not here.

She was, arguably, only a minor novelist, not a household name, and hardly known to the general public. It is surprising in a way that the British Library wanted her archives. But her novels did reflect social conditions of the times and were always concerned wholly with female relationships – mother and parents, mother and children, women and female friends. Blokes rarely came into her novels. Her memoirs, such as *Hidden Lives*, were well received, as were her excellent biographies of Daphne du Maurier and Elizabeth Barrett Browning.

I suppose it will be interesting for future English Lit students of the post-war years to study her archives. But what about the diaries? Were they not private?

Yes, I am for publication of her diaries, but then I am shameless. I have gone through life turning everything that has ever happened to me, however personal, however trivial, into copy.

My main argument is that she never destroyed her diaries, as she so often did with material she was unhappy with, so surely she must have known what might happen. Yes, they were hidden in her room and in the loft, but she never burned them, so must have known there was a chance they would be discovered.

They are not shattering, she did not witness great events, but as the adult diaries progress she does now and again refer to them as social history. Ordinary people, if they can record ordinary lives as well as she did, are part of social history. One of her bestselling books was called *Diary of an Ordinary Woman*, which was so real and graphic that most readers believed it was all true.

Even in her schoolgirl diaries there is a sense that she feels she is writing and recording for posterity – which I suspect almost all diarists have at the back of their mind, whatever they might say out loud. In her 1952 diary, she tears out the whole of September because, so she says, she was unhappy with her handwriting. If she was not writing to be read, why would that matter?

Throughout all her adult diaries she only once marks a section as 'confidential'. This was the year she was a Booker judge and was recording her forthright views on every novel she was reading – and on the other judges. So I would not allow that to be published. Even I have to respect express wishes.

We are probably in the last gasps of that long period in history in which people commit their thoughts and feelings to paper by hand. Who is going to keep all those dreary emails and computer files in centuries to come? As technology moves on so quickly, the present systems of retaining and retrieving words will be obsolete in a decade. If not next week.

But words set down on paper should last for . . . well, thanks to the British Library, hundreds of years. Margaret wrote what she wrote. And is now dead. All writing is true. All writing is not true. The people she personally wrote about in her diaries will soon also be dead, so who will care in the end?

After long discussions, with the children and the British Library, we have agreed to hand over all the original manuscripts of her books as they have already been published. The diaries are also being handed over, but are not being made available to the general public for ten years. The children feel that several people, relations and close friends, if they were allowed just to walk in and read them, which is the normal system at the British Library, would be upset. I still hope of course that edited excerpts might be published.

In due course, the children can then decide what bits can be read by all or which bits might still be embargoed. By which time, I will be gone, so I won't be bothered.

In the diaries I have come across some disobliging remarks about me. About being mean, for example, penny-pinching, late, untidy and scruffy. I don't mind any of that. She said as much to me all the time. And I just laughed.

In her 1975 diary, after fifteen years of marriage, she is wondering what has happened to me, how I have changed from the sweet innocent youth she first met aged seventeen, when she was still at school.

'At what stage', she wondered, 'did Hunter become a hustler?' Cheeky sod. Perhaps I will cut that bit out.

WISDOMS

- When you are dead, that's it, you are not here to control what happens to whatever by chance you might leave behind.
- But if you are adamant you still want some control, write it all down, make it all clear, get a lawyer to help.
- If you want to leave a personal message to your loved ones, don't shove it at the back of the drawer, down the sofa, under the floorboards or send as an email – leave

it prominently on the mantelpiece or the bathroom mirror. They are bound to spot it.

ANECDOTES

- Shakespeare left his wife Anne Hathaway his 'second-best bed'.
- George Bernard Shaw left a large sum of money to the promotion of a new alphabet.
- American businesswoman Leona Helmsley in 2007 left $12 million to her Maltese terrier, Trouble.

REGRETS

Looking back, people often wish they had written or recorded their life story, or kept a diary before it was too late, as they feel they have had an interesting life. Other common regrets...

- Marrying the wrong person.
- Not having enough sex.
- Not taking enough risks.
- Not seeing more of the world.
- Not saving enough money.
- Not telling their parents how much they loved them.
- Not asking their grandparents more about their lives.
- Working too hard; working too-long hours.
- Not spending enough time with their children.

4

Selling Up

I then had another big decision to make. I had been up several times to Loweswater to stay in our house, visit my old friends and old haunts after depositing half of Margaret's ashes in Loweswater churchyard. Her gravestone I will visit for ever, as long as I have the breath to cool my porridge, as my mother used to stay. But what was the point of going up there to stay there on my own? What should I do with a house that had been such a huge and emotional and beloved part of her life for so long?

It began on 7 May 1987, when I went up on the train from Euston to Cockermouth to an auction being held at the Globe Hotel. The hotel has a plaque on the wall that says R. L. Stevenson once stayed there, and another, more recent, marking the 2009 Cockermouth floods, when the water reached a height of 10ft in Main Street.

Only one house was being sold at the auction that day, a four-bedroom detached Victorian house at Loweswater, about 7 miles away. The auctioneer from Smiths Gore was an elderly gentleman, semi-retired, who had come back specially to handle this sale.

'Ladies and gentlemen,' he began, 'this is the most attractive house of its size I have ever sold.' Bugger it, I thought, I'll never get it now.

I had been told a guide price of £80,000. When I left home early that morning, I promised Margaret I would not go above £85,000.

For ten years we had had a very small, dark, damp but charming holiday cottage out on the open fells near Caldbeck, handy for visiting our parents in Carlisle. We had trailed up and down from London in an overloaded car several times a year with the children, at half-terms and holidays. I hate driving. And I hate children fighting in cars. Or even talking. Breathing is okay, as long as it's quiet.

In our fantasies, we would eventually move to a bigger house, in the Lake District, with lakes nearby – with lots of light, good views, a bit of height, big enough for a room each and for us to have a work room. One of the advantages of being a writer is that you can live anywhere.

The fantasy was to live in such a place half of each year when the children all left home, if they ever did. This Loweswater house being auctioned was exactly what we wanted.

There were three lakes within walking distance – Loweswater, Cummock Water and Buttermere – and it was set in lush greenery, surrounded on all sides by magnificent mountains, at the end of the Lorton Valley, about which Wordsworth had raved. It was a last-minute decision to go and bid that day in 1987. We had only recently chanced upon it, had not had a survey, and had made only one brief visit.

There were about twenty people at the sale. One of those who wanted it, I discovered later, was a well-off London solicitor who had sent his clerk to do the bidding, telling him not to go above £90,000. He obeyed his master. So I got it for £92,000.

For most of the past thirty years we had lived there half the year, roughly from May till October. We made a rule never to come to London when we were there, and vice versa. We broke it a few times, for family dramas, and of course they made visits, but it meant we only made that awful M1/M6 journey once a year. How perfect is that?

We hadn't really realised till we moved in how wonderful the views are from all sides, for the back and front of the house are alike, each with a porch and good windows. One of the drawbacks of Lakeland life, though, is how dark it can get. We could not actually see our nearest lake, Crummock Water, except in winter when the trees were bare, although it was just a ten-minute walk down a lane. Most years I went swimming in Crummock between June and October.

In each house, Loweswater and London, both by chance dating from the 1860s, our basic working life was exactly the same. We were at our desks each morning, moving words around. In Lakeland, my wife sat with her pen and ink, smiling quietly to herself when she heard me effing and blinding as the electricity went off, yet again, or the broadband was down.

In the afternoon, we walked. In London, walking down Kentish Town High Road, going for my swim three times a week, you have to try hard to breathe – not quite the same as walking alone round Crummock Water.

In Loweswater, I started my own Lakeland publishing company, Forster Davies Ltd, publishing my own guidebooks, plus lots of Lakeland books, so I needed to be there for as long as possible every year.

A few years after we moved in, I bought five fields, around

14 acres, which surround the house. I created an orchard, tree house and rebuilt the drystone walls.

I loved our little town of Cockermouth, an architectural gem, where I swam three times a week, poked around the antique shops, met local friends, had lunch. I did get upset when anyone asked, 'Enjoying your holidays?' 'Do you mind?' I'd say. 'We live here.' I liked to think I was part of the community all those years, entering for the Loweswater Show, taking part in events, getting to know everyone. It took time. Cumbrian farming folk winter you, they summer you, winter you again – then they say hello.

I did of course moan all those years about the expense of it all – paying two lots of council tax, double heating and water bills, having to have two of everything, including two TV licences. The free TV licence for the elderly only covers one home, not two. Bloomin' cheek.

For years I had two Amstrads, one in each place, for they were quite cheap. For the past ten I had an Apple computer and to save money I carted it up and down. It meant two broadband subscriptions, which has led to endless muck-ups getting connected each time. Broadband and mobile signals are a joke in the country. Yes, it is not easy or cheap running two complete homes, but of course no one wants to hear that. But I always realised how lucky we were.

In Loweswater, I always feel rural, agreeing when people rubbished London – awful place, the crowds, the dirt, the expense, the metropolitan media who ignore us, and so does every government.

Back down here I think, *Hmm, London is rather exciting and stimulating.* Everything is so handy – we can walk to the Royal Free Hospital in ten minutes.

Friends in both places always asked us which we would choose, if forced. We hesitated and said London, but only when the time comes, so we stressed. London is, after all, where our children and grandchildren live.

Alas, with the death of Margaret, the time came to decide. What would happen if I was living there on my own? Aged eighty, what would happen if I was ill, with my local GP 7 miles away in Cockermouth? As for hospitals, God knows where they are now. I did have an op on my toe ten years ago at West Cumberland Hospital in Whitehaven, but in recent years, when locals have been seriously ill, they have had to go to hospital in Newcastle or Lancaster, miles away, in a different county.

We have of course been fortunate to be able to afford two different homes. But mainly we did it for our souls, to refresh our spirits, get away from the horrors of London. I always used to say that we had the best of all possible worlds. With living up there half of each year for thirty years it was like living twice. We had an urban life. And a rural life. What could be nicer?

* * *

Some months after Margaret died, I spent six weeks on my own in Loweswater to see if I could stand it, if I could survive being on my own in a fairly large and remote house.

It was a strange feeling. In London I had grown used by now to the absence of Margaret. At first I'd think I could see her through the window, sitting reading on the downstairs couch when I came home through the back way, walking across the garden, but that soon faded. I was so busy in London, so active, so many social activities.

In Loweswater, though, during those weeks on my own, I imagined she was there, in the house with me, all the time.

Each day when I came back from my walk to the lake, or from Cockermouth, I opened the front door and I expected to find a note from her on the floor, written in her bold and impeccable handwriting. The notes normally contained one of three messages:

Do not disturb. I am working.

Answer your own bloody phone calls, it has gone non stop.

Have gone to the lake, down the Lonning, back the Scenic Way.

If it was the latter, and she had put the time she left, I would immediately turn round and go and meet her.

In Lakeland, it had always been just us, we two, at constant close quarters, in a remote rural situation. Little wonder I now sensed and saw her presence all the time. In London, we had our three children living nearby, and grandchildren, friends and neighbours we had known for fifty years, visitors for work and pleasure popping in. In London there were always distractions. In Lakeland I was alone with my thoughts and memories. So I decided to sell.

The local estate agent I contacted to do the dirty deed – well, it seems dirty to me, awfully disloyal to Lakeland – boasted that they employed a drone and a fully qualified drone pilot. The idea was to hover in the air, about 400ft high, film and photograph our lovely house, and my lovely five fields, and show the three lovely lakes within walking distance. Isn't modern technology grand?

Then everything went wrong. I leaned on my *Sunday Times* friends, the ones running 'Home', the property section, and they agreed to run a feature about the house. I told the estate agent miles ahead when the publication date would be. The *Sunday Times* did their bit on the agreed date, with a cover photo and two pages inside, with yummy photographs – but the sodding estate agent had not yet got the house on their website. Nor had the glossy catalogue I had paid extra money for arrived yet. I was spitting. After all my efforts doing publicity, attracting readers, on that Sunday nobody could find out the details about the house. I am not going to name the agent as I am still furious.

I was up there on that day, waiting for a stream of prospective buyers to arrive, storming round the house, shouting at the sheep. Nobody came. All that effort and time wasted.

A couple of days later the estate agent brought a woman along who was already on their books. She poked around in a desultory fashion and then said yes, it was very nice, but too far away.

'Too far away from what?' I asked her.

'Keswick,' she replied.

How could she not have looked at the map before she came? I was so depressed, fearing other prospective viewers would be timewasters, or nosy parkers wanting a gape.

I had wanted to show all prospective buyers round the house myself, to talk to them, find out where they were from, what they were really looking for. After all, I knew the house, knew the problems and pleasures – unlike the estate agent. The agent who had shown the woman around did not even know our area. He had come from the south and could not even identify Grasmoor, the high fell opposite our house, the local landmark.

After six days, the estate agent's details about the house did eventually appear online. Six people came over four days. It was such an intimate experience, showing strangers your bedroom, watching them lift up carpets you would rather they did not, avoiding sinks for fear of catching the plague, or entering a room and making a face at your wallpaper.

I insisted this time on showing them round personally. Four were roughly local while two had come from further afield. One was from London and the other from the West Country, both men who had left their wives at home. They each stayed overnight locally, returning the next morning for a second look. I was amazed they were investing so much time. Then I remembered that when we bought the house I had come from London on the train for the day, on my own. It could well have been a total waste of time.

Blow me, next day both men made offers – at the asking price. I suppose I could have tried to get them higher, but I was so delighted by their enthusiasm for the area, which they already knew well, and their clear love for the house.

I had cross-examined each about their finances when I had taken them round, subtly of course. I am known in our family for being subtle and discreet – har har. The one from the West Country would be getting a mortgage on his existing house while the Londoner appeared to have the cash already, having sold some internet company. It could have been a lie of course, but I believed him. He turned out to be a Tottenham Hotspur season-ticket holder, so clearly a man who was totally sensible and reliable. I don't think I could have sold it to an Arsenal fan. So I accepted his offer.

He then wanted a full survey done, which was a bit of a worry. When I bought the house at auction, I never had a survey. I decided I loved it so much that I would accept any faults. Just like falling in love with my dear wife.

But the survey was okay and the Londoner hurried me into

a quick sale, offering to exchange contracts and complete all on the same day. Usually there is a gap of about a month. It meant I had to clear up and empty the house much more quickly than I had planned.

In a way, the speed made the agony less. I was too busy to mope and mourn or have any second thoughts – which I had been having, thinking, *Oh God, what have I done?* It was not just that Margaret had died. I now felt part of me was dying as well.

I had to quickly get rid of all the furniture and my treasures – or what I call my treasures. The real rubbish I dumped, lesser rubbish went to charity shops, while some of the choicer items I gave away, such as an 1810 guidebook to Lakeland, written anonymously by Wordsworth, which I gave to Dove Cottage.

The ordinary domestic stuff went into Mitchells auction house in Cockermouth in their ordinary domestic weekly sales. That was agony, seeing items of furniture we so loved, comfy fireside easy chairs we had spent a fortune recovering, going for piddling sums. I don't know why people ever buy new stuff when you can get excellent second-hand furniture so reasonably.

Yet the price fetched for one tatty item, a stuffed red squirrel in a wooden case which was falling to pieces, amazed me. I had kept it in the fireplace in my office and looked at it every day as I sat down to work, thinking I really should repair it or at least dust it. It must have been harbouring appalling germs. It went for £60.

I didn't go to any of the sales. I couldn't bear to see any of my beloved objects being brutally dismissed, going for peanuts or, worst of all, ending up with that dreaded word beside them – unsold.

The so-called treasures in the sale, such as the Sheila Fell paintings, the signed Wainwright books, the Beatrix Potter first editions, all sold well. I like to think they will be loved by real collectors and go to good homes. I do in fact now know which home two of the best Sheila Fells have gone to.

In dealing with Paul, the man who was buying our house, I said to him, early doors, that if it all came to pass, if he completed the purchase and did not change his mind, I would give him, as a present, a signed drawing of Grasmoor by Wainwright. Grasmoor, the mountain, dominates the view from the front of the house. I always had the drawing hanging in the hall, so as you entered the house you could look at both, the image and the reality. I felt pleased, when it all came to pass, that the Wainwright drawing would remain in its home. What I didn't know till much later was that Paul had left bids at Mitchells and bought two of the Sheila Fells. So they will also be back home where they have been all these decades.

The biggest surprise and disappointment was the fate of my number-one item, the one that Mitchells made top of the bill, in the sense that it was the first of my 130 lots in the sale.

This was five letters from Beatrix Potter. The contents were not really personal or dramatic, but all to do with Herdwick sheep, which she was entering at the Loweswater Show, or judging, during 1931–35. I assumed they would have a wide local interest and would easily sell.

I bought them locally almost thirty years ago. The late David Winkworth, who with his wife Angela created the New Bookshop in Cockermouth, rang me one day to say that an old farmer had tried to sell him some Beatrix Potter letters. David wasn't interested, but he knew I was doing a Beatrix Potter Lakeland biography. (It came out in 1988 with photographs by Cressida Pemberton-Pigott, who today is Lady Inglewood.)

I went to see the farmer, who lived near Lorton. The letters had been sent, I think, to his father or uncle. I paid him what he wanted, in cash. I can't now remember how much that was – possibly £200.

In the Mitchells catalogue they put an estimate on the letters of £2,500–£3,500. Yes, it would have been a massive markup, but in the intervening thirty years there had been several films about BP – they are mad for her in the USA and Japan and 2016 was the 150th anniversary of her birth.

Guess how much they made? Nothing. They joined the dreaded ranks of the unsold.

The main reason is pretty obvious – they are not signed 'Beatrix Potter' but 'H. B. Heelis'. That was her married name, the one she always used once she came to live full-time in Lakeland. If you are a Japanese or American mogul, sitting in your snug, surrounded by your framed signed letters from Elvis, John Lennon, Marilyn Monroe, Einstein, President Kennedy or other icons of the twentieth century, you don't want to have to explain each time who H. B. Heelis is.

It seemed like a judgement, really, for trying to be greedy, so I decided to give them to a charity, the Armitt Trust in Ambleside, who already have a fine collection of Beatrix Potter's fungi paintings. I also gave the research material for my Wainwright biography to the Wainwright Society. Along with the Wordsworth book for Dove Cottage, that meant that my three, in theory, most interesting and desirable Lakeland collectable items, as well as the Sheila Fell paintings, will stay in Lakeland.

* * *

I spent the final two nights in an empty house, lying on a mattress on the wooden floor in an empty bedroom. All the contents, the domestic junk as well as the treasures, had gone.

Getting down on the floor was relatively easy – you just flop, collapse – but getting up, oh my God, that was agony. I had to roll over and somehow prop myself up with my elbow. I had not realised how low a floor is, and how high a normal bed is. Or how old I was. So I flopped back on the mattress again. I felt like a squatter in someone else's neglected, forgotten home.

I stared round at the bedroom walls. I could see the faded patches where our prized paintings had been, by Sheila Fell, Heaton Cooper, Percy Kelly, unknown to most people unless they are Lakelanders.

I stared out of the naked windows at Grasmoor, the looming fell after which our house is named. All fourteen windows in the house have stunning views, back and front, of the fells and fields, lakes and landscape. The curtains had gone as well, after the man from Mitchells pointed out they were Sandersons, in William Morris design, and would fetch some money. Good job Margaret never told me how much she had spent on them. I would have moaned.

Lying there, with my eyes closed, I could see the family and all the visitors to the house over the years. I could see John Prescott, whose autobiography I ghostwrote, and his lovely wife Pauline both sitting in our garden, with two heavies in a corner, keeping an eye on him, as he was deputy prime minister at the time. I could hear my fellow Cumbrian Melvyn Bragg admiring my conservatory, asking how I had got planning permission. I could see all our three children and grandchildren at my wife's seventieth birthday party eight years earlier.

I could also hear singing, as I lay there, on that dusty empty bedroom floor – American voices singing lustily in our house ten years earlier.

When Margaret was at Oxford, her best friend, Theo, went out with a Rhodes scholar called Van whom she later married. Margaret kept in close touch with Theo and Van all her life.

Every year the group of Rhodes scholars who had all been at Oxford at that same time – Bill Clinton, I think, was a generation afterwards – had a reunion. That year they opted to come to Lakeland, staying at a guesthouse on Buttermere.

We invited them for lunch, out on our terraces, on wooden tables and benches. The sun shone and the day was glorious. Margaret made them a great spread – home-made individual pizzas and lots of salads and tons of wine.

They got quite merry, all these elderly but distinguished Americans, most of whom had become judges, professors, heads of Ivy League colleges. Van, the man Theo married, was for a time chief economist in the Carter government.

Anyway, at the end of the meal they all started singing, very loudly, but all together. And guess what they were singing? Scottish folks songs – 'Over the Sea to Skye', 'You'll Take the High Road'. I had learned these as a boy, but I was so surprised that they, in their American primary schools in the 1940s and '50s, had learned the same songs.

I made a video of them singing but I don't need to get it out. I still hear them in my head. Still singing.

I have shots of Margaret convulsed at these elderly and distinguished American gents and ladies, bellowing away, some with tears in their eyes, remembering their own childhoods.

* * *

On my very last day in the house, our son Jake and his wife Rosa drove up from London in their car to help me bring stuff back to London – the personal bits and pieces, photographs and mementos, nothing really valuable, just things I wanted to keep. We reminisced of course about their memories of the house and of Margaret in it, such as the time, on her fiftieth birthday, she had got up at five o'clock and climbed Red Pike.

The night before, when asked what she really wanted on her birthday, she said her special treat would be to climb Red Pike first thing in the morning with me. I said great, I'll come. Alas, I slept in and never heard her getting up.

She brought me tea in bed at eight as usual and I remarked that her hair was wet.

'Oh, is it?' she said. 'Probably because I got up at five and climbed Red Pike and had a swim in Crummock. I nearly woke you, but you were sound asleep . . .'

I love this story, even if it is at my expense. It has become a family legend – the image of her going off on her own, enjoying herself so much, then gently boasting about it.

Jake now does not quite believe it. He recently got out the map and thinks she could not have got as far as the top of Red Pike and back in three hours from our house. But she had obviously been *some*where, I said. Her hair was wet. She must have had a swim. He still does not believe it.

Margaret did tend to 'improve' stories, exaggerate, but then she was a proper novelist. I plan to believe that story for ever, that she did climb Red Pike and swim in the lake on her fiftieth birthday.

And that was the house sold, thirty years of our life cleared away, packed up, gone for ever. Only the memories remain.

WISDOMS

- Living half the year in the country and half the year in the town is like living twice in the same lifetime.
- You need ample funds for a country cottage. The overheads, regardless of how seldom you are there, will come to around the same as your main house.
- But oh the warm glow, putting on your Hunter wellies and Barbour, living like a true-born country person, running down awful London, then running to the Volvo estate to get back to town as quickly as possible.
- People with country cottages always lie about how quickly they can get there. Double whatever they tell you.
- The well-off professional middle class always say it is just a hovel, a peasant cottage, don't you know, but do visit – and it turns out to be three cottages knocked into one, with two en-suite guest wings, an Aga in the kitchen the size of Concorde, a garden that takes two gardeners to tend and a heated outdoor swimming pool.

QUOTES

- 'It is my belief, founded on my experience, that the lowest and vilest alleys of London do not present a more dreadful record of sin as does the smiling and beautiful countryside.' Arthur Conan Doyle

- 'The train whistled, and chuffed out of the station. The children pressed their noses to the window and watched the dirty houses and the tall chimneys race by. How they hated the town! How lovely it would be to be in the clean country, with flowers growing everywhere, and birds singing in the hedges!' Enid Blyton
- 'Is there no nook of England ground secure from rash assault?' William Wordsworth

OTHER THINGS THAT HAVE CHANGED IN MY LIFETIME

Giving up country life is probably the biggest change in my life, but there are other things, now gone, that we have all experienced:

- Sticking photos in albums.
- Recording TV programmes on a video recorder.
- Typewriters.
- Amstrad PCWs.
- Handwritten letters.
- Using a public telephone box.
- Going to a travel agent to book a holiday.
- Using a telephone directory.
- Ringing the speaking clock.
- Owning a whole set of *Encyclopaedia Britannica*.

5

LONDON LIVING – DOMESTIC BLISS

That's it, I am never using the dishwasher again. Her instructions listed three things I have to shove in at various times: a tablet, rinse aid and some water softener. I opened it and could not work out which were the correct orifices. Or what the flashing lights meant. It would be easier to operate a spacecraft. Not my fault. Her instructions were rubbish.

What is the point of having a dishwasher anyway when I am on my own, eating on my own, usually using the same plate, mug, knife, fork and spoon?

Margaret also pinned long and elaborate instructions over the top of the washing machine, which is under the stairs in the downstairs lavatory. Not for me – for that was not my territory, a foreign place where they speak a foreign language – but over the thirty years while we were away living in Loweswater there was always some worthy but poor young person staying in our London house in the upstairs flat, rent free, keeping an eye on things, allowed to have the run of the house. Usually they were relations, nephews and nieces, or friends of our children, such as an out-of-work actress, or the children of friends from the north coming to London, the big city. Often they were doing intern-type jobs in London, unpaid, so they could not afford to rent a place, though of course their mummies and daddies were usually fairly well-off. After all, who else has the connections enabling their children to get intern work in London, and work for free, except the affluent middle classes? It was noticeable over the years how often, when we thought we were helping a poor, hard-up youngster, their own homes and lives turned out to be very similar to our own.

Our washing machine is a Bosch and Margaret did not want any dopey twenty-two-year-old, however well bred, used to being looked after hand and mouth, buggering it up.

Hence her meticulous washing-machine instructions, in her lovely handwriting – which of course I ignored, as I ignore most instructions, convinced I know how things work.

The first time I did the washing I opened the washing-machine door, thinking the cycle was finished, and water and wet clothes flooded out, not just over the floor of the downstairs lavatory but right along the hall to the front door. Oh God, how stupid. Her fault, her rubbish instructions. When you are on your own you can blame anyone. They don't answer back.

Then I did some ironing, which was a right battle. I could not open the ironing board, so I did the ironing with the ironing board flat on the kitchen floor. My back was aching like hell, with all the bending over.

Yes, I know, it is all pathetic. Even more pathetic and reprehensible is that during our fifty-five years of married life I contributed eff-all to our domestic life – neither washing nor wiping, cooking nor cleaning.

My defence, such as it is, is that when we first got married we had divvied up the domestic load and I got, well, very little. Yes, I did the driving, looked after bills and finances, attended to jobbies when things went wrong in the house, which mainly meant ringing a plumber or electrician. Till my knees went, I did climb up on the roof once a year and check the slates. I cleared drains, mended leaks, shoved black tar stuff on cracks. And I did the garden – not very well, but I did the garden.

Margaret's father had been a brilliant gardener, keeping everything wonderful and growing amazing flowers and vegetables, so I hoped I was going to get a little horticultural treasure when I married Margaret, but she had picked up none of his skills or knowledge. In my own council house, growing up, nobody did the garden, as my father was an invalid. It was left as a dump, till it got totally overgrown and neighbours would pass by either looking the other way or going 'tut tut'. Twice a year my mother would force me to go out and tackle the jungle, which I hated.

When we married in 1960, it was still that period in social history, hardly different from my father's, when men did not do cooking or cleaning or changing nappies. That was my excuse, which I clung on to for fifty-five years, despite the world and my own family moving on. All that has changed of course. My son Jake does the cooking in his house and Flora's husband Richard is the main cook in their house. Caitlin and her partner Nigel take turns. I would have called them soft fifty years ago, muttering about them not being real men.

My other defence, just as spurious, was that Margaret liked to do it. She actually got pleasure out of cooking and cleaning.

Over the bedtime cocoa, we often discussed what each of us might do if our writing were to dry up. How would we live? How would we earn money? I used to say I would have a market stall somewhere, buying and selling, starting off with selling my own collections. Margaret said she would go out and be a cleaner. There is always work for cleaners, especially someone so quick and efficient. She was not a slave to cleanliness, did not pride herself on all the nooks and crannies being dust-free, all the paintwork spotless, unlike some of our dear neighbours, but the house always looked clean and bright – mainly because it was colourful and artistic and interesting. That was all her doing. I have got no artistic leanings and am colour-blind.

During these past two years, it has been one of my biggest struggles, the cause of endless groans and moans, keeping on top of this house, trying to keep it reasonably in order.

Margaret never had a cleaner, even in the years when we had three young children, a large house and she was struggling to write her novels. She refused to have a woman in the house who might well have been her mother. She always said she did not want to boss any other woman around.

It only happened once that we had any help in the house. That was when she had her double mastectomy in the 1970s and was weeks in hospital and then a long time at home recovering. We hired a so-called nanny to help with the children, who was in fact just a friend, the daughter of our builder at the time.

But in the last year or so of Margaret's life, when she was beginning to physically tire, she did receive a bit of help from Ruby, our eighteen-year-old granddaughter, daughter of Caitlin. Ruby came in for just an hour every two weeks on a Sunday morning and did some heavy-duty cleaning, all the floors and carpets, the sinks and lavatories. It was partly to help Ruby, give her extra pocket money, and give Margaret a chance to chat to her, catch up on her life. Margaret never bossed Ruby around, never told her what she wanted done.

She just let her get on with it, come when it suited her, leave when she liked.

For about three months after Margaret died, I continued with the system, but by then Ruby, now in the sixth form, was arriving later and later on a Sunday morning, having slept in, or not having come home. By the time she came to my house I was often in bed, having my siesta, so the noise of the Hoover would wake me up.

Since 1986, I have always had a sleep after lunch every day – or a siesta, as I like to call it. This started when we went on our first trip to the Caribbean for my fiftieth birthday, Margaret's present to me, flying there on Concorde. I got into the habit in the tropics of going to bed after lunch, after too much sun and sea and drink. It is of course so hot in the tropics in the afternoons that you can't go out or do very much else, except rest indoors.

I decided it was such a brilliant habit that I have kept it up ever since, to this day, wherever I have been – in London or Loweswater, in the country or abroad. After lunch I go to the bedroom, close the curtains, get into the bed, pull the clothes up and bingo, I am off to sleep. Most of the time anyway. I stay there for thirty minutes whatever happens and, if I am not asleep, I get up feeling awfully refreshed. Half the time I fall totally asleep – normally for forty minutes. Oh, it is such a joy, such bliss. I am pleased I got into the habit when I was still middle-aged, much to the surprise of many folks, as at the time it made me sound like an old man. Now I am an old man, it does not surprise people as much.

I often say to people that with age it is surprising how I can manage with an hour's sleep. Then I pause, waiting for them to exclaim. 'After lunch,' I add.

Ruby did not quite appreciate or understand my siesta habit, or forgot about it. Finally I asked if she really wanted the job, when so often it seemed to interfere with her social life. So we agreed she could stop coming.

By chance, Maria, a Portuguese cleaner, a woman of mature years who had worked for several people in our street, lost one of her jobs when a neighbour moved. I asked if she would work for me – which she now does. She does two hours a week, arriving promptly on a Thursday morning at ten. So I know where I am, what to expect and when.

All the same, on the other six days a week, I still find myself having to do some sort of housework – clear up the kitchen after my breakfast, such as it is, tidy the couch where I have been lolling while reading the morning paper, take the rubbish out, think of what I am going to eat today. All this before I go upstairs and start working. I never realised how much time Margaret spent behind the scenes just keeping the house ticking over. I also now know how boring it is. I scream with the utter tediousness of it all.

One of the many personal services Margaret provided for me in our married life was to bring me tea in bed every morning. She would appear, as if by magic, when I was still half asleep, lean over and put the radio on for the *Today* programme, for I do find putting on the radio terribly exhausting. Then she would switch on my bedside light, carefully place my mug of tea in the correct place at the correct angle, then just as carefully exit the bedroom, ever so quietly, and close the door.

I would then hear her downstairs, grinding the beans for her cup of coffee, the only time in the whole day at which she had a hot drink. She never drank tea, ever, and only had one cup of coffee a day.

Oft times I can still hear her downstairs when I wake and am still in a half-dream, grinding her coffee. I even imagine I can smell it. Which is mad. I have chucked out the coffee grinder, one of the many household appliances I decided I no longer needed.

But the best, most lovely thing she did for me and which I miss terribly was to run my bath. Well, she ran it for herself. After bathing, she would then return to the bedroom, clutching her towel, and I would get up and go into her bath, which was then at a perfect temperature for me, as she did like it a bit hot.

For some reason she never liked me telling people this – that I used her bath water. As if it was somehow disgusting, that I was using dirty, second-hand water. But you are the cleanest person I have ever known, I would say to her, your bathwater is pristine. Just like you.

I also liked the fact we were saving money, helping the resources of the country. George VI would have been very pleased. During the war he used to tell all British families to use just 6 inches of water in their bath to help win the war. I was never sure how that worked. Would the Germans give up when they heard we had saved all this water? We did not in fact have a bath or hot water in our house, so the message was hardly necessary.

Oh, I did so love going straight to have my bath, getting in without having to run the water. Today, it is probably the single most annoying thing that hangs over me every day. The moment I get my eyes open, check I am still alive, then roll back under the blankets again, it then slowly dawns on me that I will have to run my own bath. Oh God.

Our boiler is a right pain. The hot water in the bath tap seems to have a life of its own, suddenly running cold for no reason, turning itself off, or it is suddenly so scorching hot you can't touch it and have to have the cold on as well to get it right. Margaret was quite content to sit there, for the whole five or six minutes it takes, to stare out of the window, keeping an eye on the water to regulate it till it was perfect. I don't do sitting. I don't do waiting. I have no patience. I have gone through life always in a hurry.

And yet I desperately need my bath, every morning, to get ready for the day, ease and soak my limbs. Many folks I know have their daily bath last thing at night, but I have never fancied that. Seems such a waste, going to bed all clean and soaked and fresh. Seems better to be clean and bright and ready for the day, not the night.

For weeks after she died I tried to sit there stoically, waiting in the bathroom for the bloody bath to fill up. Then I decided to go off and do some little household jobs, rushing back and forth to see it had not run cold. Now I seem to have got some sort of system, setting the hot and cold taps at the right level, then rushing downstairs, opening the curtains, getting the paper out of the front letterbox, putting my muesli into a bowl. Then I rush back upstairs to the bathroom, check the water has not overflowed, altering the cold tap if necessary. I then rush into my office and turn on the computer, look to see if any interesting messages have come in overnight. Sometimes I get distracted if they are too interesting, forget about the bath, then belt like mad to the bathroom to find the water up to the top, which means I can't get in without flooding the floor. Or behind my back the bath has filled itself with totally cold water.

The worst thing of all is cooking for myself. I hate it. I come home, go into the kitchen, look in the bread bin and think, *What should I make for supper? I know, I will just have some toast. Toast is nice. Toast is good for you. Toast is easy.*

Toast is one of the things I have always been able to make. If I have the recipe book in front of me. Joke.

Actually I did create my own toasted delicacy called Hunter's Special some forty years ago when my wife had that spell in hospital. It consisted of ham and cheese on toast, with a poached egg on top. Yum yum. I gave it to the children every night when they came home from school till they were screaming for mercy.

Finally, when I open the fridge, thinking, *No, I can't make toast for myself yet again*, there is often something lovely inside, which wasn't there before, left by the food fairies.

My three children, and also two of my neighbours, have keys. When they have made something for their evening meal they often do an extra portion – of lasagne, bolognaise sauce, quiche, stew, nut roast, or whatever it is they are having. I usually eat half for my meal that evening, then put half in the freezer for another day.

All the same, unless I am going out for dinner, which I try not to do as I have gone off going out in the evening, there can be six nights of the week when I have to make something for myself, however humble. If I have been out to lunch, which I love, saying yes to all invites and lunching out at least once a week, in the evening I usually just have a salad or pasta or a sandwich. When out for lunch, I usually order meat. I like to keep my meat intake up, but I don't like cooking meat at home. I now dislike the look of meat and its smell.

This happened to Margaret. In the last few years she had practically become a vegetarian. It was not on any moral principle about eating dead animals, but because she could no longer bear to look at red meat or handle it or cook it. So we had mainly fish, chicken pasta, salads. But once a week, as a favour to me, she would cook meat of some sort, such as fillet steak, which I loved.

When she was in the hospice during her last four weeks, and I was struggling to cook for myself at home, I bought some fillet steak. Not cheap. The next day when I went to visit her I got out my notebook and asked her how she cooked it, what sort of pan I needed, what were the things she cooked with it, how would I know when it was ready ...

'Oh spare me,' she said. 'I am too tired to think about anything like that. You will manage. You will be fine.'

I had left it too late. If only during our married years I had watched her carefully or, even better, attempted to cook things myself when she was around, I would surely have learned enough to do simple cooking.

I did cook that very expensive fillet steak, and it was horrible. I burned it, yet the onions were still raw. I have not bought steak since.

I do eat a lot of salads, but very often, especially if the tomatoes are half decent, I don't put any dressing on. I do know where the balsamic vinegar is. Found it by chance at the back of a cupboard. Probably four years old, coated in a black sludge. But I can't remember how she mixed her salad dressings, so normally I do without any sort of dressing these days.

Partly it is because I am such a messy eater. I tend to sit on the couch reading the evening paper while I have my evening meal and knock back the wine. I usually manage to drop or spill something onto my shirt or pullover – and if it is salad dressing, that is a killer. And I have to do the washing these days, worst luck.

During those last four weeks in the hospice, when I was first struggling to feed myself, I decided to buy a microwave oven. Margaret never had one. She refused to consider it, believing they were an insult to proper cooking. She was a bit of a snob, in many things, and could not be shaken when she had dismissed certain things.

When I confessed I had got one, and was using it, in *her* kitchen, she was appalled.

She immediately told her next visitor, who was Valerie Grove, complaining to her about what I had done and giving a very long sigh.

'So that's it,' said Margaret. 'I will never be coming home now.'

And of course she didn't.

* * *

All our married life I lolled on the couch from six to seven each evening reading the evening paper and having a drink, in total silence, while Margaret got on with her magic in the kitchen. I would not even ask, 'What's for supper, pet?' I liked her to surprise me. And not to interrupt, please, I am still reading the paper.

I still try to re-create that hour from six to seven, having a drink. Being in the garden in the summer I love best of all. I still often forget I am on my own, and have no idea what it is I will be eating for supper, when I have finished the paper. Apart from another drink.

When I do make something, and catch myself sitting eating it alone, in my own house, in silence, I think to myself, *How did this happen? How do I come to be here, alone in this house?*

When I am washing up, clearing away, I often stop myself in my tracks, look out at myself, and again think, *What happened?* I am still taken by surprise by my situation. I wonder if that will change as the years go on. Will I become used to being on my own, forget to catch myself unexpectedly?

Making supper for myself is exhausting enough, but then afterwards, clearing up, I think, *Oh no, I will have to go through all this again tomorrow*. The trouble with making food is that someone always comes along and eats it. In this case me.

Margaret gave up drinking in the last few years. The chemo and the drugs seemed to affect her taste buds and she no longer had the desire for wine. In the old days, we had a bottle every evening and would fight over who had had most, marking with pencil on the side of the bottle if she had poured herself a particularly large glass. Since she died, I have gradually upped my wine intake, drinking for her as well – in her honour, in her memory. Every day, all round the year, I now consume a bottle of wine. I drink a large glass at lunchtime and three in the evening – one before the meal and two during. Sometimes more, if I have been out, though I try to limit myself to a litre a day. I do have limits.

I never miss meals. I always eat something, even if it is just a frozen pizza. Actually I now hate frozen pizzas so have stopped buying them. The taste in my mouth seems to linger on long afterwards. Margaret always made her own pizzas, which were delicious. All ready-made supermarket meals seem to leave an aftertaste and a coating of fat and preservatives on the roof of my mouth. And they are so full of salt and sugar. Is it age? Have my taste buds changed? Or have I got more sensible?

I get tempted now and again in Morrisons or Marks & Spencer by two meals for £10, or whatever it is, and the lasagne looks so tempting. Then I regret it and usually end up with items I don't really like or want. I now just want simple, fresh food.

I don't buy or cook potatoes, which Margaret always did for me, as I loved them. Except chips – we never had chips. I can't be bothered now with any potatoes. I also don't eat bread with every meal, which Margaret did. So perhaps cutting down on spuds and ready meals accounts for my weight loss. I hope that is all it is.

I read the other day that with age men's ears grow bigger. I don't believe that for a moment. I think it is just that they have less hair. But I do have a theory that people, especially men, get thinner with age, regardless of what they eat. I suppose it is the lack of physical exercise, or their body receding, getting smaller.

I long to speak to Margaret, show off my tum, and say ah ha ha ha, look at me, look how slim I am, yet I am drinking twice as much, you was wrong, ah ha ha.

* * *

If Margaret did come back – and I often think she will pop in to check on me, and her house – she would be appalled by various little domestic changes I have made. I now leave the clothes line up, with all the pegs still on, all the time. She always took down the clothes line, once the clothes were dry, rolling it up neatly and putting it away out of sight, hanging it away on the branch of a tree. She hated looking out of the back window and seeing a clothes line, even if there were no clothes on it. I thought she was potty, taking her aesthetic tastes and sensibilities to silly levels. It does not offend me, seeing the clothes line up all the time. In fact, I am not aware of it.

The plates and mugs and glasses are more stained and grey than they used to be. I put the dishwasher on only once a month. If that. I tend to wash my plate after a meal in cold water, just a quick rinse. If the plate is too dirty, I have found that using my fingers, my bare fingers, without plastic gloves, to wash and clean it is just as effective and quick and easy as using a dishcloth or a brush. After all, your skin is the most miraculous creation. It lasts longer than any cloth and does not stink and harbour germs the way Spontex cloths do. I was always buying new ones. Now I am saving money by using my own hands. They dry so easily.

I am sure there are many other ways in which I have let her standards slip, not doing things the way she did them. But she is gone. It's just me here.

* * *

Since she died, I have spent a lot of time in the garden, looking after it, caring for it, making it nicer.

For thirty years we were never in London in the summer, being up in Lakeland from May to October. It was a strange feeling in 2017 to be here all summer. In 2016, the year Margaret died, I was up north a few times, such as the six weeks selling and clearing the house. Now I am London-based full-time.

On the whole, I don't like it. London gets horrible in the summer, with all the tourists and the dirt and the dust, especially Kentish Town, our local shopping area. I go to the local baths for a swim three times a week and when I stand in the high road, in all that squalor, waiting for the bus home, I think, *What am I doing? Why I am in London and not in Loweswater? I can live anywhere. I don't need to be here.* But I have already made that decision. My children are here. My life is here, from now on, such as it is.

So I now spend a lot of time and get a lot of fun out of growing stuff in the garden. We always had apples and pears, plums and damsons, but they all fell while we were away and had turned mushy on our return, covered in wasps, and everything was overgrown. Now I care properly for the fruit trees and have also put in raspberries and strawberries and potatoes. I planted the latter with my two younger granddaughters, Amarisse and Sienna. They were amazed four months later when we dug them out. They could not believe that each soggy, funny-looking old seed potato had spawned a massive family of sweet, fresh dinky white potatoes with skins that just fell off. They carefully washed off the soil, scrubbing like mad, totally soaking themselves – and then we ate the new potatoes. Oh the joys of grandchildren. One of the many pleasures of age. As long as they don't stay too long or get too boisterous or pick my best tulips in the garden, eat what they are not allowed to, swing on trees, break branches, pick the magnolia buds just because they look so pretty, bring mud and grass in from the garden or put on horrible pop music. Which is when I say, 'Is it not time to go now, my little darlings? Won't Mummy be waiting for you?'

As well as the summer house, where half Margaret's ashes are, I also put in two arbours, mainly for the look of them. I do have some aesthetic tastes, after all.

I have also done a lot of work in the house, doing things I should have done ages ago. It began with clearing out the loft when looking for the manuscripts of Margaret's books for the British Library.

I realised there was no proper insulation or flooring – no wonder the top floor had always been freezing every winter. So I had proper floor insulation installed, plus a Velux window to replace the old broken trapdoor onto the roof to give light. The builder who did it also sanded some floors and patched up some ceilings. Altogether, his bill came to £8,000. I could have bought a Georgian gem for that, back in 1963.

But the big achievement, which has given me such pleasure, is a downstairs shower. Wow! You should see it. It's so gratifying. I open the door under the stairs and stand there, in a daze, ogling it.

There were two periods in my wife's life, after operations and treatment, when she had to spend three months sleeping on the ground floor, unable to walk upstairs. We have always had a downstairs lavatory, under the stairs, which turned out to be handy when she was ill, but that was all we had.

The space under the stairs, like all such spaces, is small and awkward, but somehow, twenty years ago, we also managed to squeeze in the washing machine. When my wife was ill, I suggested we should somehow add a shower downstairs for her to use. She told me not to be so stupid, it would ruin the house. Anyway, she didn't need it. She would manage till she could get upstairs again. When she did, we of course forgot about it.

Being at home most of the summer, and doing lots of gardening, it struck me that I could do with a shower when I got hot and sweaty. We gardeners, eh? It would be so handy to have one on the ground floor, so I could go straight into it from the garden. And there was another reason I wanted a shower downstairs. I have noticed with elderly folks that one of the first things they can't manage is the stairs. I plan to stay in this house, always, till they carry me out. A shower, therefore, would make my downstairs quarters complete. My children don't like me talking like this, and change the subject when I bring it up.

I contacted Grant, a plumber we have had for twenty years – and his father before him – and he hummed and hawed, said no chance, a shower would not fit in that little space under the stairs. Too much in it already. I said not an off-the-peg, a specially built shower. I want you to take the washing machine out and create a shower from scratch in that funny, titchy space.

Where did the washing machine go? I moved it – I mean Grant moved it – into the kitchen, replacing the freezer.

And where did the freezer go? Into the dining room, of course.

It amused Amarisse and Sienna to help me wallpaper and tile the freezer. It now looks like, er, a freezer covered in wallpaper. I plan to leave it to the V&A.

'How will you stand up in the shower?' Grant asked.

'Don't you worry,' I replied. 'I can crouch.'

Another thing I have noticed with age is that we all lose height as well as weight. I can in fact stand up, just as long as I don't forget and go to the back of the shower and knock myself out on the sloping roof. I might lie there for days, till one of my children comes, or a neighbour or a lady friend.

Having finished, Grant was covering the shower walls with white tiles before I could stop him. I didn't want it looking like a public toilet. I rushed into the garage and found some old broken Portuguese tiles, forty years old, which I knew one day would come in handy. I told Grant to fit as many in as he could, just randomly, any old where. It is my house, it is my shower. I don't care what it looks like.

Grant charged £200 a day for labour, plus his materials, and managed to do it all in five days. Altogether, it came to £1,600. A snip, I thought, for a unique, designer shower.

* * *

So it turned out rather expensive, that first year living on my own, with the summer house and garden and inside work.

Over £10,000 went down the plughole, well . . . some of it did. But what pleasure and purpose I will get out of it in my dotage. Not to mention the pleasure in knowing I will never spend any more on this house, ever ever again . . .

One of the minor domestic changes I have made – a habit rather than a physical alteration – is in my bed, in my sleeping arrangements.

Throughout our married life, Margaret slept on the left of our large king-sized double – as you look at it, standing at the bottom – and I was on the right. I can't remember how or when this began. Most long-time couples are the same – you get into habits and routines. Once established, you never change. Your body has adapted to it, puts itself down on the bed each night. You naturally fall into bed, any bed, in a hotel or a strange house, on your own side. Cuddling will seem strange otherwise, you tell yourself. You won't sleep unless you are in the correct, long-established marital positions.

I remained on my own side of our bed for a few weeks after Margaret died, without thinking about it really. Then I realised, I don't have to do this, crouch to one side. I can take over the whole bed, control the whole empire of the land of counterpane, as R. L. Stevenson described it in writing about his childhood bed. So I moved into the middle, stretched out, commandeered all the sheets and duvet and pillows.

By being now in the middle, I did not know at first which side to get out of – my old one or Margaret's. I had slept on the far side of the bed, near the window, while Margaret slept on the side nearer the door. This had been jolly handy in the years in which she got up first and went quietly downstairs to make my tea.

She would never do that again, so I decided to move right

over to her side of the bed, handy for the door, handy for getting up in the middle of the night. I have always got up at least once in the night for the lavatory, but now, as an elderly gentlemen, it seems always to be much more frequent.

So after a series of progressive nocturnal moves, I am now established on Margaret's side of the bed, nearest the bedroom door. I have got used to it, doing it without thinking. My body knows its new place.

Then one night I began daydreaming, or night musing: what if I ever meet a chum and we get into a sleeping situation, hmm hmm, and it turns out that she has gone though her life sleeping on Margaret's side of the bed? Where will I sleep? What will we do? Will it be non-negotiable? Will that be the end of a relationship, even before it has begun?

WISDOMS

- Living on your own you can cut corners, do bodge jobs, leave everything a mess, don't bother to tidy. Who will tell you off? The only inspector is yourself – and you don't care to do any inspecting.
- After a month without dusting the house, it gets no worse. Just more artistic. And it does provide a good protective coat for the furniture.
- You can save on dishcloths by only ever using your bare hands to wash up and clean the pots. Hands don't wear out or smell or go yucky and need replacing.

- What is the point of cooking a meal? Someone always eats it. So you have to do it all again.
- I would rather loll on the couch than clean underneath it.
- A garden is like a house: it does not need to be tidy. A clear-up once a season is quite sufficient. Do not let yourself become its slave.
- Cover everything in the garden in weeds – then you don't have to do any weeding.
- 'There is no need to do any housework. After the first four years, the dirt doesn't get any worse.' Quentin Crisp

JOYS IN OLD AGE

- A walk in the park.
- A walk on the beach.
- Grandchildren coming.
- Grandchildren going.
- Silence.
- Standing up without groaning.
- Sitting down ditto.
- Suddenly finding a lift.
- Or a handrail.
- A bus driver who lets you on or off between stops.

FACTS

- There are now 7.7 million single households in the UK – homes lived in by one person. In 1991, there were 6.6 million. The biggest increase in singledom is in the 45–64 age range – people who got divorced, a partner died or they never married.
- People who do not drink alcohol are more likely to take sick days off work than those who drink moderately. Obviously total boozers will not be able to get out of bed in the morning, but for we – er, hmm – moderate drinkers, knocking back three glasses a day perks us up to work and is a treat when the work is done.

6

MONEY MATTERS

One of the surprising things that has happened in my lifetime is that the elderly appear to have most of the money. Obviously this does not apply to all the elderly. There are loads of old people in poverty, totally dependent on the state or their families or charities. But thanks to the increase in property prices over the past fifty years, any homeowner, with almost any sort of home that they have managed to buy and pay for in their working lives, is sitting on a good lump of capital. This did not happen to the same extent to the generations that have gone before. In the case of my family and Margaret's, they never owned their own house, so they never accumulated any capital. Before the war, the majority of people rented.

Owning a house is in one way theoretical capital. You can't really spend it, just feel a small glow of contentment and pride and smugness every time you open your own front door and enter your own house. If you sell it, you will have to go and live somewhere else – and elsewhere, if half decent, will also be expensive. But of course you can downsize, as so many of my contemporaries have been doing, especially around this area of London, cashing in on the astronomical increase in house values, moving to a mansion flat beside the Heath, or moving to a smaller house further away, and giving the spare money to their children. You can of course spend it on yourself, blow it on wild living, mad self-indulgence, though people I know rarely seem to do this, apart from a cruise or a luxury holiday somewhere exotic. Alternatively, you can do good with your good fortune, which people often say they will do, then usually don't.

I did give £50,000 to Marie Curie after Margaret died. It was one of her last requests, nay, demands, as she felt so grateful to them, as did I. I promised to do it, so I could not very well go back on my promise. Anyway, with selling our Loweswater house, I did suddenly have some capital, which was half Margaret's anyway.

It was the same amount I had given a couple of years ago to the Cumbria Community Fund, an umbrella charity that distributes money quickly to other Cumbrian charities at times of need, such as when floods or foot and mouth hit. I was able to direct roughly where my donation would go. I said I wanted it to go to education and the arts in Cumbria, such as the Lakeland Book of the Year Awards. I began them over thirty-five years ago, and they now have a life of their own, with other folks doing all the real work.

At my age and stage in life, more money is not going to make much difference to me or what's left of my life. Margaret and I had a long innings, producing books for almost fifty years. I have also done journalism as well for most of those years, currently hanging on to three columns (once a month in the *Sunday Times* on money, in the *New Statesman* on football, both of which I have been doing for twenty years, plus a monthly column I have done for ten years in *Cumbria Life*. I also do six travel features a year for the *Mail on Sunday* Travel section). But mainly I look upon myself as a book writer. I've had a total of 100 books published so far, including children's books and books that are merely collections of my columns. Margaret always dismissed them as non-books.

Some of our books did well, others did averagely, quite a few in my case were total disasters that lost the publisher money. Authors do not lose if a book does not sell well, as they keep their advance anyway, but of course the publishers don't fall over themselves to commission another.

Margaret had no real failures, which is why she stuck with the same publisher, Chatto & Windus, for almost all her books. I have been totally promiscuous, often having three publishers on the go at any one time. If one turns an idea down, I try one of the others. If a book sells badly, I don't go back to that publisher, not for a while, hoping they will forget or new people will be in charge when I go back.

Being in work in my eighties is still a surprise. I never expected it would happen to me. I assumed by the time I got to seventy I would be well retired from most of my work, that my various publishers and newspapers and magazines would have given up commissioning me. I would be living on my pension and savings, trying not to upset the horses or be a bother to anyone, least of all my children. Now I boast all the time about how much work I have – which Margaret hated me doing, said it was appalling at my age, all this showing off. Do grow up, be your age and a bit more dignified.

I felt a small pang of jealousy in February 2018 when the *Sunday Times* hired a new radio columnist, Gillian Reynolds, who had done the radio for the *Telegraph* for over forty years. Hurrah to hiring elderly people, especially women. Should be more of that. Then I thought, *Hang on*. I did meet Gillian many years ago, and knew her husband at the time, Stanley Reynolds, who used to work on *Punch* with me. She must be, well, my age. So I contacted her, and it turned out she was born on 15 November 1935, making her two months older than me. Drat it. I can no longer go around boasting that I am the oldest columnist on the *Sunday Times*.

One reason for keeping on working is that I don't want my children to look after me, at least not financially. I hope to be totally self-sufficient and pay for my own care, till my old mind and old body have no idea what either of them is doing. Margaret and I looked after our parents from when we got to the age of fifty. We bought bungalows for them to live in, enabling them to leave their council houses, and paid all their bills from then on. We organised care when they got weak, or, in my mother's case, Alzheimer's. From about the age of seventy she needed constant attention. Eventually we brought her to London, moving her into a flat in our street where she had round-the-clock care. She died at seventy-eight.

I was in Venezuela at the time, working on a biography of Christopher Columbus. I called home to find out how things were. Margaret said my mother had just died. I am supposed to have said, 'You're joking.' I was never forgiven for this callous reaction.

My father died at fifty-three, after twenty years as an invalid, suffering from MS and becoming totally bedridden, so when I reached fifty-four it was a milestone in my life. I felt so pleased to have got there. And even more when I managed to make it to seventy-eight. Now I feel every year is a bonus.

However, if I don't get at least to eighty-four, which is supposed to be the average age for men like me these days, I will be furious and want my money back.

Money does make things run smoothly. Having money does make most people happier. So many of the boring day-to-day problems that most ordinary folks face are to do with money – for food, clothes, transport, heating, the children. So those problems are solved or lessened if you have money. But of course having money does not change your innate character. A depressive will still be depressed. I am still as mean and penny-pinching as I have always been, despite having money in the bank.

I often stand in the horrible filth and fumes of Kentish Town High Road after my swim, waiting at the bus stop with all the other poor, pathetic people dependent on public transport. When a black cab chugs past with someone lolling inside, or a chauffeur-driven Bentley glides its way up to Highgate, I tell myself I could afford that. Well, perhaps not the Bentley or chauffeur – steady on – but a taxi to take me home, every day, for the rest of my life. People in the queue don't know that, but I could. Oh yes, I have the money.

That impulse lasts about ten seconds. Then I sober up, remember who and what I am, and how I expect I will always be.

I always buy cheap stuff, special offers, two for one. I often have to wipe the mould off the two-punnets-for-£1 raspberries, and even throw away one whole punnet, but I still feel pleased with myself, having got a bargain.

So I remain at the bus stop, moaning about the long wait, looking a proper tramp in my horrible clothes, which I always wear when going swimming, though I rarely buy anything new anyway. I could probably buy my own bus and a driver and a conductor to escort me to my seat. But I can't do it – I can't recklessly spend or impulse-buy.

I used to blame my penny-pinching on being brought up in the war, with rationing, no bananas, wearing cardboard shoes, eating turnips for treats, keeping your clogs in the bath as there was no hot water, being urged by the king to waste not want not.

I often tell younger people that it is no wonder I ended up being pretty tight-fisted.

I could not of course ever say this in front of my wife. She had exactly the same upbringing as me, at the same time, in the same sort of house, yet she was totally the opposite of me when it came to money. She was not a spendthrift by any means, but if she wanted something, and it did not seem to her extortionate, she would pay the price.

She used to get furious with me for trailing up and down a high street looking for 50p less, even if I had already seen the exact thing I wanted three shops earlier. She would point out how much time I had wasted trailing around, all for 50p. It was false economy.

Whenever I was sent for the weekly shopping, which did not happen often, I would be given a list which always had at the top, underlined in her best handwriting: NO BARGAINS. NO SPECIAL OFFERS. NO THREE FOR TWO. I had to buy exactly what she had requested, at the price marked, and if there was none, on no account was I to buy anything else. She would manage.

Our three children are roughly like her, not really interested in money. The one most like me is probably Caitlin, in that she has always enjoyed charity shops, jumble sales and car boots. These days, now I am in my eighties, I hardly go to charity shops. The excitement of the chase has lessened, the stuff in charity shops now is all plastic rubbish, the bargains have gone. The shop manager can now go on eBay and see what stuff is worth, and put the prices up accordingly. But mostly it's because I now have no space. Having sold our Loweswater house and brought some stuff back, my own rubbish is already covering every surface. I really must start clearing out soon, or I know what will happen after I die. They will say the same as my wife would have done: 'Straight to the dump.'

And yet I do splash out on some things, such as lots of holidays. I always go club class on long-haul flights and travel first on Virgin trains when I go up to Cumbria. For the last eight years of her life Margaret was unable to travel, but before that, unless we went club class, she would not go anywhere. I seem to have picked up that disgustingly flash habit. 'I'll come to want,' as my mother used to say.

* * *

I realise all the time how fortunate I am. Imagine having to sell your own house, in which you have lived all your life and brought up all your children, in order to fund medical expenses or a decent care home in your dotage where they won't neglect or abuse you.

I am assuming that will never happen to me, that I will stay here, in this big house – far too big now for me of course – and when the time comes, I will use my untouched National Savings Certs to pay for my own expenses.

About thirty years ago my wife was walking along our street. She caught up with two men standing talking on the pavement. One of them was pointing out that further along the street someone had climbed onto a skip and was going through all the rubbish.

'See that bloke,' the man said to the other. 'You wouldn't think he was a millionaire.'

It was only when she got nearer that she realised the scruffy bloke was me – the one rummaging in the skip. My wife often told this story. To my embarrassment.

My own fault really. Not the fact of looking for treasures in a skip, which I still do, and am proud to do, but allowing people to believe I am well-off.

I first felt well off in 1960, the year I got married. I felt I had won the lottery, not in money but in luck and love, full of hope for us and the future. It was also the year I joined the staff of the *Sunday Times*. So I had a wife and wages.

In those days, most of the staff got a personal and confidential letter from the editor each Christmas saying we were being awarded a pay rise, usually another £100 a year. The implication was that it was private. You did not reveal it, or go around boasting. Which I always ignored. I felt it was a management con to keep us in our place. So if I got a raise, I always told everyone.

It was only after about ten years, having saved up each month to buy the usual domestic possessions – a bed, a couch, a car and then a house – that I began to feel wealthy financially.

By this time we had each done a novel which had become a feature film and I had also done the Beatles biography. We had a two-year spell we knew would never be repeated. And it never was. Tax at the top rate was 95 per cent. We saved a bit by going abroad for a year. When we got home we did what flash, newly well-off, working-class gits have always done – we treated our parents.

And then I foolishly went around telling friends that I no longer worked for money, which was stupid, pathetic showing off. What I meant was that if I really wanted to do a certain book, however niche and specialist, I was prepared to accept whatever piddling advance a publisher might offer. Between us we wrote ten books for no money at all – handing over all the proceeds to worthy bodies, such as Marie Curie, Shelter, the Multiple Sclerosis Society. So during those years, we worked for nothing.

Again, I went around letting it accidentally slip out, or boasting as it is often called, to my wife's fury. She never boasted or showed off in her life. It was mainly her idea anyway, pushing me into being generous.

The first week I ever got any wages, which was £14, back in September 1958 when I joined the *Manchester Evening Chronicle* as a graduate trainee, she said I must send £2 every week from now on to my mother – after all she had done for me. With my father an invalid, I still don't know how she managed.

I protested, saying, 'Not now pet, give us a break, it's my first ever money, I will do it soon, promise.' She said no, you must start as you intend to go on. So I did, posting two crisp pound notes to my mother every week. I put it up, year by year, as I got increases. Never once did it get lost in the post.

And of course I always let my generosity slip out, boasting as usual, hoping folks would say, 'Ahh, what a kind son he is, oh, bless.'

So, over the decades, I have brought it upon myself, boasting about how well-off I must be, hence friends and neighbours still go round muttering behind my back, 'Old Hunt, he must be worth a bob or two, lucky beggar.'

It isn't really true, of course. I am only comparatively well-off, not *really* well-off, not more than loads of our neighbours, for our area has come up over the years, with QCs and people who own their own publishing companies. But of course they don't boast.

I was unaware, till I came to London, of the middle-class pretentions of poverty, of never talking about money, except to deny it, moaning about the cost of a cleaner, or two ski holidays, or gosh, I just don't know how we are going to afford to send all three children to private schools. Which they always seem to manage.

I go mad when people say to me, 'Oh well, you can afford it.' I have two friends who are always making catty comments. 'Off on club class again, eh? Okay for you, wish I could afford it.' They titter and snigger and think they are being awfully amusing. Yet I know each is just as well-off as me.

Trouble is, I have told people for so long that I am well-off that I can't alter their perception. Too late now.

When I come back in life, next time round, I am never going to mention money, ever.

* * *

Since Margaret died and I have been living alone, life should in theory be much cheaper than it was living as a couple. But is this true? Is your outlay as a single really much less than as a double?

There is of course one new expense I had never had before – a cleaner. I could do it all myself, but it is so boring. It's the sinks, lavs and the bath that are the bugger. I do try to give them a quick wipe, when I remember, but I can never get them as clean as Maria does.

Even though I am shopping less and less, I have a Marks & Spencer card, a Morrisons card and a Co-op card. I always fall for the fantasy of getting points and free vouchers, in other words getting 2p back when I have spent £200. Oh rapture. But I rarely use any of my cards. I tend to pick up stuff at Lidl on the way home from swimming, depending on how the queues look. I press my snotty nose against Lidl's window then think, *Nah, I'm not waiting there, half of Kentish Town is already waiting inside. I'll just have toast when I get home. Yum yum.*

While I save money on buying food, I am spending loads more on caffs and restaurants. I reckon at least £30 a week goes on cappuccini – with a mid-morning one and afternoon one. I can get one in South End Green for £1.90 but it is a bit of a trek, so I stick to my two regular places round the corner, where it is £2.20. Oh no, breaking news: Bistro Laz beside the Heath, my favourite, has put their coffee up from £2.20 to £2.50. How will I cope?

Now and again I get caught out by one of those organic veggie hipster beardy places which look rough and ready and cheap – then the cup of coffee turns out to be £2.90! And titchy. By the left. I don't go there again.

I have lunch out locally around once a week with a friend, often a lady friend, and I usually talk them into going to the Bistro as it is so handy for me.

I try not to go into town for a meal, even though I am a member of the Groucho Club, and have been since it opened. I resent losing two hours of my life on public transport, even though it doesn't cost me anything with my Freedom Pass – hurrah.

Living on your own, the basic bills of course, like gas and electricity, are just the same – the meters don't know or care how many are in the house. My council tax has gone down a bit, I've forgotten by how much. I did fill in a form to say I was now a single occupant.

Spending that £8,000 recently on internal work was a one-off expense. It will never be done again. That's it. The house can now fall to pieces. But I will probably continue to spend money on the garden, such as £25 on a bougainvillea and £15 on a white wisteria. That is all indirectly the result of living alone. Being here all summer I want to brighten up my outdoor life. And myself.

I am drinking twice as much – a bottle of Beaujolais a day, or similar – now that there is no one here to say, 'Stop it, Hunt.' So that must be an extra £20 a week.

I am only cooking and eating for one, but I find I eat out more, spend more. Counting the cost of the cleaner, it roughly works out at around £100 more a week than before. Being alone is proving more expensive. Good job I have money.

But there are some very handy financial perks of being elderly, such as free travel on the bus and the London Underground, a free TV licence and the winter fuel allowance, for which I got £300 last year. With age you do feel the cold more.

But there are also extra expenses when you get old, such as car insurance. They practically double it if you get to eighty. Soooo unfair. As for travel insurance, they often won't even quote. Don't bother us, they say. Why don't you just stay at home and die?

All the utility companies try to take advantage of the old, which is also so unfair. It is a nasty surprise to get to this age and realise that loyalty is a dirty word. After all we went through – air raids, blackout curtains, Arthur Askey, rationing, saving waste paper in order to win the war.

People of my generation who were loyal to their country went on to be loyal to their gas and electricity suppliers, pension companies, railways, phone companies, insurance companies. And a lot of good it has done us. Being loyal, never changing or swapping, means we are treated as simpletons, there to be taken advantage of. We trusted them, believing they would always be fair to us. When we realise we are being conned, that we should take our business elsewhere, and the experts tell us to shop around, we do not have the knowledge, the time, the dexterity or desire to go online. The government should step in. Make it mandatory for loyalty to be rewarded, not penalised.

I do nothing – never swap or change, but just accept whatever they say the increased cost is now, out of inertia, laziness, not understanding or knowing how to go about changing. I can't face going online, getting in a state, wasting time when I could be profitably working. I reckon anyway that, as I have savings, I don't personally have to worry about being ripped off. I am a lucky one.

* * *

Should I give some of my money now to my loved ones, when I am still alive, and get the pleasure of seeing their little smiling faces? It is such a natural human thing to want to do this at a certain age, at a certain stage, as the end approaches.

My wife was always against giving or leaving any money to our children. Let Marie Curie hospices have anything that is left. Or the government, she said. I am sure they will know how to spend it wisely for the good of us all.

No, that wasn't her joke. She did not believe in inherited wealth.

I did agree with her, for a long time. We inherited nothing, bought our own house, and the car, and the tortoise, from scratch by working and saving. Why shouldn't our kids do the same?

For many years, in my twenties, I felt aggrieved when friends and colleagues acquired sudden sums, enough to put down a deposit on a house much better than the one we were struggling to buy. Not fair. Shouldn't be allowed. It was partly jealousy, of course.

But slowly I have changed my mind. Obviously I am not talking about mega sums, which will affect their lives, take away the pleasure of working and saving. No sensible person wants to do that. But I do now want to give them a little help from their friend – i.e. moi – a treat along the way.

Not sure I can explain the reasons, even to myself. I still feel guilty, that it is somehow morally wrong, should not be allowed. Yet it seems a natural, understandable desire to help your own flesh and blood.

I have brought them all into this life, and a pretty nasty place it is sometimes turning out to be in many ways, socially and economically and politically.

So how do I justify to myself changing my mind, and being willing to help my grandchildren, which I am sure Margaret would have been against?

The world is so different from when I was first married in the 1960s. Together, my wife as a supply teacher and I as a young journalist saved £1,500 in two years, enough to put down a one-third deposit on a house. Today, a similar young working couple would have to work and save for, I dunno, about 120 years, possibly 1,200 years, to acquire an average one-bed London property, possibly in Croydon. That is the first rationale I used to persuade myself. Secondly, they did not choose to be born in London. We brought them into the world here, so naturally their roots and friends are here. They would like to remain. While we never spent a penny on their education, we did end up giving them a middle-class lifestyle – while of course stoutly denying it at the time – with skiing holidays when they were young, a country cottage for weekends, wine at the evening meal. Their standards and expectations in life were dramatically different from our own, brought up during the war in Carlisle council houses.

I remember when one of our children returned from ten years in Africa, with a young baby and nowhere to live, she moved back in with us, to her old bedroom, for six months. She put her name down for a council flat – and I was desperate for her to get it. Not to get her out of the house, certainly not, but because I could go around boasting – council house to council house in just three generations. But then she found a flat.

The third rather specious argument is that millions of people, of all classes, rich and relatively poor, are currently helping their children or grandchildren get a foot on the property ladder. It is less unfair than it used to be, less elitist, in the sense that so many are managing to do it. Still does not justify it, but it is common practice. The Bank of Mum and Dad is now the biggest in the world, so up your bum, HSBC. The only bank that will soon be bigger is the Bank of Grandma and Grandpa. In the UK, it is how the housing market works. It would collapse otherwise.

I have talked in recent months to many folks of my age about giving money to their grandchildren and the same worries always crop up. What if they find out, and know what is coming, however small? What if they spend it on what you consider worthless, self-indulgent pleasures, wasting the money you sweated so long to acquire? Or, worse, some dodgy partner, male or female, comes into their lives and goes off with half – or all – of it?

I have several friends with their own companies who long ago made their children directors and shareholders, which is an easy way of helping them, but I haven't got a company and don't want to start one now.

I thought for a while about setting up a family trust, but I have an aversion to lawyers, accountants and tax advisors. They would charge. Then where would they invest it? All investments these days are rubbish. It would mean meetings and documents. I was appalled to be told that with a trust I might have to pay 20 per cent inheritance tax up front.

Buy to let? Put something in their names, till they are older and could run it themselves? That would teach them how the world works. No, too much of a faff.

Shares? That would be good, even though I personally have no shares, have never fancied them, yet I know from reading the Money pages that in the long run shares always do well, so they say. But they are too young for all that, at eighteen, nineteen, nine and ten.

National Savings, which I have loved all my life? I still approve of them, despite the low rates. By investing in them you do help the government and the old country, who need all the help they can get. And that's what I decided on.

With the younger ones it was easy. As a granddad, I was able to fill in the forms and send off the money in Investment Accounts, without them ever knowing what I had done. The interest at the time was piddling, only 0.45 per cent, but safe. With the older ones being over sixteen, I could not do this, so turned to Income Bonds, which at the time were paying a better rate – 1 per cent. They will provide an income every month, possibly £20, which I have told them will be my allowance to them, during their college and early working years. If they ever get to college, if they ever get any work. The capital would stay safe till I revealed all to them.

Alas, the world of investment has gone mad, and the fear of money laundering buggers up every transaction. I even had trouble moving my own money out of my own bank. I had to prove the young ones existed, with their parents submitting birth certificates. With the older ones, their banks at first refused to issue money drafts, made out to NS&I, demanding to know what it was all about.

Everything has now gone through and seems to be working, apart from a few hiccups. I have written a personal and secret letter to each grandchild, to be opened sometime in the distant future, full of jokes, funny things I was doing that day, which was New Year's Eve 2016. I explained that was the year their grandma died, so this in a way was partly an inheritance from her. I have put the same sum for each into NS&I, which will earn interest for a few years, and then in due course the capital will act as a modest deposit on a modest property – but only when they are in work, earning enough to pay a mortgage. I imagine this will not be until they are thirty. Perhaps sixty. Perhaps never. I won't be here of course, so their parents, and the letter I have left for them, will explain what my plan was, and my hopes and ambitions for them.

Have I done wrong? Am I spoiling them? I can hear my wife groaning.

But 'tis done. All I have to do now is live another five years. Wish me luck.

I have always been interested in money, but really it is such a boring subject. I have now decided I can't waste time earning money or thinking about money. I have better things to do. Such as living.

WISDOMS

- Count your blessings, not your billions.
- You can't take it with you – but you can shove it in some nice, worthy, amusing directions and die with a warm glow.
- You can never be too rich or have too many corkscrews.
- The nicest position in life is to be able to afford to not waste time making money.

QUOTES

- 'All things are obedient to money.' Horace, 68 BC
- 'Money is round and rolls away.' 1619 proverb
- 'The rule is not to talk about money with people who have much more or much less than you.' Katharine Whitehorn
- 'Business, you know, may bring money, but friendship hardly ever does.' Jane Austen
- John F. Kennedy was campaigning for the Democratic presidential nomination in 1960 and visited a coalmine:
    'Is it true you are the son of one of our wealthiest men?' asked a grizzled old miner.
    JFK said yes.
    'And you have never wanted for anything?'
    JFK nodded.

'And is it true you have never done a day's work with your hands in your life?'

'I guess so,' said JFK.

'Let me tell you something. You ain't missed nothing...'

- 'Money is like muck, not good unless it be spread.' Francis Bacon

- George Bernard Shaw was negotiating to sell the film rights of one of his plays to Sam Goldwyn. After long discussions, Shaw decided not to sell: 'The trouble is, Mr Goldwyn, you are interested only in art while I am interested only in money.'

- George Raft, the film actor, earned and spent $10 million in his working life. 'Part of it went on gambling, part on horses, part on women. The rest I spent foolishly.'

- 'There are few ways in which a man can be more innocently employed than making money.' Samuel Johnson

- 'No man but a block head ever wrote except for money.' Samuel Johnson

- 'Money can't buy you happiness but it does bring you a more pleasant form of misery.' Spike Milligan

- 'If you want to know what God thinks of money just look at the people he gave it to.' Dorothy Parker

- Tommy Cooper, after taking a taxi, would shove a tea bag into the cabbie's hand with the advice, 'Get yourself a drink, mate.'

- 'It takes a lot of money to live a simple life.'
  Johnny Depp

BUCKET LIST

If elderly people had the money, these are some of the
things they think they would like to do:

- Go on a cruise.
- Treat their children.
- Help their grandchildren.
- Drink more.
- Eat more cake.
- Spend it on the garden.
- Travel more.
- Wear purple.
- Give to charity.
- Find a toy boy/young lady friend.
- Deliver some home truths to their family and friends.

7

CHANGES IN MY LIFE

So what did I do with the money realised from the sale of our Loweswater house? Give it all to charity, having boasted I am so frightfully well-off? Well, I did give away those two lump sums. But not all of it.

Our Loweswater house was jointly owned by my wife, so I felt in a way the family already had a stake in it – and in the proceeds. I had offered it to the children to own it and run it, but none of them has got the same connection with the Lakes as we always had, though they did love it when they visited us.

After capital gains and others taxes and expenses were paid, I decided the money left from Loweswater should go into another house. And why not a seaside cottage for a change, after all these decades with a Lakeland cottage? And for a real change, why not somewhere on the south coast?

It was the south coast bit that made me feel slightly embarrassed and disloyal. After all the raving I have done about Lakeland in articles and books all these years, and all the books that Margaret wrote with a Cumbrian connection, surely I could not abandon the Lakes now, our birthright, our love heart, our joy for so long? It would feel as if I was sleeping with someone else if I turned my back on Lakeland now.

But then, I thought, the death of Margaret is the death of owning in Lakeland. I will still go up every few months, which I have done, and always will, on Margaret's birthday in May for example, which we always celebrated in Loweswater. I will visit her grave, see my old friends in Loweswater, in Cockermouth and Carlisle. I can still do all that, but why not also have a change of direction and scenery, culture and geography, go somewhere that is new to me, with which I and the family have no connection? In football, I always feel that English players should go and play abroad for a while. It benefits them as players and as people. A change is as good as a stimulant.

It would not be my sole decision, where we would look for a southern seaside cottage. I made that clear to the children from the beginning. This cottage would be in their names, they would have to pay the bills, look after it and run it. I might visit now and again, for the odd weekend, if invited, if allowed. All I would have to do would be to live for seven years, to save on inheritance tax. So they had better look after me, keep me alive. But where should we buy?

My first criterion was that it must be no more than one and a half hours on the train from London, preferably St Pancras. That is the most civilised station in London and very handy for my house. And I wanted it on a direct line, so as not to have to change trains, which immediately cut out nice places like Rye. Wherever it turned out to be, I never wanted to drive there. Done driving. All those years slogging up the M1 and M6 to Cumbria was often a nightmare with roadworks and traffic jams. Oh it can be such a fag having a country cottage – which is just how the middle classes always manage to moan about their incredibly fortunate, easy, well-upholstered two-house lives.

Would I be spoiling my children? Been through all that with Margaret over the years. She was against helping them. Nobody helped us, blah blah.

Margate was in all the property sections of the papers: the new groovy hot spot, artists flooding in, period cottages being practically given away. Tracey Emin came from Margate, now it has its own Tate gallery, there will be a boom soon, you'll see, so anywhere in Margate will be a marvellous investment. That's what the world and his wife and two nice children and their Range Rover were discovering about Margate, according to the property pages.

But I was not thinking of an investment. In my mind it would be a seaside cottage for the family, and all the grandchildren, and their children to come, and would stay in the family and be the family seaside cottage for ever. That was my fantasy, being a capitalist pig, with delusions of immortality.

However, we all went in turn to Margate, had a poke around, looked at several houses. Caitlin loved an open-air sea pool, as she is a passionate wild swimmer, and also loved a funny hotel she visited, but the others were not so keen. Margate did seem a bit depressing – only a small part of it was really nice.

We then looked at Whitstable. We had had many great outings there when the children were young. The brother of one of our neighbours had an apple farm nearby and we went down each year to pick apples and go on the beach. Whitstable is a lovely town, with a lovely main street, but I had forgotten I had never liked the beach. No real sand, mainly pebbles and mud, and the sea itself all seemed cloudy and muddy. And not cheap, compared with Margate.

I did like one house, right opposite Whitstable harbour. I rang up and made a bid to see what the reaction would be. It was on a busy road, so would be noisy during the day, and dangerous for the young ones. The agent selling it said we would have to pay their fee, the agent's fee, something I had never come across before. What a cheek, what a nonsense! The normal deal is that the vendor pays the estate agent's commission, not the purchaser. Anyway, the children did not like the house and I withdrew the offer.

Next we looked at Ramsgate, which I really liked, with its most interesting and active harbour, a long sandy beach and some handsome period houses. I made a bid for a Regency house in a perfect Regency square with a tennis court in the middle, not far from the front. There was a bit of a hill down to the harbour and beaches, which I might find difficult in the years ahead with my poorly knee, but I felt I could cope. It seemed an amazing bargain – just over £300,000 for a four-storey Regency house. Incredible compared with London prices.

The children turned their noses up. 'It's just like Islington,' one said.

'What's wrong with Islington?' I replied. 'You are such snobs.'

What sort of children have I got, I wondered? They should have been brought up in a council house during the war in the north. That would have fettled them, oh yes.

But I could see roughly what they meant. It was not the fantasy version of a seaside cottage they had in mind, something cottagey and seasidey. This was more like a London town house. They also pointed out that there was no back garden, not even a yard, just a sort of well at the back, all dark. So where would you sit out, to have your drinks in the summer as you do in your London garden? I hadn't thought of that. So I withdrew that bid as well.

Next we looked at Broadstairs. Margate, Ramsgate and Broadstairs are a linked trio of seaside resorts on what is called the Isle of Thanet in the county of Kent – all of it new to me. I had vaguely heard the name Thanet at election time, but didn't know exactly where it was. It is not an island, though presumably once was, or at least a peninsula. The three seaside resorts, in a line right on the south coast, three pearls on a string, have been popular with Londoners of all classes since Victorian days and the arrival of the railways. I did not know any of it.

The first surprise was the Thanet beaches – so many excellent ones, so much sand and space – unlike Brighton, which I have been to many times over the years. Brighton is attractive and lively, but the beach is a joke, totally pebbles. I could not believe it the first time I visited. Why had no one told me?

We all agreed Broadstairs was the nicest place we had visited – a proper seaside town, with a wonderful beach, promenade, sea walks, restaurants and handsome period houses. You walk out of the little station, turn left and catch a glimpse of the sea. You are on the main street, leading straight down to the beach. That's how seaside towns should be. At Margate and Ramsgate, the stations are awkwardly situated, the walk into town not as attractive.

Broadstairs has connections with Dickens, as it was his favourite seaside place, and was where Edward Heath was born – not that that is much of a recommendation.

We thought of course we had discovered Broadstairs on our own, but we soon discovered it is locally considered the nicest town in Thanet, with a better class of resident and better sort of tourist. So we were told. We also discovered almost at once that all the houses we fancied were 50 per cent more expensive than in Margate or Ramsgate. All the family loved it, and so did I. We made endless trips all that summer.

One day Jake and his wife Rosa rang to say they had found a cottage they absolutely adored and were sure the rest of us would. It was not in Broadstairs itself, but on another adjoining beach, just a fifteen-minute walk along the esplanade. No, there was no sea view, except if you leaned out from an upstairs window. And no, it was not actually on a beach. You had to walk for five minutes through a gap in the chalk cliff to a brilliant beach, just as big, just as sandy as Viking Bay, the main beach in Broadstairs itself, but much quieter and emptier.

I was intrigued by the name – Tait Cottage. The owner did not know why it was called that. Caitlin and I did some investigating, as we do love that sort of research. It turned out that the big period mansion next door was once the holiday home of the Archbishops of Canterbury, Canterbury being not too far away. In the mid-nineteenth century, a prominent Archbishop of Canterbury called Archibald Tait had been resident there. When a coach house was later converted into a cottage, it was named after him. We then found that Archibald Tait had come originally from Scotland, as I did. And that at one time he had been Dean of Carlisle, my home town, where Margaret was also born. Well, that clinched it. So we bought it.

It is their house, in their names, they pay the bills, they look after it. As I had intended, I am just an occasional guest. They all always drive there, which I hate. The one time I did drive there with one of them was on an August bank holiday and it took three hours. When I go on my own, and now sometimes with a chum, I go out of my back door, jump on the 214 bus to St Pancras, get the next train to Broadstairs, and I am there, door to door, in just over two hours.

So that is it and will be it for many years to come, as long as I have the puff and the knees.

It has been the biggest, most obvious single change in my life. So far. There could be more soon. Who knows? But Broadstairs has proved a new and fascinating interest, a new outlet, a new sensation, a new place to explore. Isn't that what we would all like to happen in our eighties?

* * *

Meanwhile, at home in London, I planned to make some changes to the house there as well. Which might or might not turn out to be just as monumental in my future life.

If you are going to consciously, willingly, want to make changes when you are into your eighties and suddenly living alone, you have obviously got to get your skates on. There might not be much time left, squire. Little point in sitting and moping, looking back at all the good times in the past. You have to work hard on the future, see it as an opportunity, a challenge, not a problem – which is the awful cliché they use in business and politics when something goes horribly pear-shaped.

Back in January 2016, when my wife was in the Marie Curie Hospice in Hampstead, I noticed one day that four beds were empty. It was the first time I had noticed even one bed vacant.

When next I met Philip, the palliative care consultant in charge of my wife, I said how surprised I was.

'Yet people must be dying to come into this hospice,' I said.

He sighed wearily. An old joke he must have heard many times.

He explained that the problem wasn't a lack of potential patients, but a lack of nurses to look after them. They could get doctors and also cleaners and basic care staff, but nurses were harder. Nurses, like schoolteachers, can't afford to live in London, hence many commute from miles away, living on someone's sofa during the week, going home at weekends, considering it worth it for their career. Till they can't face it any more.

After Margaret died, the top floor of our house hung over me – the waste of space, the guilt of spare rooms when London is full of homeless people. I read recently that in the UK there are 71 million unused rooms.

So I decided to ask Derek, an architect friend and neighbour, to draw up plans to make the top floor self-contained.

It was a flat when we first bought the house in 1963, but it was not separated from the rest of the house, and a sitting tenant lived there, which was how we managed to get the house for £5,000. Totally empty it would have been £7,500. It was lived in by an old woman who drove us mad. She had a kitchen, but not a lavatory or bathroom, so used to pad down all night long to use our lavatory, spraying it afterwards with some awful cheap Woolworths spray, so it smelled like a Turkish brothel – not that I know what one of those smells like. She had to use our front door and go up our stairs, which was another awful annoyance and inconvenience.

By the time we had three children, she had pro rata more space than we had, with the whole of the top floor. I eventually managed to buy her out, or at least get her to agree to move to another flat which I bought a few streets away.

For the next twenty years or so our three children lived on the top floor, each with their own bedroom, lucky them, plus a bathroom and shower.

When they all moved out, and we started going to Loweswater for half the year, we added a proper kitchen, out of the smallest bedroom, and made a proper flat in which we let people stay for free while we were away, to look after the house. It was still not separated – they had to come through our front door – but as we were not there, that didn't matter.

So the top floor had long had its own kitchen and bathroom, a bedroom and sitting room. All it really needed to make it a proper and separate flat was its own entrance, which we could easily create by installing an outside iron staircase in the side passageway, at the side of the house. The house is semi-detached, though it looks from the front as if it is in a terrace. I would lose the side passage, which would be a shame as it has been ever so handy all these decades. My neighbour next door had already installed an outside staircase, though she doesn't use it these days, so there was a precedent.

It needed a draughtsman to draw up plans for the whole house, with detailed drawings of every room, which I thought was potty, when almost nothing inside the house was being altered, so did I moan when I had to pay a cheque for £763. Then I had to pay £365 to Camden's planning department, just for them to get off their bums and be kind enough to consider my application.

But I did feel a warm glow, thinking of the good I was going to do when it was all completed and would be able to help someone.

Which was why I jumped the gun and contacted Philip, the consultant at the hospice. I told him that very soon I would have a flat that one of his nurses could have, rent free. He was well made up.

A few weeks later, still glowing with the warmth of my own virtue, I heard from Camden. Their traffic department was recommending refusal of my application. You can have fifty guesses at the reason, but I bet you still won't get it right.

It was because my application to separate my top floor had not indicated where space for four covered bike stands would be. Yes, *four*.

I don't have a bike, not with my dodgy knee, and I don't expect some poor shattered nurse coming back from her night shift will have a bike either. Yet Camden wants me to provide covered space for four.

The official letter from the planning officer said:

As per the London Plan requirements, each flat must provide 2, step-free, secure and fully enclosed cycle parking spaces (4 in total). In addition, the facilities must meet Camden's CPG7 requirements. This document can be found at the hyperlink below ...

I gave up reading at that point. Derek, the architect, just sighed and bunged in a proposal for four bike stands in my garage, hoping to meet their requirement.

Camden had described my plan as 'creating two flats', which rather threw me. It was technically true, but in my head I was not doing anything like that – I was simply adding a separate entrance to the existing top floor, and not changing any of the house internally. Very simple, so I had assumed.

I realised I had entered a mind field, I mean mine field – or do I? I could see ahead endless planning bureaucracy, health-and-safety laws, traffic regulations.

There would doubtless have to be two separate council tax bills, which obviously would come to a lot more than the one I pay at present. Then more rules and controls, fire and other regulations which I can't even imagine.

By this stage I had begun to fear that the shape and

CHANGES IN MY LIFE

atmosphere of the whole house would be spoiled by creating two separate flats. To keep Camden happy there would have to be a proper fireproof partition at the top of the stairs to the top floor. I would also lose some light on the staircase itself.

Whoever lives in the house in the future would of course turn back whatever I had done, making it one house again. They always do. People round here want whole houses, which is why all the sitting tenants have gone. Back in 1963 the street was full of them, with almost every house having at least one flat.

The estimate for all the work that would have to be done to separate the flat and install a complicated side entrance – if I ever got planning permission – was creeping up to almost £20,000. There was nothing in it for me, no financial returns. So I packed it in. By which time I had spent £2,000 on the draughtsman, architect and planning applications – all now wasted.

I then had the awful job of confessing to Philip at the hospice that the deal was off, the offer withdrawn. Why on earth had I jumped the gun and told him? Big Head, that's me, showing off, always wanting applause.

My wife always said I was a boaster, which I always denied. When asked how her work was going, she would change the subject. Ask me and I can go on about the amazing projects I am doing or about to do till you fall asleep.

Or, in the case of the upstairs flat to help a hard-up person, a project I was no longer doing.

A minor advantage of having someone in the flat upstairs would have been extra security. We had had people staying there for those six months when we were away in Loweswater not just to help them but to keep an eye on the house, make sure nothing had gone wrong. It was vaguely at the back of my mind, now I was living on my own, and often away, that it would be a good thing to have someone else in the house again.

I think one of the single most annoying, irritating and time-wasting elements of living on your own is having to stay in for parcels, gas engineers, workmen, Amazon deliveries. They never turn up when they say they will or when they are expected. Even when Margaret was ill in the last few years, and practically housebound, she was always in, never out, and able to open the front door – with a struggle.

It makes me so mad and furious when I come home and see a duplicated red note in the letterbox from the Royal Mail or some delivery man saying they have been and I was not in. Of course I was not in. I have a fucking life to lead. I think I swear more about that than anything else these days. But then we all swear more these days than we once did, particularly the elderly, particularly women. Oh yes. I have heard them, the most well-dressed, well-brought-up, ladylike women suddenly letting out all these expletives on the bus or in a shop. Initial shock and surprise is followed by amusement. I do think posh people swearing is funny.

When I have to collect an undelivered parcel, I have to trail down to the Kentish Town sorting office. I could ring up and arrange new delivery times, but it takes for ever to get through. Then the chances are I still won't be in when they call. I hate having to rely on neighbours to take my stuff in, for they have busy lives or are at their country home in the West Country or on hols in Tuscany.

So having someone else living here, upstairs in that empty flat, would help them and help me. They would be able to take stuff in and increase security.

* * *

One day, about six months after Margaret had died, I parked my car in my garage at the bottom of the garden and walked slowly across the lawn, carrying some of my shopping. I had been to Morrisons, my monthly Big Shop, the biggest item being thirty-six bottles of Beaujolais. As always, they said to me at checkout, 'Having a party? Can I come?' And, as always, I said, 'No, it's just for the weekend.'

I noticed a plank of wood up against the back door. *How strange. It wasn't there when I left*, I thought. *Has Jake, my son, come round to do some jobbies?* The back door was locked, as I'd left it, but the moment I stepped inside I noticed my iPhone had gone from the dining table. I remember having thought, *Should I take it?* And then thinking, *Nah, I don't want to be bothered*. I hate carrying things – don't even like wearing a watch – so I had left it on the table.

My iPhone was clearly not there, but had I perhaps forgotten where I'd put it? Or had someone got in and taken it? But how?

I went upstairs and immediately realised my new MacBook Air laptop, which had cost me £900, had gone. Bloody hell. What had happened?

I went into my bedroom, looked out of the window and there was a pane of glass lying neatly on the flat roof of the back addition.

I rushed downstairs and saw there was a gaping hole in the roof of the back addition, where one of the glass panels had been taken out. Yet I had not noticed.

So began a lost week, seven days in my life I hope never to be repeated, in which I grew more and more stressed as I tried to cope with the boring, routine aftermath of a very simple, very basic, run-of-the-mill burglary.

They had got in by breaking down the door to the side passage of the house, gone round the back, then climbed up on the back addition roof, removed a glass panel and jumped down into the kitchen. No damage was done in the house itself, not even to the glass, which was why I had not noticed.

I had been out just two hours, between nine and eleven on a Saturday morning, and none of the neighbours had noticed or heard anything. The burglars were so brazen and daring, and yet so neat.

As well as the iPhone and laptop, they had taken the front door keys when they let themselves out, and also for some reason my spare remote key to the electronic garage door. Not much really. They must have been in a hurry, realising I was not far away.

I dialled 999. One officer arrived in ten minutes, a forensic expert, who said sorry, he could not stand on a chair. 'Health and safety.'

A police constable and a policewoman soon followed, upset that they had been beaten by forensics. They turned out to be ever so helpful. The policeman went up on the roof, without any moans about safety. He put the glass panel back in its place, without being asked, and did a temporary seal with some gaffer tape. He then went to the garage and brought in the rest of my shopping, which I had still not taken out of the car. So kind. Being eighty, and looking it, can prove a plus. I find if I stand around looking confused and dopey, people do help.

The policewoman turned out to be from Carlisle, my home town. We chatted about where her mother lived. And yes, she does read *Cumbria Life* – never misses an issue.

After the cops had left, I spent the next ten hours on the phone and the computer, effing and blinding, shouting and moaning. I was trying to get through to O2 about my phone, my insurance company LV, a locksmith, a glazier, plus my bank and Visa card people, fearing I had left vital details on my mobile phone.

It drove me furious, trying to get any human beings to answer. Most had an automatic response, which fooled me every time, making me think, *Hurrah I have made contact*, saying your call is vital, we will respond as soon as possible. Which turned out to be rubbish. It was a Saturday, so all humans had left the planet. Being burgled on a weekend is like going into a hospital at a weekend. You pray it will never happen to you.

It was all made doubly annoying by being on my own. There was no Margaret to moan to, share decisions with, tell me not to be so manic, get it in proportion. Most of all there was no one to stay in when I had to go out, wait in for cops to come or for the glazier to eventually turn up.

It was not the money that really mattered – around £2,000 worth of stuff taken – but the hellish drag of trying to cope, my mind in a whirl, not knowing what to do next, who to contact.

When the locksmith did eventually come, I rushed downstairs to answer the door, forgetting that I had been on the computer in the middle of a so-called internet chat with O2. When I got back upstairs, I had been cut off, logged out. It had taken me ages to get through to them.

I started trying to play the glad game – the house had not been wrecked, they did not take the iMac computer on which I do all my work. Too big to carry, I suppose. And ten years old, so hard to sell. I did not feel scared that they would come back when I was in the house alone. Just furious.

I was still counting my blessings six days later when my younger daughter Flora arrived with my two younger granddaughters, bringing me meals on wheels, one of my wonderful food fairies. She put the food in my fridge and offered to change the sheets on my bed, which I hate doing. I said there was no need, I changed them two months ago … okay then, go on.

Sienna, then aged eight, was looking at my shorts, which I was wearing as I now do most of the time from May to October, whatever anyone ever says. Margaret never liked me in shorts, but hard cheese. She can't say anything about it now.

'You've got young legs, Humper,' said Sienna.

'Humper', a combination of Hunter and Grandpa, is used by all my four grandchildren. It's their own invention, which I rather like. Sometimes they spell it in notes to me as 'Humpa', sometimes 'Humper'. The *Oxford English Dictionary* has not yet decided on the precise spelling.

'Oh, thank you,' I replied. 'What about my face? Have I a young face?'

Sienna paused, giggled, looked a bit embarrassed.

'No …'

It reminded me of our son Jake when he was seven. One day he said to his grandmother, 'When are you going to die, Grandma?'

'Soon, I hope,' she replied.

While Sienna and I were idly chatting, Flora suddenly reappeared downstairs, clearly very distressed. She announced that Mum's wedding ring had disappeared.

I had been handed Margaret's ring by a nurse at the Marie Curie Hospice the day she had died. The nurse was laying out the body and asked if I wanted the ring. She sprayed the finger and eased it off. I brought the ring home and put in on the mantelpiece shelf in our bedroom. My fantasy was to offer it to the first of my four granddaughters, if and when they ever got married.

It is in white gold, not very valuable, rather a broad band, with a sort of leaf engraving. I dug out a photo of my wife wearing it and sent it to my friendly policewoman from Carlisle. Would it ever turn up? Who knows? The kids who did the robbery probably threw it away, or sold it for 50p.

The insurance company, after a lot of forms and faffing, agreed to pay me the full value of the stuff stolen. But of course the ring was sentimentally and emotionally valuable. No money is going to make up for that.

After the burglary, I decided I had better be sensible for once. Over the fifty-five years here we have been burgled three times, which is a low rate for London and this area. Once it was our fault, leaving a bedroom window open in a heatwave. Another time we had workmen in and they left a makeshift front door which was easy to push in. Another time I had left the front door wide open and some chancer walked in, cleared the hall shelf of keys, a camera and a phone.

Nothing serious was ever stolen – as we don't have expensive things in the house. In the past I have had valuable items in the house, though it would have taken someone really knowledgeable to identify them, such as my nine Beatles manuscripts. They have long gone to a safe place, the British Library, in the manuscript room next to Magna Carta, Shakespeare, Beethoven and Wordsworth.

But I don't want anyone breaking in again, whatever piddling stuff they might steal. So I decided I would have to have a burglar alarm.

What a mistake that has been. I now hate it, almost as much as being burgled. It seems to go off all the time. The children and neighbours are regularly being rung up when I am away. An automated message gives them a telephone warning. They come round and find no one has broken in. When they tell me later, I have to grovel and apologise.

Maria, my cleaner, can't cope with it, refuses to take in the password or instructions, so when she is due to come I can't leave it on if I go out.

I have tried to cancel it, but apparently I have taken out an eighteen-month contact and I will still be charged a monthly fee even if I cancel. I have another year to go. Can't wait.

I am surprised burglars can be bothered these days to get out of bed and leave their homes and trail around the streets searching for some easy-looking house to break into. Mine must have been pretty stupid ones, unable to do anything else to make easy money, such as sell drugs or, even easier, so we are led to believe, commit some sort of cybercrime. I have had my Visa account broken into and about £2,000 taken from my account in two minutes. Almost everyone you speak to these days has been the victim of some sort of internet fraud. You just yawn when they start to tell you. It's as boring as their bad back.

The burglary made it more disappointing that my plan had collapsed to have a nurse living on the top floor, coming and going through her own separate side entrance. It would have helped with the security of the house. And been an interesting experiment.

Then, out of the blue, old friends of ours who live in York, whom we had known from our schooldays in Carlisle, contacted me about their daughter. She was looking for a London flat for two nights a week for a year, as she was being seconded to London on some medical research project.

Hmm, did I really want some young woman coming through

my front door, going up my stairs? What if she sang when she came home late, or staggered, or smelled of cheap perfume? I hate all perfumes. (Sauvignon Blanc, that would be okay.) Or brings a bloke back?

I had met her, some years ago, and knew she was very respectable, but all the same, when I invited her to come and see the flat I made it clear that there was to be no singing, no dancing, no pets, no entertaining. Oh, I can be a right sod.

She has been living with me now for a year – and it has worked out perfectly. She has her own house in the north-east, comes down on the train early on the Monday morning, goes to work, then comes home to my flat in the evening at about six-thirty.

I often don't hear her come in, as I am sitting reading the paper and having a glass or three. When I go upstairs to watch the football on the telly I can sometimes hear vague movement in the room above. I thought at first it was mice, or burglars, forgetting I had a lodger. She leaves at eight in the morning, when I am in my bath, and I hear the front door close. Just two nights a week.

She is a doctor, doing research at some government medical centre in north London. I thought, *Brilliant, just what I want*. She can have a look at my back, check my hearing, make herself generally useful. It's what all elderly single blokes fantasise about. Not a dancing girl living with them, but a doctor or nurse on tap.

I am charging her a small amount for the nights she stays, as she does have two rooms, a kitchen and bathroom to herself – a modest contribution towards the heating and cleaning. Surely she would be willing to share some of her expertise? I hung around the front door a few times in the early weeks, before she went upstairs, and said, 'Er, like to join me for a drink in the garden, pet?' Then I brought the subject round to bad backs, how she ever dealt with them.

Turns out her speciality is public health. Bloody hell. No good to man or beast. I don't think she has looked at bad backs for years, since she was at medical school. Should I be about to start a national campaign to help AIDS sufferers, or launch a new form of flu jab, I am sure she would prove jolly useful.

So, alas, I am not getting medical help. But I am getting a warm glow from helping a medic. It is one of the changes in my house, and in my life, which has 'worked out champion', as Margaret's father always used to say, whenever he was pouring HP sauce onto his bacon and eggs or his sweet peas were coming into bloom. It all 'worked out champion'.

More and more young people choose to live alone. Older people are usually alone through circumstances. For whatever reason, half of single people have a spare room, not used full-time.

CHANGES IN MY LIFETIME FOR THE BETTER

- More diseases are treatable.
- Housewives do not live a life of domestic drudgery.
- There is less poverty in the world.
- Smoking is banned in most public places.
- Smog has gone from London.
- Computers.

- Emails.
- Enormous choice of TV channels.
- Dads are more involved in family and domestic life.
- More female equality and less prejudice.
- Cheap foreign travel.
- Better, wider choice of food.
- Mixed marriages (In Britain, it is now reckoned there are more interracial marriages than in any other European country.)
- We live longer. Well, we did till this year. Now longevity appears to have peaked or reached a plateau. Since the last year, every decade average life expectancy for all men and for women has gotten longer. Five years ago it had reached eighty-two for women and eighty for men. Since then, there has been no increase. Some even expect it to start to go down. It could be because of austerity, poverty, cuts in NHS spending, obesity, diabetes.

SOME THINGS ARE NOT QUITE AS THEY USED TO BE

- Streets were so quiet, with few people having cars.
- You could play out till dark and feel safe.
- Bobbies on the beat.
- Families ate together at mealtimes.
- People were politer and had more respect for each other.

- Life was slower.
- Free university education.
- Things were made to last.

8

HOLIDAYS

I was in Bequia in the Grenadines on hols. I went into the little harbour at Port Elizabeth and bought four pretty postcards and stamps to send to my four granddaughters. How caring, how thoughtful.

Except I had forgotten their addresses. I sat there, licking my pen. I know one lives in a street beginning with an L and it's number 96, or could be 76. As for postcodes – no idea. How could I not know, when they all live just a few streets away from my London house, and have done all their lives?

The answer is that Margaret did all that. Just as she knew all their phone numbers and mobiles and dates of birth. In her head, she carried about fifty phone numbers and about fifty dates of births, including those of all the royal family. Gone, all gone.

Yes, I know it is mental laziness, but it was one of the jobs we divvied up. I drove the car and she remembered the names and addresses and phone numbers and dates of birth of the relations we were going to see. Then, when we had parked, she would remember where we had parked.

Bequia was one of several holidays I have had since she

died, in which I've missed her in so many ways. I missed discussing with her all the people met during the day – Goodness, what was she wearing? What a bore that bloke was ... Or the food ... I shouldn't have had the flying fish, you chose well, pet, picking the barracuda, my fish was horrible. On your own, nobody knows, nobody cares what you have seen, what you have eaten.

I have always specialised in overheard conversations, bringing them back from bus stops or train rides, bits of chats picked up while meeting folks. I have acquired so many on my recent hols on my own, but I cannot unload them. They were piddling anyway, nothing that in twenty-four hours I hadn't forgotten, but they lie in the dark at the back of my brain, unloaded, unheard.

Eating alone I don't find such a hardship, at least not when I am on my annual January trip to the West Indies. We went to the same hotel in Barbados, Cobblers Cove, from 1986 onwards, the one we went to on my fiftieth birthday. Because of the time difference, and because we went by Concorde, we got to Barbados before we left London and were able to have two breakfasts on the same day.

But in the last seven years of her life, because of all the horrible treatment and drugs, she could not travel in planes any more. She insisted I still went in January on my birthday to Cobblers Cove in Barbados, or the Bequia Beach Hotel in Bequia, our number-one favourite Caribbean island. Because we had been going to the same places for so long, we knew all the regulars.

Going there on my own, I am always looked after by the regulars, some of whom I have known for twenty years, who invite me to join them at supper.

But since Margaret died, I have branched out, been to quite a few new places, or places where I know nobody. Having a holiday on your own and in a strange place is hard for most single people.

Should you find yourself alone in a hotel restaurant, try to get in early. The waiters will make a fuss of you, serving you quickly, as they want you out, sharpish, not hanging around cluttering up the place, looking pathetic, setting the wrong tone. Pretending to read a book is also pathetic, but writing occasional stuff in a notebook is good. I always do that, whenever I am on my own. In most cases, anyway, I will be writing a travel feature. The waiters don't know this and worry you might be a management spy.

Sleeping alone on hols is of course sad. On the other hand, you can go to bed when you like and have all the bed to yourself and you don't get woken up by someone snoring. Margaret did sometimes snore, but she always denied it.

Probably the best thing about having a hol on your own is that you are always open to offers. If someone suggests something, anything, any time, I always say yes. My wife's first response to almost all social invitations was to say no, managing to think up an immediate and totally convincing lie about why she could not make it.

I, on the other hand, always reply yes, lovely, without really thinking it through, or checking my diary. I now constantly find myself not just double booked but triple booked, having to rush round like an eejit or forced to cancel something. So often, when the times come, I deeply regret what I have agreed to do.

On your own, you can go off without consulting your partner if someone suggests a jaunt, a sail, a walk, an expedition, another rum punch. You have no one else to consider or to point out that you have already had two rum punches today and it's only eleven in the morning.

On your own, however, there is the burden of having to sparkle, to entertain, to pay your way by being good company. With your loved one you can just slump, or drone on about the same old subjects – Do you think I have put on weight? I think my tan is peeling. I am sure this filling has come out, I'll open wide, please have a look, oh go on, I'll be your best friend.

Being poorly on hols, that is a real drag on your own. Two years ago at Cobblers Cove I spent two whole days in bed being sick and feeling hellish. For the first day, nobody knew, nobody cared that I was too ill to move, till I started pathetically ringing fellow guests and asking them to bring me some dry toast please.

On your own, there is nobody to moan to about a spot or a sore bit or a cold coming on which you are sure is flu. What do you think I should do, pet? Should I take something?

Oh just shurrup, that's what you should do, was usually my wife's reply. She often asked me to do her a favour and not talk for the next half-hour.

On that Bequia holiday, with the postcards, I solved the problem of not having the address of my grandchildren by sending a text message on my mobile to my son and two daughters saying, 'Quick, what is your address and your full postcode? I want to catch the post.'

My wife could not have done that (not that she needed to). She never used a mobile, or a computer, or sent an email or text in her life. All the information she needed was in her head.

* * *

The new places I have been to since she died have included Thailand, which was a press trip, to write a feature for the *Mail on Sunday*. If she had been alive, I might not have gone all that way, especially in the last year or so when she was getting weaker.

So I have been freed, if that is the right word, to go as far as I like, and as often as I like. I can't remember them all, but this last year I have also been to France, Greece, Italy, Mallorca, Portugal, Grenada in the West Indies, plus my normal January West Indian jaunt to Barbados and Bequia. I hope to be able to visit Bequia every year for ever, as it is my favourite Caribbean island, but I have given up on Barbados. Last year was my last visit to Cobblers Cove, after thirty years. It is too expensive. Yes, I can afford it, but it is not worth it for what it provides. Barbados has lost its charm; so much of it just feels like the Med, or Chelsea. It all began to change when they stopped growing plantations and started growing golf courses.

I said I would never go on a cruise again. For lots of reasons. It is a cliché, and also pretty true, that the elderly love cruises – they are so simple, so organised for you. I had been on three over the years, in order to write travel features, all of them five-star cruises, one of them on a proper sailing ship. All were incredibly luxurious, but I felt so bloated afterwards. You can't really have a proper walk on a ship, however big, and the swimming pool, however luxurious the ship, is rarely bigger than my bath.

And also, well, they are pretty nearly always full of folks like me – old. I can meet those at home. I do like a variety of ages in my social life.

So I told myself I was never going on a cruise again, not at least till I am really old – which, blow me, I now am. Not just old, but also a widower. So when the suggestion recently came, I thought, hmm, I would give it another chance.

It was with Oceania, a cruise company I had not been with before, on a ship called the *Rivieria*, noted for its high-class food and for holding 1,250 passengers and 800 staff. If you had never been a cruise before, your first impression would be, *Wow, what a whopper, wouldn't like to see that parked in our street.*

On the way there, on a Ryanair flight to Pisa to board the ship at Livorno, I had a bit of a disaster. I had my pen round my neck, my best Hi-Tecpoint rollerball, not cheap. I rarely wear a jacket, so I always have a pen round my neck on a string in case someone says something amusing, informative, wise or really stupid, so I can lift it and use it in a column somewhere.

The plane zoomed up in the usual way planes do, the air pressure became intense and my ears popped. Then my pen exploded all over my suit. Yes, I was wearing a suit, a rather natty lightweight from Marks & Spencer, bought only twenty years ago. I was told that on the *Riviera* not only would the food be fab but we had to look smart for dinner.

Not a good start. I wondered if I could sue Ryanair for, er, not sure what. But it meant for the four days on board I had to keep my hands over my groin to cover the two huge pen blobs.

As usual on a cruise, I spent the first two days lost. With fifteen decks and corridors the length of Wembley, all looking much the same, I could never remember my deck, which way to turn out of the lift, or the number of my cabin. Correction – luxurious veranda suite. Cruise liners do have poncy titles these days. In fact, on the *Riviera*, all the suites have verandas, which is a huge plus. They also have a resident artist. Very arty.

As ever, about the best fun on a cruise is waking up as you

sail into a new place – looking at the new harbour, new city, wondering how you got here.

In four days, I did Italy (with a chance to explore Pisa and Florence), Monaco, Marseilles in France, ending in Spain at Barcelona.

We old cruising hands know from experience you don't have to join an organised excursion. In most ports, you can just walk into town, or use their little boat, then get a taxi, or the ship's shuttle bus, if they have one, and explore on your own. Far better than being herded around with a bossy boots holding up a flag and talking non-stop, half of which you can't hear and the other half not understand.

Another nice thing about cruising is sailing off again, into the sunset, while you have your cocktails or stuff your face. Cruise liners do tend to sail at night, not day time, so you don't have to stand around all day looking at that boring flat watery thing, or the sea, as it's often called.

The cruise entertainment, as ever, was a good laugh, like 1950s Butlins. The crooners and young dancers were ever so energetic and wholesome, never rude. And I should think not. We oldies don't like rude. Behind the scenes, though, goodness knows what might go on.

So I did quite enjoy it. I had only one complaint – the awful piped music round the pool, too loud, too crappy.

Would I go again? Yeah. But not on my own, and only when I get really, really, *really* old. Such as next week . . .

* * *

I have also travelled quite a lot in the UK this past year or so, mainly to literary festivals. I had decided to cut down on them in recent years, feeling I had outgrown them. Over the decades, I had been to most of the main ones at least once, such as Edinburgh, Cheltenham and Hay on Wye.

Margaret gave them up long before me. About twenty years ago, she had it agreed with her publisher that she did not need to go to them, ever again, or do any signing sessions or visit bookshops.

But on my own, after she died, I started accepting most things, if half decent. A big attraction was that everything was organised for me, so I didn't have to go online and try to book hotels and trains, which I hate. I may be a techie compared with Margaret, but I still make a mess of ordering stuff online and get in a froth.

So I found myself last year going to book festivals in Cheltenham, Stratford, Hexham, Chiswick, Durham, Kew and probably another two I have forgotten.

Book festivals have seen a massive growth in the past ten years and there are now about 500 in the UK, often in remote, isolated towns, hellishly complicated to get to. Hay, for example is a nightmare to get to, yet that is one of the biggest and best.

I think the main reason they are so popular is that in this age of wall-to-wall, screen-to-screen, round-the-clock packaged entertainment, people like to get off their bums and go out and see and hear someone performing in the flesh.

Readers fall in love with authors, or are intrigued by them, want to see what they are like, if only to say, 'What a scruff, much fatter than I thought and what a bighead.'

Why do authors do it? That is not quite so obvious. Vanity of course. Getting out of the house instead of sitting alone looking at the screen or more likely out of the window.

Publishers push their best authors. The book festivals look at the catalogues for the next season and say to the publisher's publicity department, 'Oh, I would love to have that mega-famous author' and Publicity says, 'Yes, I might be able to arrange it, but I would like you to take this brand-new unknown novelist as well.' So there is some horse-trading.

The economics do not quite make sense. The publisher will probably pay £200 for the author's train journey to, say, Carlisle, as star authors insist on going first class, while the book festival will pay for the hotel, meal and drinks, which can easily be £200. Yet even big names rarely sell more than twenty books, resulting in no more than £40 in royalties for the author. Publishers tell themselves it is worth the money to promote the author, raise his or her profile in the local area.

Book festivals pay the author a fee – usually £100–150. (Borderlines in Carlisle pays £200, hurrah, but Keswick's Words by the Water pays nothing, boo.) The Society of Authors insists authors get paid – in the past not all did – despite charging around £10 for a ticket and hoping to get 200 in the audience. Many book festivals are now big business, with at least one person paying themselves a full-time salary all year round.

In her early writing years, when Margaret did go to one or two, she felt afterwards it was a waste of her time and energy. She did not like the part of herself that enjoyed performing, talking about herself, showing off.

I quite enjoy that bit, especially now I am on my own – much more than the old literary lunches.

Lit lunches were the main public performances for authors back in the 1960s when we first got published. You would slog up to Leeds for the Yorkshire Post Literary Lunch, have an awful chicken lunch, sitting beside some local councillor making inane conversation, waiting for your turn. They usually had three authors and each had fifteen minutes to push their latest book or at least attempt to amuse the ladies of a certain age in their best frocks. It became an unspoken competition to see which speaker sold most, the winner usually being from the telly, someone really famous, a soap actress or weather forecaster. They did not put you up for the night, so you dashed for the train home, having sold three books, vowing never to do another.

Book festivals are much better. You perform solo in the main, have an hour to make your pitch, in a theatre or similar, as opposed to a hotel dining room, and it can be quite jolly. There is usually a green room, where you can eat and drink and meet other authors. In the case of Borderlines, the annual book festival held in Carlisle, I had the pleasure of meeting up with my daughter Caitlin – and also appearing with the string quartet of the Liverpool Philharmonic Orchestra.

What? Yes, you heard. I hope you are not getting as deaf as me. I performed on stage with a top string quartet.

We all look back in life and remember the turnings we never took, the possibilities we spurned, the girlfriends/boyfriends we missed, the jobs we might have had if we had had the Latin. I sometimes – well, for about ten seconds – imagine I might have ended up being a violinist, if life had panned out differently, if I had been any good at it.

I find it hard to believe it now but when I was a boy in Carlisle I went to violin lessons. If I had to meet that lad today, coming down Caird Avenue on the St Ann's Hill estate carrying his violin, I would simply not recognise him. Not just the look of him, but what was in his mind, what he was thinking, what he was hoping for in life. I suppose that applies to most people. The past is a different place. And we were different people.

Goodness knows how my mother could afford it. More

mysteriously, why did I go for so long when I was so useless? I think it was my mother's wish. Her dad had played the fiddle, self taught, and she wanted me, as the oldest child, to do the same. My violin teacher was called Alf Adamson. His day job was delivering packets of Rington's tea, door to door, in a little van. I think when he realised my mother's situation, he probably either did not charge her anything, or very little.

One year he put me in for the Carlisle and District Music Festival. I came fourth in the under-fifteen violin section – out of four.

During those five years or so struggling with the violin, I did eventually become awfully keen on classical music. I played in the school orchestra, went up each year to the Edinburgh Festival and down to London for the Proms to see my heroes, Isaac Stern and Yehudi Menuhin.

In the 1950s, rock came in. Then the Beatles arrived. And that was it. I turned my back on classical music. For ever.

Until, in 2017, out of the blue, a cellist at the Royal Liverpool Philharmonic Orchestra contacted me to say their string quartet was doing a concert and would I like to be involved.

I thought for a moment they wanted me to play the violin, wondering how on earth they had heard I once played. Turned out they wanted me to talk, not play.

The result was a concert at the Liverpool Philharmonic Hall in March 2017. The quartet played Beatles tunes and I introduced each one, telling the stories behind each song. They could have sold out the tickets three times.

I was so pleased to have done it, to have said yes to what appeared a bizarre request, something I had never done before. There were five musicians in fact, for the four string players were joined for our Beatles concert by a keyboard player, Mike, a GP in real life who was about to begin a degree in music at Liverpool University. He played the keyboard and the mouth organ. Which rather ruined a joke I had been labouring over for my introduction.

We were going to play 'Love Me Do', the Beatles' first record, to begin our concert, and of course a feature of that was John Lennon on mouth organ. I said I had wondered how a string quartet was going to manage it – then remembered they were the Liverpool Philharmonica Orchestra. That was the joke, in case you missed it. The audience did laugh, then I had to reveal that the musicians that day did include someone on a mouth organ.

We all enjoyed it so much, myself and the musicians, that afterwards we vowed to go on a world tour. Getting a bit carried away. But we did do a UK tour, starting with Carlisle, my home town, appearing at Borderlines in September 2017. The festival is centred round the Crown and Mitre Hotel, the poshest in the city, with imposing bars and a wood-panelled dining room, which I was too nervous to venture into as a boy. It also has a grand ballroom, and it was here on 8 February 1963 that an unusual incident happened in the early touring life of the Beatles.

They were on tour, but down the bill, not yet getting the girls screaming. 'Please Please Me' had been released but was not yet at number one. The tour was topped by sixteen-year-old Helen Shapiro. They played that evening at the Lonsdale, then a big cinema, now demolished, and afterwards the Beatles walked a few streets back to their hotel, the Crown and Mitre.

They realised when they got into their hotel rooms that they were starving and so went looking for something to eat – and wandered into the ballroom where the annual dinner dance of the Carlisle Golf Club was in full flow, with all of the guests in evening dress. The Beatles helped themselves to some food and Ringo started jiving with Helen Shapiro. The good golfing folks of Carlisle were appalled by the look of these scruffy, uninvited interlopers, with their long hair and leather jackets, and they were soon asked to leave. The story made the northern editions of the national papers. The Beatles were described as 'Helen Shapiro's backing group' who had got themselves ejected from a provincial ballroom. It has since gone into Beatles mythology, known about by most true fans.

So it seemed neat to be going to play a Beatles concert in a ballroom where the Beatles had been and perform there with four gifted musicians from Liverpool.

I wondered if I should take my fiddle and my bow, check the strings? I think they are still in the loft somewhere. And check if I still have any resin, that funny block of what looked like hard Pears soap which you used on your bow, rubbing it on the block, producing a sort of grey dust. I loved doing that – it seemed so professional, and I loved the smell it created – far more than playing the actual violin.

The quartet members are all top professionals. My new friend Hilary, the cellist who first wrote to me, is deputy lead cellist, while the violinist Jim is leader of the whole orchestra – a body some ninety musicians strong.

And yet beforehand I still had a fantasy that one of them would get lost or delayed on the way up from Liverpool to Carlisle. Is there a violinist in the house? So the cry would go up. I would modestly step forward. With a bit of luck I would be able to spin out resining my bow while still talking about the Beatles for the whole concert.

For this second appearance in public with the Liverpool

String Quartet I also performed. Oh yes. It meant I had to join the Musicians' Union and the Fire Brigades Union. Joke. But during the playing of 'Penny Lane' I was the one ringing the fireman's bell. Not easy.

Then I did an event with my daughter Caitlin, the only one of our three children who is an author, with ten books published. It was the first time I had appeared on a stage with her. The subject we talked about was Margaret – her mother, my wife, who of course came from Carlisle.

Caitlin appeared a bit nervous, which at my great age I never am any more. My theory is I am only going to talk about myself, so why should I be nervous? I am an expert on me.

I told her it was the job of Roger Bolton, who chaired our event, to make her good, so relax, pet. She did and was excellent, especially at the end when she read out some excerpts from Margaret's 1954 sixteen-year-old-schoolgirl diary, which is set wholly in Carlisle, the one which was published in December 2017.

It could have been the chlorine from swimming in the Crown and Mitre Hotel swimming pool, but I did feel a bit tearful sitting there listening to my daughter reading out the words written by my dead wife ...

SOME GOOD THINGS ABOUT CRUISING

- Seeing different countries, different places, without having to drag your case around with you.
- The food, which is almost always good, and plenty of it, is mostly included. Sometimes the drinks as well.

- On board there is always a massive choice of food places, bars, caffs, and there are entertainments and activities of some sort almost all the time.
- On shore, when you land, there are lots of organised excursions to the local tourist sights, some quite expensive, so take care not to book too many.
- Cruises are good value. Considering what you get, in either the high-class cruises or the mass market, they are mostly worth it. You would be hard pressed to eat and enjoy yourself and see so much if you stayed at home and went out every night.

SOME NOT-SO-GOOD THINGS ABOUT CRUISING

- You eat too much and can come back fat and bloated. Even more than when you went.
- And lumpen – being stuck on board, sealed off from real life, not being able to have a proper walk, does make you a bit of a zombie.
- You get herded around, being lined up, counted, especially disembarking, becoming a number, not a person.
- Your fellow passengers will tend to be, er, on the senior-citizen side. Nothing wrong with that, being one myself, but it does limit the company and variety and dictates the sort of old-style entertainment they provide.

- You can feel trapped – your life taken over, your individuality gone, your freedom taken away. You have been captured. Though of course it is the sort of luxurious, cossetted captivity that most humans dream about.

QUOTES

- 'We travel not to escape life but to escape ourselves.' Anon
- 'Man cannot discover new oceans unless he has the courage to lose sight of the shore.' André Gide
- 'He travels the fastest who travels alone.' Rudyard Kipling
- 'Old and young, we are all on our last cruise.' Robert Louis Stevenson

9

PARTIES, PARTIES

Parties are great things to look forward to, at any age, and with age you should cram in as many as possible, just in case. Parties are also great to look back to, so the older you are, the more you are likely to be able to recall, to see again in your mind, to cuddle and caress. And enjoy, all over again.

I had a big party for my eightieth birthday on 7 January 2016. Margaret was still alive, though in a bad way, doped with morphine, but she insisted I went ahead with my plans, knowing how much I loved parties and how long I had spent planning this one. After all, getting to eighty seemed to me to be an enormous achievement, one to celebrate. And I did it all on my own. The NHS hardly helped.

Even if she had been fit and well, Margaret would not have gone as she didn't care for parties. But she was determined to hang on, not collapse, to stay alive, until my Big Party was over. She was looking forward to all the children, in turn, coming to her bedside and telling her blow by blow what a pain I had been, what I had done, how embarrassing, what stupid things I had said. She knew each of them would have a different slant, a different take on my behaviour, and different stories about all the guests.

Margaret did hang on and heard all about it, blow by blow. Then the next day she collapsed. She went by ambulance to the Marie Curie Hospice where she died, four weeks later. I always thought she had hung on by sheer willpower, forcing herself to cling on to life, not wanting to spoil my party.

It's strange that I have always loved parties, yet I have no memory of birthday parties as a child, or any other sorts of party. We did not go in for such extravagancies. There was a war on.

I don't even remember attending any street parties to celebrate the end of the war – VE Day on 8 May 1945 and VJ Day on 15 August. I was aged nine at the time and living in Dumfries. Did we not have any? Or was I not invited? Damn cheek.

Nor did we ever go on holiday, stay in a hotel, eat out at restaurants, have hot water or central heating, a car, TV, fridge or telephone, but goodness, we did have a lot of mince and tatties. And toast. Oh, the buttered toast in front of a hot coal fire with the blackout blinds closed. It was delicious. I can taste it now, the hot buttered toast. What could be nicer? Crouching in front of the fire, surrounded by sodden clothes permanently draped on the clothes horse in front of the fire, coughing and spluttering, enveloped by the rising steam from the clothes plus black smoke from the fire, but jings, that toast was rare, that toast was the boys. Funny how when I look back to that scene I start speaking Scottish, which is how my parents spoke.

Naturally, when I got to twenty-one I wanted to lash out, make up for the years of deprivation – no, not deprivation, we never thought of it as that, just the years of not having parties. Just toast.

I was twenty-one on 7 January 1957. I remember it well, for I was there, but also because of the cost. Did I moan about the cost. Can't of course remember now exactly what it *did* cost, but

I remember regretting that I had decided to pay for everything and be Big Mick. That was one of my mother's expressions, when someone foolishly shows off in some way, usually by being unnecessarily generous.

I could not expect my parents to pay for my twenty-first, which seems to be normal today. My mother would have jumped at the chance to entertain my friends at home, as she always maintained she had bags of food, just as she maintained she had bags of money, bags of room. All were fantasies. A pound of mince and a bag of tatties can only go so far.

Over the Christmas of 1956, like scores of other students throughout the country, I worked at the Post Office, doing extra hours and extra-long shifts in order to pay for a slap-up do. And if not slap-up, then a do, some sort of do, with or without slaps. But where to go in the depths of 1950s Carlisle?

The revolution in food has been one of the biggest changes in my lifetime. There has been a transformation in eating and cooking at home and in restaurants, across all classes, all ages, all regions. But dear God, Carlisle in the 1950s, or any provincial town in the 1950s, was a wilderness.

In the middle of the town there were chip shops like Brucianas, where you queued in a side alley and bought chips, mushy peas and pies. And there were some dusty, old-fashioned tea shops, where ladies in from the country went after they had done their shopping, sitting with pots of tea in the window, wearing their tea cosy hats and sensible coats, and scoffing scones and cakes.

All such tea shops and cafés closed at five o'clock, as did all the other shops. At five o'clock each day, retail Carlisle signed a suicide pact, gave up the ghost, died a sudden death. The centre of Carlisle then became a morgue till morning.

The only place you could go and eat after six o'clock was one of the hotels. Even the crummiest commercial hotel had a dining room with waiters who wore soup-stained dinner jackets, dribbled at the mouth, staggered about, and if you arrived for lunch at one minute past one they wouldn't let you have a table. As for the food, well, that was mainly soup, tired watery cod and vegetables boiled until they screamed for mercy. In the better-class hotels they were dumped on the table in silver tureens which you opened and had no idea what sort of vegetable had originally been plonked inside.

I was too intimidated by the Crown and Mitre to contemplate having my coming-of-age party there, so I decided to book my twenty-first dinner at the County Hotel. This was a fairly rundown commercial hotel on the Viaduct, popular with sales reps.

I invited my girlfriend Margaret, my best friend Reg Hill (later the crime writer Reginald Hill) and his girlfriend Pat, Mike Thornhill and Margaret Crosthwaite. I paid for everything, gritting my teeth.

I then went mad and told my second-best friends, the ones I could not afford to invite to dinner, that I would buy them a drink beforehand at the Friars pub, which was where the loucher grammar school masters and upper sixth formers used to go.

'Anything you like,' I announced. 'It's on me, this first round.'

All but one chose a half of bitter. State Management bitter, which was very cheap. But there was one boy, whose name I am not going to mention as it still rankles, who asked for a whisky. The bloody cheek. He knew how I had to scrimp and save my money all over the Christmas holidays, yet he went and ordered the most expensive drink. I never spoke to him again.

The meal, of course, was appalling – horrible soup, then

chicken, followed by ice cream, a set meal, which was the cheapest available. I was in a sulk all evening. Margaret was furious with me.

Oh if only I had become twenty-one just ten years later. It was in the 1960s that things began to look up, foodwise. Chinese and Italian restaurants began to arrive in Carlisle. Out in the Cumbrian countryside, gourmet dining started at Sharrow Bay on Ullswater. It was first opened in 1948 by Francis Coulson, arriving from Euston with saucepans on his back, later joined by his partner, Brian Sack. In the 1960s, it became nationally famous. Miller Howe on Windermere came a bit later, in 1971. Together, these two wonderful hotels with their marvellous food attracted the local and then the national quality for the next few decades, spawning many imitations.

Eating out in Cumbria had become fun. And it still is to this day. But not, alas, in January 1957. But I was pleased, while moaning, that I did manage to take my closest friends to a real hotel, with waiter service and white tablecloths, hardly any stains, to celebrate my twenty-first. And paid for it.

* * *

I was a student at Durham, from 1954 to 1958, which was roughly when skiffle arrived in the UK. In January 1956 Lonnie Donegan's 'Rock Island Line' became a surprise hit and spawned hundreds if not thousands of skiffle groups all over the country. On Merseyside, we discovered later, there were about ten million skiffle groups being formed, so they all claimed later.

The attraction of skiffle was that you did not need to be at all musical. You didn't have to play an instrument, or even *have* an instrument. There was room in a skiffle group for people rubbing a thimble up and down your mother's washboard, or plucking a string attached to a large tea chest, the sort that Lipton's threw out.

Going home to Carlisle in the hols in 1956, I joined in one evening with an impromptu skiffle group who were playing in the pitch dark beside the suspension bridge. All I did was rub a washboard, which is harder than you'd think, and tough on your knuckles. We did it for a few evenings, and planned to find somewhere proper to rehearse, but nothing came of it.

Back in Durham, in my third year, I went to pubs to find that skiffle groups had taken over all the back rooms. I thought they were wonderful – full of energy and life, however rough, and far preferable to the phoneys in blue shiny suits who sang pop songs to us in a mid-Atlantic accent.

There was one group called the Blue Devils who had just won some local skiffle competition and were calling themselves the North Eastern Skiffle Champions. I decided to book them for a skiffle party, having discussed it with two of my friends.

One was my new room-mate, John Davies. We had decided to share a room for our third year, and we were fortunate to get excellent rooms in what was called Hall Stairs. This was right in the heart of the Castle, up a broad wooden ancient staircase behind the Great Hall. It was above the college library, so handy for studying, har har, with a large bay window overlooking the college courtyard. You could see everything going on, who was bringing girls in through the porter's lodge, or sneaking them out later than they should have done.

John was a scientist reading chemistry, and had recently become advertising manager of *Palatinate*, the student newspaper. He came from Newcastle, lived in a private semi, and his father was an electrician who worked at Kemsley House in

Newcastle. We didn't have a lot in common, but went drinking together, though not of course to excess, as in my early, silly first year.

My other new friend was Michael Bateman, not a Durham student, but an Oxford graduate who had recently arrived in Durham working on the local paper, the *Durham Advertiser*, as a graduate trainee. He had been given the task of writing about university affairs, which was how I had met him.

The three of us clubbed together, tracked down the Blue Devils and offered them money to perform at a private party for us. We went to the Wearmouth Bridge, a large pub in the middle of Durham City, which had big upstairs rooms. We talked the landlord into letting us have the function room for free, explaining that we would be bringing in so many students that they would make a fortune on the drinks.

I can't remember how much we paid the Blue Devils, but we worked out we would easily cover their fee by charging our friends for entrance. We printed tickets, with rather arty blue printing, designed by Michael who was very good at drawing. The evening was a huge success. We filled the room and made quite a bit of money. I still have one of the tickets to this day, with all our names on.

A lot of students, over the decades since, have discovered or created careers for themselves by organising student hops, student discos, then going on to do similar but bigger things in the outside world. It never occurred to me at the time that anyone could ever make a job out of what we had done. Skiffle seemed a phase which would pass; no one could possibly make money or a career out of it, either playing it or promoting it. It was for our own amusement, to see if we could do it.

We never held such a party again. That skiffle party was

the first and last I ever did. I moved on to other things, other amusements. For me, that meant starting to write articles for the student newspaper, *Palatinate*, eventually becoming editor and then, oh joy, becoming a proper journalist. In 1958, on leaving Durham, I became a graduate trainee on the *Manchester Evening Chronicle*, part of the newspaper group that included the *Sunday Times*. I don't remember giving parties in Manchester. Or going to any. Perhaps I was never invited.

I eventually joined the *Sunday Times* in 1960 and was on the full-time staff for the next ten years, then came back later for a few years, part-time.

I gave a lot of parties during my *Sunday Times* years, for different reasons – to rally the troops, raise morale, bond us all together. That was the excuse. It was really to have good times and spend the paper's money. God, newspapers had so much money back in those days.

We thought it was just us, in Fleet Street, but when I talk to people of my age who were in advertising, or the City, or the law during the 1960s and '70s, they were having grand times as well, lunches that went on for hours, dinners that lasted till the next day, massive expenses, jollies in hotels, staff outings, staff parties, throwing the company's money around, mainly on themselves, but calling it 'entertaining contacts'. The poor sods today, in almost every profession or office in the land, can't even put a cup of coffee on expenses and get sacked if they look up from their computer.

In 1970 I went back to edit the women's pages, or the *Look* pages, as they were called. Harry Evans, the editor, was trying to give them a broader appeal, and also hoped that Ernestine Carter, the grande-dame fashion editor, would pack up, disgusted by the changes I was being encouraged to start introducing. I tried my best straight away, with series like 'Me and My Vasectomy'.

I inherited a new columnist called Jilly Cooper, a failed secretary whom Harry had hired after she had written a funny piece in the magazine. I took her out to lunch and discovered her husband Leo had been married before, so I encouraged her to write a personal piece about being a second wife. She became the most popular writer on the whole paper – much to the astonishment of the Insight team. They thought readers bought the paper for Insight.

My time on *Look* was the most fun I ever had. Well, since I edited *Palatinate* at Durham. Apart from Jilly, there was Molly Parkin, Lucia Van Der Post and Lesley Garner. Oh, the lunches we had – they went on for days, and we were in hysterics all the time.

And the parties. We only had a tiny room at first, but I managed to bag another room and called it the *Look* Suite. We even had a fridge, which I paid for. When I left, carrying it out, I got stopped by the doorman who was convinced I had stolen it.

Early on in my spell on *Look*, I created a novel, *I Knew Daisy Smuten*, written along with my friends on the paper, partly as a bonding exercise for the new *Look* department. Daisy was a photographer who had suddenly got engaged to Prince Charles and everyone wanted to know who she was. The name Daisy Smuten was an anagram of *Sunday Times*. We even sold the film rights. It was the first time in print in a book for Jilly and most of the other contributors.

To celebrate the book, which was edited by Tony Godwin, then the editorial boss at Weidenfeld & Nicolson, we persuaded George Weidenfeld to hold a *Daisy Smuten* launch party – at his house. He must have been potty. I invited all the contributors, and their partners, plus friends in publishing, friends in newspapers, assorted hacks, plus there were dozens of gatecrashers.

It was the most chaotic, awful, yet incredible drunken party. A lot of George's carpets and furniture got wrecked and a valuable painting disappeared – later recovered.

For about a year, it was still being talked about in Bloomsbury. That was how we used to describe the publishing world, just as the newspaper world was known as Fleet Street. George never gave a party like that again in his own house.

* * *

I then did two years as editor of the *Sunday Times Colour Magazine*, which was not as much fun. When I finished on the *Sunday Times* at the end of the 1970s, for ever, or so I thought, I was so relieved not to have to go to an office ever again, not to have to waste all that time travelling, listening to people chuntering on, moaning about their secretary, their expenses, the size of their office, their dopey ideas for an amazing story which would mean them flying to Cuba, this very afternoon.

But after a few months at home, writing away every day, all on my own, I began to realise there was one thing I missed – lunch.

I was moaning on about this when Margaret said, 'Why not organise your own lunches?' I had organised my own football team, Dartmouth Park United, which played only a few hundred yards away on the Heath, at a time of my convenience, with me as captain, picking my own team. I think they allowed me to score lots of goals as well.

I sat down and in thirty minutes had made a list of forty writers I either knew or knew of who lived within 2 miles who were all working from home and probably, like me, interested in a lunch with fellow hacks, in which we could rubbish agents and publishers.

Only two out of the forty said no. One was A. J. P. Taylor, who said if I was organising a regular dinner, he would come, but he no longer ate lunch. David Cornwell (John le Carré) said he would rather meet his fellow writers in the next world, not this one.

I booked a room in a cheapo Greek restaurant at Camden Town, near the Tube, which I thought would be handy for most people. The idea was that once invited, you were invited for ever, on the last Wednesday of every month, even if you never showed up for months or even years. And you could bring another writer.

The first lunch was packed, with lots of drinking and shouting and eating. I see from a letter I got them to sign that those at the first lunch included Margaret Drabble, Joan Bakewell, Kingsley Amis, Eva Figes and John Hillaby. Later writers who attended included Martin Amis, Julian Barnes and Salman Rushdie. One of the visiting authors was Jessica Mitford, over from the USA.

After the first lunch, I got a distraught phone call from a young novelist, who had just had her first novel out to great acclaim, to say she would not be coming to the next lunch. She could only afford £5 a week to keep herself alive – and she had spent it all on that one meal.

To keep it simple, I had decided at the first meal that we would divide the whole bill exactly by the number of people. What I had not realised was that Kingsley Amis had drunk whisky all the way through, practically doubling the drinks bill. From then on, only the food was divvied up. You had to pay for your own drinks.

The lunches went on every month for several years – though

it had moved by then to a Hampstead restaurant in the High Street called Fagin's. The hardcore members by then were mainly Hampstead-based, and mainly women, such as Bernice Rubens. I had given up attending by then. I had got a job presenting *Bookshelf* on BBC Radio 4 and our recording day became Wednesday, so I could never make the lunch. The literary lunches fizzled out after about ten years. But they were such fun while they lasted.

* * *

When our children were young, we always gave a lot of children's parties – so different from my own dear childhood. Flora, our youngest, was born on Halloween, which gave us a brilliant excuse to have a themed birthday every year. I mean, gave Margaret an excuse. Because she did it all. I only wish I had made videos of the parties.

Margaret disliked adult parties, especially dinner parties, though in our early married life I did talk her into going to a few, and even holding a few, moaning. But she always absolutely loved organising birthday parties and Christmas parties for our children.

She once converted the whole ground floor into a witches' coven. You had to crawl through the front door, down the hall, round corners, avoiding beastly traps, webs and spiders, before you got to the safe area.

We did the usual dipping for apples and turnip lanterns and lots of games. One game Margaret invented was called 'Strip On' – as opposed to 'Strip Off'. Two teams lined up. At the end of the room was a massive pile of our old clothes, or in my case, clothes I was still wearing, which included coats, jackets, jumpers, trousers, frocks, socks. In turn, every kid had to run to the end, pick up an item, put it on, run back, and then the next one in their team ran and did the same. When all the clothes had gone, the teams stripped off the clothes they had put on, the items were counted, and the team with the most items won. The clever ones quickly sussed out that it was better to put on socks rather than an overcoat.

For Jake's birthday we once turned the climbing frame into a castle, covering it completely with lining paper, then painting in battlements and turrets with red paint. The guests all got given cardboard swords. One team defended the castle, one attacked. In the end, they were allowed to destroy the castle.

It can sound cringe-making now, and so awfully NW5. And I suspect the children themselves probably can't remember all those parties.

With age, we polish up our memories, especially of our children, their parties, their little ways and their little sayings, improve them over the years. Margaret and I used to swap stories of our children's parties, then argue about what year it was, how old they were, who came.

For about ten years, we always had a Christmas Eve party for all the neighbours plus children. I organised the games – all of which were very competitive and intense and often embarrassing, such as a version of Mr and Mrs. Couples, in turn, had to answer personal questions about their other half, the answers to which I had found out beforehand.

I always did a quiz, with rubbish prizes. The questions were either personal, about our family and relations, or about the street, the area, local people, just to check how observant they had been in the previous year.

When the children were young, I endlessly cross-examined them after every walk, every meal, every outing. What hat was the woman with the ice cream wearing? What did that man with the dog say to us? I had it in mind that if they become spies or detectives or journalists, I had at least trained them to be observant.

Now they give *me* parties. At Christmas they take it in turns to have the whole family to their house, which is what Margaret did for so many decades. I am so pleased when one of them does a family quiz, the sort I did, all those years ago. Handing on the baton, carrying on the traditions I created.

* * *

For about ten years, I changed my birthday. Instead of 7 January, I made it 7 August.

January is and was always a rotten time to have a birthday. Rotten weather, boring fag-end time of the Christmas hols, too near to Christmas itself to expect a half-decent present as no one had any money left.

The reason for changing it to 7 August was that for many years we were always in Portugal in the summer. I woke up one day in the 1980s and thought, *I know, I will have my birthday now, in August. What a good excuse to have a birthday party for our Portuguese friends.*

I got the idea from Robert Louis Stevenson, that birthdays can be transferred, could be moveable feasts. When I told my mother my birthday was now on 7 August, so save my birthday card till then, she was not at all amused. It was good enough for her, having me in Thornhill Maternity Hospital in Johnstone, Renfrewshire, on 7 January 1936. Why change it now?

* * *

In 1985 I got two letters in the same week, each asking me to invest money. Both schemes were classed as British Enterprise Scheme, or some name like that, which meant you got a tax advantage by investing in a new start-up enterprise.

One letter was from Jeffrey Archer, whom I had never met, who was part of some group setting up a company to convert and run the Playhouse Theatre. I have no interest in the theatre, but it seemed a worthwhile venture, helping a new project. Mr Archer was known to be awfully smart, so I put in £3,000.

The second letter was from some friends of mine, Carmen Callil the publisher and Michael Sissons the agent. They were beginning a club for women as well as men in Soho, mainly media types, all informal, not at all like the Garrick. It was to be called the Groucho Club. I put £3,000 into that as well.

About six months later the Playhouse project collapsed. For years afterwards I got endless documents saying if money was ever recovered I would get around one penny in every pound. I never got nowt.

But the Groucho proved a big success. I began to get around £1,000 a year in dividends, plus reduced subs as a founder member. In 2001 there was a takeover bid. I had to sell my shares, for which I got £30,000. Amazing. Today I have no shares, on principle – the principle being I could never be so lucky again.

In 1985 we held our silver wedding party at the Groucho. As a founder member, I thought I would do my bit to get the new club off the ground. Margaret was not all that keen. She said our own relations and neighbours would not want to go to Soho, and certainly would not want to mix with my media friends. So we had two silver wedding parties. One was at home in our house for our local friends and family. The other at the Groucho Club, for my work friends.

I think the room I booked at the Groucho was called the Blue Room. It was still being decorated the day before and in fact the club had not yet officially opened. Our old Cumbrian friend Melvyn Bragg was there, and even made a speech. So was a new friend of mine, Shiva Naipaul, a brilliant young novelist, brother of V. S. Naipaul (Shiva died suddenly, just two months after the party, in August 1985).

Also there was Robert Robinson, who had been my boss when I joined the *Sunday Times* in 1960 on the 'Atticus' column. He too is no longer with us.

I even made a video film of the event. I was writing a column at the time in *Punch*, 'Father's Day', and for some reason a company had given the *Punch* staff the free loan of a state-of-the-art new super video camera. It was my turn that week to take it home and try it out. So I brought it to the party. It was a hefty thing and needed proper lights, which I didn't have, so everything came out a bit dark. I still have it, somewhere. When the Groucho Club does its centenary I hope someone will dig it out.

Our silver wedding party at the Groucho was held on 14 June 1985. I didn't realise it at the time, but it turned out to be the first private party held at the Groucho. Historic stuff. Just like my eightieth ...

So that was why I thought it would be neat and apt and fun and jolly to have my eightieth birthday party at the Groucho Club – on 7 January 2016, on my very birthday day itself. The real one.

I decided to invite my nearest and dearest, along with some of my media friends from newspapers and publishing. Margaret groaned at the very idea, pleased she was not coming.

All my three children were there, and partners, and four

grandchildren, plus my brother and his family came down from Carlisle and my sister from Leighton Buzzard. My media chums, some of whom I had known for over forty years, included Joan Bakewell (who the previous year had invited me to her eightieth), Jilly Cooper and Melvyn Bragg. The newspaper people included Martin Ivens, editor of the *Sunday Times*, and Becky Barrow, who was then still editor of the Money section, where I have written a so-called Money column for twenty years, plus Jason Cowley and Kate Mossman of the *New Statesman*, where, again, I have a long-established column. Got to keep in with them. Publishers included the one and only Iain MacGregor of Simon & Schuster and also Alan Samson of Weidenfeld, for whom I have done many books over the years.

Live music was by the Quarrymen – the original Quarrymen, the ones who were founder members of John Lennon's school skiffle group at Quarry Bank High School in 1956. When John met Paul and then George, the original members went their separate ways in life. But forty-odd years later they met up and started playing again.

It was a sit-down do, a proper four-course menu, served by nice waiters and waitresses at nice tables, none of that standing around. Aged eighty, I don't do standing any more. I also dislike buffets of any sort and barbecues and anything that means eating stuff with your fingers while standing.

I did a quiz with fab prizes and created two unique going-away presents for everyone, as if it was a children's party. One was an inscribed china mug to celebrate the event and the other was a limited-edition twenty-six-page booklet written and printed specially for the occasion, *My Life In Parties* (and from which I have lifted material to use in this chapter in this book. Waste not want not. I was brought up in the war . . .).

There was dancing and singing. Melv sang, or at least shouted, 'Twist and Shout' while the Quarrymen played. I also persuaded Alan Samson's wife Joan Rodgers CBE, who is a well-known opera singer, to stand up and sing 'Yesterday', despite being totally unprepared. Oh, it was grand.

I like to think Margaret would have enjoyed talking to all the people, if she had been up to it, if I had been able to persuade her to come. Over the decades I used to talk her into things she did not really want to do by saying, 'Please, please, I'll be your best friend . . .' That used to work, now and again.

* * *

I have been determined since I turned eighty to keep giving parties. I feel you should carry on doing all the things you have enjoyed doing in life, if you can. Age should be no barrier. Nor living on your own. Why should parties be seen as being mainly for young folk? We oldies can be as embarrassing and shameless as everyone else. And dance on tables, if required. Life itself will soon catch up with you, call a halt, blow the whistle, so get on that table while you can. Or at least stand up.

In this past year I have given three parties. I have been taking so much hospitality from so many people, friends and neighbours, since being on my own, with people feeling sorry for me – poor old soul, I wonder if he is eating properly, let's give him some bread and gruel – that I decided I should reciprocate, give my own party and invite them all back.

In the summer of 2017 I gave a garden party with loads of food and drinks with my granddaughters helping to serve. I always think it is boring when a party is just a party, neighbours who meet each other all the time, just standing around talking and nibbling. In that case, all the organiser does is provision. No original or creative thought or real work gets put into it. I like to think my parties, as Margaret's children's parties were, do have some thought put into them.

I organised a treasure hunt with loads of clues, and loads of prizes, which had everyone, parents and children, rushing round the garden and then down into the mews behind the garage, following all the clues. I also had a quiz with equally fab prizes.

During the summer, I gave another garden party, this time for fifteen Japanese people. They were all members of the Beatles fan club of Japan and won me in some sort of competition, or at least won the chance to meet me and see my Beatles collections.

I got the older granddaughters this time to serve tea and cakes and food – and paid them. One of the things I did was a Beatles quiz. Each of the guests had to write down on a piece of paper the names of five Beatles songs with a woman's name in the title. All of them got at least three. Some wrote the answers in English, some in Japanese. I kept all the Japanese writing as it looks so pretty. It has now been added to my Beatles archives.

The number of Beatles songs I would allow with a woman's name in the title was twelve. Hurry hurry to the end of the chapter to see how many you can manage.

At Christmas 2017 I gave a film party, showing a Super 8 film I made of the 1977 Queen's Jubilee street party, the one which was held locally in our adjoining streets, forty years earlier.

Super 8 films were amazing at the time – so clever, so ingenious, so state of the art. But what a faff. I was well into them in the 1960s and 1970s, thinking I was such a techie.

You bought three-minute blank films produced by Kodak in little yellow envelopes. You shot the film, in my case on my EUMIG camera, then sent the film back to Kodak to be developed. The cost I think was £3 each, or perhaps less, which covered buying the film and having it developed. I showed it on my EUMIG screen using my EUMIG projector. Or that was the theory.

In practice, I always had trouble showing the films. They often got stuck, or turned out to be full of blanks, or showed acres of bare floor as I had unwittingly left the camera running.

You could splice the short films together, as showing each three-minute film, one at a time. It took for ever, by which time most of your expectant audience was asleep or in bed. Much better to join ten together and create a continuous thirty-minute film. I bought the gear, which consisted roughly of some glue and a reel, and joined lots together.

The trouble was, I often made a mess of the glue part, so every three minutes the film jammed, having got to a lump of glue joining one film to the next. It would go round and round, showing nothing, get red-hot, steam would rise and, if you were not quick enough to turn it off, it would burst into flames. That did amuse the children when they were young, and scared all the adults.

As the decades went on, I eventually transferred many of the original Super 8 films on to DVD. When I show them you can still see, every three minutes, the original burn marks. Very genuine.

I have long lost my EUMIG projector, and the screen, so for my street party film party at Christmas 2017 I had to get Caitlin's partner Nigel to acquire a modern digital projector for me and I borrowed a screen from a neighbour. I arranged the whole of the ground floor with seating in rows, and had my two younger grandchildren acting as usherettes, tearing up the tickets and going round with a tray of popcorn and choc ices hanging from their necks.

The invites were very clever, thanks to Nigel, printed like a reel of film, with burn marks. All the food was supposedly traditional cinema-type food, hence the popcorn, along with hot dogs, pizzas and crisps. And loads of wine, of course.

I also showed a very short Super 8 film I shot in 1968, showing Paul McCartney and Linda at our house in Portugal. He had recently met her and brought her out, with her daughter Heather, to stay with us for ten days. The filming is a bit arty as both Paul and Linda took it in turns to do it, turning the camera sideways and upside down. Historic stuff, though I have never made the film public.

So three fab parties last year, all in one year, at my great age. Well, it does keep me happy. Something to look forward to.

I wonder how many more I will have? Will I manage to have the strength and energy, time and inclination, desire and delight to be bothered to organise any more? My ninetieth birthday party? My one-hundredth? If the latter, you are all invited. Don't bother with a present . . .

BEATLES QUIZ

Beatles songs with the name of a woman in the title. In this list of twelve, I have allowed the last two, though it is a bit of a cheat. One is the Queen – well, she *is* a woman – and the other is not a woman but the name of a street, which sounds like a woman . . .

- Dear Prudence
- Eleanor Rigby
- Sexy Sadie
- Julia
- Lady Madonna
- Lovely Rita
- Lucy in the Sky with Diamonds
- Martha My Dear
- Michelle
- Polythene Pam
- Her Majesty
- Penny Lane

HOW TO GIVE A GOOD PARTY

- Invite people – I always think an empty room with no people ruins a party.
- Do proper invitations, and print them. An email is cheating. People do like a stiffy on their mantelpiece.
- Food and drinks, obvs, but do try to think of an extra attraction – a quiz, a treasure hunt, a film show, a game, a record player with vinyl records from the olden days, i.e. the 1960s.
- People don't have to take part. They can just sit and watch, scoff and mutter how naff, then possibly how funny, what a good idea, puts my party to shame and yes, I will have another glass.

- Going-away presents, original, but cheap and amusing.
  Remember that most oldies are children at heart,
  except for their bad back.

10

MOTORING MATTERS AND MODERN LIFE

When your car insurance or your house insurance policy comes up for renewal, those thoughtful people often write and tell you some good news. 'You need not do anything, we will renew automatically.'

My first reaction has always been, *How kind, that will save me thinking about it, I can now get on with other stuff, such as, well, living.*

Then I think how stupid, allowing them just to take my money.

Then I have a third think, thinking is it worth it, arguing the toss, shopping around, to save a few measly quid? With age I have been trying to keep calm, keep life simple, carry on much as I have always done, which means keeping the paperwork down and doing as little on the internet as possible.

I do totally trust the government's National Savings and Investments whenever they say my fixed-interest cert will automatically be renewed for another term. The government would not con us. Of course not.

But with my building society investments I have become more suspicious. When they tell me a bond has matured, but don't worry, I can invest it in their excellent limited offer, hurry

hurry, new issue, just sign here, I immediately suspect something. Then when I look at the new rate, which I don't always do, being lazy, being busy, I see it is 0.5 per cent and I burst out laughing. Who do they think we are? Total mugs? Spot on. That is what they are banking on.

One of the benefits of age, or perhaps a handicap, is that we can remember what interest rates used to be. Only yesterday, so I tell myself, I was getting 5 per cent. I even have a memory, decades ago, of getting 12 per cent. Can I have made that up? Then I tell myself that all investment rates, everywhere, are totally rubbish today, so what is the point? You can't beat them. I will just leave it with them. Then I forget for another five years.

But with my car insurance I moved on from being increasingly suspicious each year to being furious. It just seemed to go up each time, yet I was driving it less, and the value, after all these years, was going down and down. I had been with them for years but of course the last thing they are interested in is your loyalty.

When these companies say you need do nothing, they are relying on the elderly, the relatively well-off, the plain lazy, the awfully busy or the totally feckless to do nothing. I now realise I happen to be all of those.

But suddenly the worm turned when I got my car insurance renewal letter from LV. It was the wording that set me off. If I was happy, so they wrote, I could do nothing and relax, knowing I was covered.

For five years I have had a basic Golf, now six years old. For the past year I drove it 2 miles once a month to Morrisons for my shopping. That's it. I don't drive anywhere else, now that I have given up going to the Lake District, though even then

I was rarely doing more than 2,000 miles a year, most of it the journey up and the journey back.

Despite now doing such a paltry number of miles, I was informed the insurance premium for next year was going to be £684.81.

I eventually got up the energy to see what I paid last year – which was £567. They had put up the premium by almost £120. I know I could have shopped around and got it down a bit, but I have not the time nor the energy for that.

While I was thinking about what to do, I rushed out one morning to do my monthly trip to Morrisons and found I had a flat tyre. Oh God, it hardly leaves my garage, so how can that have happened? It cost me £150, including VAT, to get the tyre mended.

Twice over the past winter it wouldn't start. I had not been in it, or starting it up, for so long that the battery had gone flat.

The joker mechanic who came to restart it, on my insurance breakdown cover, so I didn't have to pay, talked me into spending £75 on a new battery. He explained in words of one syllable, as if to a child, that car batteries, like people who are getting on in age, i.e. me, cheeky sod, do tend to get weaker as they go on, so they need to be recharged or replaced. I don't know about being replaced, though I have got a new knee, but recharging, God, I am trying to do that all the time. I charge around everywhere, constantly. Though getting up in the morning, dragging myself to the bathroom – that is often enough recharging for one day.

Then I realised my MOT was due, and that cost more money. It passed okay, but when I looked at the paperwork I saw that in the past year I had only done 79 miles. Only 79 miles! Yet the basic cost of running the stupid car was around £1,000, with servicing and repairs. Plus another £1,000, possibly £2,000, on depreciation.

So should I get rid of it? Not having a car would mean I wouldn't have to pay parking fees any more, or fines when I overstayed in the Morrisons car park, which I did in Penrith one year and they charged me £80. Or speeding fines. I was done several times on the M6 in Cumbria where they lie in wait for you, having nothing else to do. Or petrol, though I can't remember when I last filled up. Possibly last year. Without a car, I could be up to £3,000 a year better off. Plus there'd be no more worries about going into my garage and finding the tyres or battery flat. No need to clean it either – not that I ever did, except once a year at a car wash in Penrith.

If I lived any sort of rural life, as we did for those thirty years, then like all country people I would be lost without a car. In Loweswater, I needed it to go shopping and swimming in Cockermouth 7 miles away, on outings to the coast or the Central Lakes, or into Carlisle. Now, that life is long over. Getting to Broadstairs – that will always be by train.

I always hated driving anyway. On long journeys when the children were young I would not let them talk. I couldn't concentrate if they did. I always moaned about the traffic, the other drivers, the queues, the boredom, driving in the dark, driving in the rain, driving on a strange road, being stuck captive in my car behind a steering wheel, the total waste of valuable time when I could be, well, not driving, doing other stuff, such as sitting on a train reading. Oh God, now I remember how I was always moaning about driving.

And with age, I was beginning to fear my nerve would go eventually. We had a neighbour in Loweswater who was an ace driver, totally fearless, who during the war drove officers around at very high speed. She suddenly decided she was scared to drive into her own garage, fearful that she would bash her car.

I still have my nerve, so I told myself, but I had noticed that reversing the car was becoming harder. My neck has got stiff, my eyesight not as good. I was bashing the sides of my own garage more often, leaving dents on my car, as if I cared. I had become hesitant doing any reversing, avoiding it if I could. Hard to go round the block for ever, looking for a large enough space to drive into – almost impossible to find in London.

I had become unwilling to drive anywhere I had never been before, knowing I would get in a panic about the route, the roads, how to get there. I could have got a sat nav, but do I want to start learning new tricks? Can't even manage the ones I am supposed to have mastered, such as this iMac computer I am working on now. Stuff keeps on appearing at the top of the screen, covering half of what I am trying to write, which I did not invite, and certainly don't want. And there is a loud buzzing sound from inside. What the hell can it be?

But a computer, as long as I have books and columns to write and emails to send, is a necessity. I could not possibly hand-write stuff, not the way Margaret did. I would not manage more than a paragraph without my wrists seizing up, and no one would be able to read my writing anyway, least of all me. But a car I can do something about, immediately solve the problem for ever – don't have one.

I realised I had grown to really really hate the car, all cars – not just generally moaning about them, not just driving them, but being driven anywhere by anyone. And now the expense had suddenly got out of all proportion to the pleasure and use, especially with the wonderful Freedom Pass, which now exists all over the country for elderly folks. I can hop off and on buses and Tubes all day long, for free – whether I want to go anywhere or not.

And yet … and yet … while telling myself I have always hated cars, I was oft lying awake at night trying to remember all my motors in my long-legged life. In fact, one night, while lying awake, I was vaguely thinking, *You know what, instead of getting rid of my car, why don't I change my boring Golf for one of those new nifty, natty Minis? Remind me of my youth, how my driving life first began? I can afford it. Why not have one last motoring hurrah?*

* * *

The first car I had was in 1960, when we got married, a 1947 2.5 Riley. It looked beautiful and smelled wonderful – of leather and wood – but was hell to drive and was always breaking down. It cost £100. I did not have £100 at the time and the sods at the Midland Bank at Kings Cross would not lend it to me. Fortunately I got a car loan from work.

It was Mike, our so-called best man at our wedding, who persuaded me to buy the Riley, saying, 'How classy.' The day before the wedding I failed my driving test, so Mike had to drive us in my car on the first day of our honeymoon.

I then bought a brand-new Mini, price £500, in 1961. I used to wonder at how a car so small could have such space inside. I said it was blue. My wife said it was green. We had an awful row about it one evening and stormed out in the dark to check. She was right. That was when I first realised I was colour-blind.

I was once interviewing Aldous Huxley, who was very tall and going blind, and offered him a lift across London to his publisher in Bloomsbury. At a traffic light, the wheels of a double-decker bus suddenly towered over us, and he tried to jump out, scared he was going to be crushed to death.

Then I had a Mini Traveller, a long version of the Mini, with wooden batons down the side. I never cleaned it and eventually it started growing grass.

I had a Citroën, forgotten why, and it would never start. Then a white Triumph Herald, convertible, rather snazzy, but I sold it almost as soon as I'd bought it as we went abroad for a year.

The only sort of sports car I ever had was an MGB GT. By then we had two children and a cottage in Wardington, Oxfordshire, whizzing up the M1 at weekends. It didn't have proper back seats, just a low bench. When I realised the children were growing up with flat heads I decided to change to a Volvo estate.

I felt suitably middle-class and middle-aged with my Volvo, as if I had stepped up a class. It was orange – at least I called it orange. It could technically have been yellow. You could spot it five streets away. Volvos are supposed to be solid and safe. It felt solid enough but I never felt safe in it. On the M1 doing 70 mph the steering wheel used to vibrate. But I never said anything to Margaret, not wanting to frighten her. We got extra seats fitted at the back, sort of bucket seats, in the boot, facing the back window, and two of the kids always used to fight to sit there. So they at least enjoyed it.

For about ten years I drove a series of Ford Granada Scorpio estates, automatic, black leather, which were excellent, never let me down. The first got stolen from outside my house. Then the second got stolen as well, at the same time on a Sunday afternoon, when I was watching football. The insurance paid up, no bother. For another ten years I had ancient Jaguars, XJ something, never did get the exact model, all bought second-hand, long and low, smooth and elegant, which were lovely – perfect for going up to the Lake District. It was like gliding, not driving.

The image of a Jaguar driver had always been of someone quite well-off, an English gentleman, someone with taste and discrimination. That was the old stereotype, when I was growing up. Once I had one, I discovered it had changed. I felt a bit flash in my Jag, like a second-hand car salesman or drug dealer. My exact model, equally bashed up, became the motor of choice for north London drugsters. But I did love it, and felt safe and comfortable in it, till it began to fall to pieces and the replacement bits proved so expensive. It also drank petrol like an alcoholic.

It was six years ago when I traded in my last Jaguar, getting peanuts for it, and bought an almost-new Golf, transferring my personalised number plate onto it. People were always surprised I had a personalised number plate. Not the sort of thing I would do, having no interest in that sort of status or show, or even in cars.

It happened by chance, about fifteen years ago. A dealer wrote to me offering me the number plate M2 EHD for £350. I was amazed. How did he know my wife's initials were M and that my full name is Edward Hunter Davies? I have never ever been called or used Edward in my whole life.

I rang him up and he explained that he had bought a list which had been compiled from the UK electoral registers. He had gone through it and found ten people with the initials EHD whose partner, husband or wife had a first name beginning with M. Then that list was whittled down to five using the national postcodes, and he only wrote to people who appeared to live in fairly affluent postcode areas and who might be daft enough and rich enough to want their own personalised number plate.

I was so fascinated by his research that I said I would write about him and mention his firm's name. I got him down to £300 and wrote the story for the *Sunday Times* driving section – the first and last time in my life I have ever written for a motoring section. I got paid £400 for the article. So I made money – and got myself a personalised number plate.

It proved very useful as I got older and my memory was not as good as it was. It was not a matter of being forgetful or mentally wandering, like my poor old mother, but being mentally lazy, preoccupied with other things. I tell myself that there is no room in my bursting brain to remember trivial things like my car number plate. But I could always remember M2 EHD, so easy, and mostly I was able to find it in car parks.

One reason for buying a small car like the Golf was that the children had now grown up and left home. It was just the two of us going to the Lakes on our own, so we did not need a big car any more. The Golf was very economical compared with the Jags, neat and sensible enough but, oh, so totally boring.

It was a combination of the car insurance going up now I was eighty, the car having a flat tyre yet again, no longer going up every summer to Loweswater and living on my own that made me finally decide, *This is silly – I don't need a car*. Very often when I decide I have decided, I then decide to change my decision. This time this was it, end of the road.

I then wondered what to do with the car. Give it to one of the children? Then I can lean on them to take me shopping, though of course they would do that anyway. But none wanted to change their present car. But my nephew Ross, son of my sister Annabell, heard I was getting rid of it. He did a test run and we agreed a price of £4,000, which was quite a bit less than the listed value, as it was in good nick and had only done 12,000 miles. He is on a good salary and is a director of one of these many media tech companies that suddenly on paper are worth millions, so I did not see why I should give him the car for free. He then changed his mind, said he did not want it after all, was saving for something else.

Then Shirley, an old friend from my *Sunday Times* days, a former picture editor, came for lunch. She noticed my Golf in the garage as we walked through the garden on the way to lunch. She said she too drove a Golf, but it was twenty years old, and she really should get a newer one. I said she could have mine for £4,000. She gave me a cheque without driving it or even sitting inside. I worried that she would be disappointed, or something would go wrong when she got it back to Chelsea and that she'd want her money back.

She did ring up about a week later to say there was something funny about it – a light seemed to go off and on all evening. I said that is the security system, pet. It has come in since your ancient Golf was new. She still has my Golf, with my personalised number plate on it. I couldn't be bothered to put the old one back on, even though I could have sold the personalised one for a few hundred quid. I could not face the paperwork and, anyway, a dealer would take half. Shirley still appears very happy with it.

But not as happy as I am not having a car. What a relief it has been. People said, 'What will you do if you want to go places out of London, visit family and friends in the north or wherever?' I said the train. Marvellous invention. I love trains. You can read in comfort on a train, stuff your face and drink all the way, or just doze.

On long trips up to Penrith or Carlisle, going first class, Virgin supply red or white wine almost the whole journey, as much as you can manage. You have to put up with their ever so jokey announcements in the lavatory when you lift up the seat, warning you not to flush newspapers, sanitary towels, goldfish or your hopes down the pan. It's funny the first time, but not if you go to the lav all the time, as I seem to do more and more.

I feel that giving up the car has in fact given me more independence, not less. I'm not just saving money, but saving on paperwork, forms, fines, bills, annoying phone calls, buying petrol, getting it cleaned, remembering to have it serviced and MOT'd. And no more flat tyres or flat batteries to worry about when I go into my garage.

I then had the nice problem, sorry, challenge, of what to do with my garage. I did not want to rent it out, which I could easily have done in this area, not wanting the money or the involvement with someone.

I thought at first of turning it into a Spurs museum. I moved in several hundred old Spurs programmes from the 1960s and '70s, which are worth little. I do have a lot of pre-war ones but they are too good and valuable to store in a garage. I am hoping eventually they will go to the Spurs Museum, in the new stadium, along with my 2,000 othe bits of Spurs memorabilia. I don't want money. I want two free tickets in the new stadium for life – or longer. We are still discussing it.

I also hung up four large Spurs flags from the ceiling of the garage. All fans at the last game at White Hart Lane in 2017, and the first one at Wembley when the new stadium was being built, got a free flag. I went to each game with my son Jake and bagged his flag as well.

Then I put a table in with a colourful plastic tablecloth and chairs. When my two younger grandchildren, Amarisse and Sienna, visit I have usually given them a meal or at least a snack. Now we all sit munching in the garage, which amuses them. And me.

I recently found in our street, newly dumped, a drum kit, a proper one, with a foot pedal and a cymbal on top, probably owned by some teenager whose mother had got fed up with it. I dragged it home and put it in the garage. The girls play with it when they visit me, along with a keyboard that plays recorded backing tracks at great volume, which they are not allowed to have in their bedroom at home. In my garage, right at the bottom of the garden, they can make as much noise as they like. No wonder they like coming to see Humper.

So, I have not only saved a fortune by dumping my car, saved myself endless aggravation and time, avoided worse problems which I am sure would have come while driving in the future, but something nice has come out of it all as well.

Cars have had their day anyway. Sales are falling, diesel cars are being banned, electric cars are in, and any moment now driverless cars are coming. The government has said that by 2041 they will be commonplace on all UK roads. They have been boasting and proclaiming how driverless cars will be a godsend for the elderly and the ill. I am not sure how this will be such an amazing benefit. People like me, who don't like being driven anyway, will not find being driven in a driverless car all that much fun. And a hell of a worry, I should think. And you will still have to tax and insure them.

Far better not to have a car at all. Every day I smile as I go through my carless garage, not having to worry about starting a non-existent engine. Buses and the Tube are free. If you have children you can lean on them to drive you or get your shopping for you. God knows, it's the least they can do, after all I have done for them, what all we oldies have done for them, the next generation. Did we not make them, bring them into life, feed and clothe them for all those years? Well then.

I wonder if I will be alive in 2041? Hardly, as it will mean I will have got to 105. It would be nice to be here to see if driverless, electric cars do come to pass, but I can't quite believe they will.

I am also sceptical about global warming. Not that it is not happening – I do accept the facts – but I find it hard to believe we on the planet are the sole cause of it. It surely has often happened in the past. Obviously we are polluting our own immediate environment, and something must be done about that, just as we were causing London smog by all our coal fires. Getting rid of the London smog was one of the best and most dramatic improvements in my lifetime. In 1960, driving home from work, I often could not find my own house, or even see my hand in front of my face.

But my mind can't take in the notion that we are causing the whole globe to warm up. When you go on long-haul flights, you can stare out of the window for ten hours and see totally nothing on the ground – no habitations, no people, just tens of thousands of acres of empty, harmless landscape. I like to believe the globe is big enough, old enough, experienced enough, with enough checks and balances to fight back against any little regional difficulties we may be creating. Surely it can adapt, accommodate, as it has done so often in the past.

Meanwhile I am waiting for what all the experts have been telling us will happen – that global warming will warm up our winters, which would be nice. Yet it seems to me the last few winters have got colder if anything. At least the summer of 2018 was a beezer. When the world does regularly warm up, and we become a tropical island, I won't be here to see it, alas.

But I can look back and think of all the changes in my life-time. Nobody had a car when I was young. We played football in the streets, all day and all evening, knowing no cars would ever appear. The only car that was ever spotted in our streets was the doctor's. Now every street in the land is jam-packed with cars. Households often have two, three and four members, each with their own car.

I missed the beginning, as petrol-engine motor cars first appeared on our roads around 1900, but I saw the height, which was in the post-war years, beginning in the 1950s, when people suddenly had more money and motor cars became mass market. Petrol-driven motor cars, if they go by 2041, will have survived for just 100 years.

Canals had an even shorter run. The modern, commercial version began in the 1770s and within fifty years were taking over the whole country, the whole economy, with millions of navvies digging them out, everywhere, and the nation's heavy goods being trundled and dragged through thousands of lock gates. Then, in 1825, the first steam railway arrived, the Stockton to Darlington. And that was it. Almost overnight, canals had no future. Long live steam. Now steam has gone, though we still have railways.

Planes have now taken over as the main means of transport for those going abroad. Will planes go as well, when we all have our own miniature flying machines, driverless drones to take us wherever we want? When I was young, the comics often had scenes of people in little aeroplanes, buzzing over the houses, over the streets. It never happened.

Now we are led to believe that Artificial Intelligence will take over and perform everything. Robots will do our work for us, probably our living for us as well, which will save us having to grow up, learn things, get a job, have a family, grow old. Where will the fun be then?

I grew up with a manual typewriter, bashing away, and the noise of the keys could be heard out in the street. Then electric typewriters came in. I bought an expensive electric one, which became obsolete when Amstrad word processors arrived.

I loved my Amstrad PCW dearly. Over ten years I wrote millions of words on it. I did not want to give it up. It served me so well. But then email came in. I'd been happy enough to use a fax machine, after I had printed out copy on my Amstrad. Even Margaret learned to use a fax machine, sending out her handwritten material instantly. 'What is a fax machine, Humper?' My grandchildren asked me that the other day. How could such a clever, useful invention as a fax machine come in and go out so quickly? But having a computer with email was clearly much better and quicker. Offices then stopped using fax machines, leaving them to get dusty in a corner. So I was forced to change again, if I wanted to send copy to publishers and newspapers instantly.

I acquired an Apple iMac and had to learn new skills. Which ten years later I still have not properly mastered. But I am grateful for my computer, and use it all the time, live on it.

I also have an iPhone. I hate mine. Mine is not a mobile phone, in the sense that I never take it out with me, unless I am going somewhere new. I don't answer phone calls on it. I never know what to press and I can't hear when they do get through. But I do read and send emails and texts on my mobile when I am on hols, which is handy.

It is an accepted wisdom these days, trotted out all the time, that modern technology has totally transformed our lives. People always nod ritually in agreement. I don't see it, personally. My life is very much as it was in the 1960s – getting up, going to my desk, writing stuff, going to bed. The fact that I do my work using a slightly different machine is pretty much irrelevant. I am still me, doing the same sort of work. It takes me the same time to write 1,000 words and the newspapers and magazines I write for still come out at the same time. Books get published no more quickly today than they did fifty years ago, or 150 years ago.

My case is not typical, but when I am on the top deck of a bus looking into office windows, I see rows of vaguely human beings sitting silently at tight desks in front of identical computers, a scene I could not have seen when I first came to London. At that time, they sat at rows of typewriters, just as cramped, if a bit noisier. So what is the real difference? The process might be different, the technology and procedures non-existent only yesterday, but it is still work, still sitting in cramped offices, moving words and figures and messages around.

I don't really value the so-called enormous benefits modern technology has brought us – apart from emails, which I am grateful for, meaning we are able to communicate instantly. But who really needs all that? Most of us don't. Emails just seem to have generated more work. Everyone in an office moans each day about finding fifty emails when they arrive at work, most of them stupid or pointless, which they have to open, just in case, before they can get down to starting their proper work.

Postcards, which I still send, were fine, attractive, personal and unique and the contents last for ever, unlike stuff on computers. Technology changes all the time. Our present-day computers and systems will become obsolete, making it hard to access the contents now on them. That's what happened to my Amstrad. I still have dozens of discs I can't play.

I threw out my original Amstrad PCW, which was probably a mistake. I should have kept it, just as I should have kept my first motor car, the 1947 Riley.

Oh, I wish I had it now. It would look great, gleaming away in my garage. I could turn it into a motor museum, not just a Spurs museum.

I am amused rather than irritated by modern technology, considering that AI must be a joke, and all the other even more wonderful wonders about to happen to us, if we live long enough, probably won't actually happen.

There are so many running dramas, rows, horrors, horrible leaders across the world, which I don't really need to worry about as I won't be here when they do their worst.

I do think life, all round, has genuinely got better in my life-time, but when I think of all the billions that have been spent on Brexit, and of all the clever people who could be spending the best, most productive years of their lives doing something good and useful to society being lumbered with the job of sorting it out, I think, *Thank God I won't be here when it all comes to pass, whatever it is which eventually does come to pass.*

REASONS NOT TO HAVE A CAR

- Car insurance costs a fortune, especially for those over eighty.

- Plus tax, MOT, servicing, car parking, speeding fines – and petrol.
- With depreciation, it probably costs the average motorist £3,000 a year before they take their car out of the garage.
- A garage. You have to keep it somewhere. In the street means it could get vandalised and the council will charge you.
- Things going wrong – from piddling things like flat tyres, battery failure to bashing into things – often self-inflicted, when you get older.
- Driving is so boring. You are stuck there, a victim, a prisoner, desperate for release.
- Being driven – almost as boring, and you might get car sickness.
- Having to listen to motor heads talking about their dreary cars.
- Having to listen to people when they tell you which route they used to get here.
- Polluting the environment, ugh.
- Cars are dead, yesterday's technology. Who needs them? Get rid of it now.
- Cars, when we were young, might have had some pulling power. But come on, having £3,000 more a year to spend on someone – isn't that more attractive, hmm? Environmentally sound? Rather sexy?

SOME MODERN THINGS I
COULD DO WITHOUT

- Automatic checkout points in supermarkets.
- Recorded messages that tell us our custom is important, har har, pull the other one.
- Banks that have no manager.
- Banks that don't exist, have been closed, now exist only in the sky.
- Investments and payments and transactions that can only be done online.
- The death of chequebooks.
- Booking flights online.
- The built-in obsolescence of all Apple products.
- The price of a cup of coffee.

11

DAY-TO-DAY LIVING

I go through the garage all the time, and rarely use my front door, which Margaret thought was potty. In wet weather my shoes get wet and muddy from the grass. I have to take two keys, the remote control for the garage door as well as the back door. She maintained it saves no time at all. I maintained it is the scenic way.

It leads onto a mews, with bushes and trees and plants. I can imagine I am in the country every time I walk down it. When we first moved here in 1963 there was a woman in the mews who kept a horse. At night we could hear it neighing. Now we just have owls and foxes and squirrels, awfully sylvan, considering it is only 4 miles from Charing Cross, which traditionally marks the centre of London.

I walk down the mews wherever I am going, whatever the time, even in the dark, which my children tell me is dangerous. It gets me quickly to the 214 bus stop, just two minutes away, very handy when I am rushing to get to St Pancras to catch the train to Broadstairs. Or going for a swim at Kentish Town Baths. Or trailing to Camden Town for the nearest HSBC branch. I was furious when the HSBC bank in Kentish Town closed. It was so easy to walk to. All the custom I have given them over the decades. Banks are just another example of modern multinational firms having no thought or consideration for the convenience of their loyal customers.

I find with age I am becoming a creature of routine, though Margaret said I always was. I am probably worse now. On your own, you have to have a routine or you forget what you are doing, where you are, who you are.

I created a column in the *Sunday Times Magazine*, 'A Life in the Day', which is still there after over forty years. In my obit they will say, 'Oh yes, did he not begin "Life in the Day"? I wonder if he did anything else?' The point of that column was to take a person, well known or otherwise, through not their working day but the boring, humdrum, piddling, trivial non-working part of their day. Everyone, well known or otherwise, still has to go through the same sort of thing each day, from when they wake up each morning. In that domestic day, there is a life and a shape and routine of its own.

I have always asked people about the routine of their day – what time did they get up, who did they sleep with, spouse, partner or no one, did they have tea or coffee, who made it, did they lay their clothes out the night before or decide what to wear on the day depending on the weather or their engagements? All riveting stuff. So here goes. My turn.

I wake at seven. I switch on *Today*, then the kettle. Nowadays I always have a kettle plus tea bags in my bedroom, being on my own with no wife, partner or staff. Before I go to bed the previous night, I bring up a mug with milk in it. Sometimes I forget. In the morning I stagger around, looking for it, moaning like hell, and have to trail all the way downstairs to get it, ruining my own time-saving arrangements.

I drink my tea in bed, propped up with two pillows, while reading a paper or magazine, either one left from the Sunday papers or the *New Statesman, Oldie, Private Eye, Cumbria Life, The Author*, all of which I have on subscription and come by post. I do have a daily paper delivered, but I save that for over breakfast. Anyway, I am still listening to *Today*, so I am up to speed with the day's excitements, tragedies, plane crashes, hurricanes, political rows and the death of an American actor/actress/TV star/country and western singer of whom I have never heard.

I wait for *Thought for the Day*, then quickly leave the bed, rush into the bathroom, which is on the half-landing, turn the tap on for my bath and add a very small amount of cheap bath foam which is supposedly dermatologically tested. It has been a real test of my temper and concentration to run the bath for myself, after decades of Margaret doing it. While it is running, I go downstairs, open up the curtains and shutters, and put some of my home-made muesli in a bowl with a banana and loads of soft fruit, ready for when I come down later.

It is the same recipe Margaret used – just porridge oats with raisins and pine nuts, not much of a recipe. We used to add proper nuts, like walnuts, but I maintained it brought out a filling, hence we stuck to this harmless pap ever afterwards, suitable for invalids or the elderly.

I go mad if for any reason I run out of bananas or soft fruit. This has been one of the hardest things I have had to learn, to permanently be thinking ahead and provision for myself, which of course I never did before. I still forget to keep an eye on lavatory paper, washing-up liquid, Spontex cloths, all so boring but necessary. I either suddenly find I have run out or I have overstocked, continually buying the same stuff and ending up with twenty packets of raisins. And of course if there is a bargain offer at my favourite stall at Kentish Town Tube Station, like two punnets of raspberries for £1, I buy four, three of which go mouldy before I have finished the first one.

I either have too much milk or too little. I never seem to judge it right. We – I mean I – get milk delivered, one pint three times a week. He comes in the dark at about four in the morning on an electric milk cart. I have seen him, if I am unable to sleep and am wandering round the house, looking idly out of the window. I stare out into the dark, hearing his bottles rattling, the front gate closing, and imagine I am back in Victorian times, when everything was delivered, when thousands of people were working all night long to keep London ticking over, with bread and rolls, vegetables and fish, coals and logs plus five deliveries of post a day.

People in Loweswater always found it strange that we got milk delivered despite living right in the middle of London. It would probably be much cheaper to stick to supermarket milk, but I like the romance of it, the history, keeping an ancient trade going. With age, having it delivered is a boon. Now I am so weak. Have you ever tried to carry milk home? It weighs a ton.

In the bath, I soap my face before I get out, rub it then wash the soap off, then I have a shave. I picked up this habit from our first landlord, Mr Elton, in our first flat in the Vale of Health in 1960. He was a non-speaking, non-communicative elderly bachelor, so I can't imagine how we came to have a conversation about shaving, but he told me that soaping and softening your bristles before shaving helps to make it easier. And it is true. I always had a heavy growth and often, when I was younger, I would have to shave again in the evening if I was going out.

I have a wet shave, using a cheapo Bic razor. I am so furious that the old-fashioned shaving sticks have been discontinued. I am now forced to use an ordinary bar of soap which is nowhere near as pleasant.

Back in the bedroom, I do my exercises. I used to do quite strenuous ones, getting down on the floor, doing push-ups, pulling my legs up behind my back, but now I fear if I get down on the floor I might never get up again. So I just do bending down, to ease my back. In theory I do it ten times, trying to touch the floor with my hands, but I cheat and rarely manage it these days. Who's watching? Who cares? Then I get dressed and go down and have my breakfast – the muesli, followed by a cup of coffee.

I loll on the couch while eating and drinking and read the newspaper. I dearly miss *The Independent*. When they ceased as a proper newspaper we tried *The Times* for a few weeks, but neither of us liked it. Then *The Guardian*, but that was so self-important. But I do get *The Guardian* on a Saturday. I like their magazine and several of my friends write for the paper, such as Ian Jack, Tim Dowling and John Crace. I also like their sports section, especially Barney Ronay.

Then I go to work. Down the coal mine, sorry, words mine. I aim to be at my desk by nine o'clock, and instantly start bashing away, trying not to be distracted by any emails till half time. These days I force myself to stop at eleven, go for a coffee round the corner, perhaps a short walk on the Heath, otherwise my arm and wrists go funny and my back aches and I feel knackered.

Every day is a working day, with the same basic routine. On Saturday and Sunday I am a journalist, writing my columns. Weekdays I am on a book. I religiously stick to this territorial divide, trying not to allow either occupation to overlap into the other's territory.

Thinking of what to eat is a right drag, but it has to be done, so I have started once a week cooking a large dish of something or other, such as a bolognese sauce with mince and vegetables, or a purely vegetable dish of aubergines, red peppers, red onions, tomatoes and garlic. I eat it two days running, then freeze what's left for future lunches. Margaret would be so proud of me. Not just coping but being so sensible.

For Saturday lunch I always have the same thing – a tuna fish sandwich on fresh brown artisan bread, bought at the local farmers' market, plus tomatoes and a large glass of Sauvignon blanc. In the evening I try to have something hot, either a stew or nut bake, which one of my kind neighbours or children has made for me.

It is very easy just to eat the same food or make the same dish all the time, over and over. It saves thinking. It all goes down the same way anyway – then you have to start all over again. I often wonder, when I catch myself trying to cook something new and interesting, why am I bothering? Who cares? It's just food. Who will know if I just have toast and cheese – again?

Being on my own I can of course change my routine at any time. I will drop everything and sunbathe in the garden if it is really sunny, but then I feel guilty. I have gone through life with self-imposed targets that I can't stop creating for myself, deciding in my mind what column I will write by a certain day, or how many chapters I will complete by a certain month. I find it hard to skive off when I have not completed my targets. If I do, I then have to make it up, put in an extra shift.

I remember when Margaret's father Arthur was widowed and living on his own for the last ten years of his life. We would often trail all the way to Carlisle from Loweswater to see him, thinking he would be delighted by a surprise visit.

But he would greet us at the door suspiciously, clearly annoyed, saying we had caught him on the hop, he was busy doing something. He would then try to usher us out of the door as quickly as possible.

In the front garden, we would peep through his window and see he was settled down watching the horse racing on TV. Nothing wrong with that. It was his routine, his pleasure, what he always did at that time of day. He had been working towards it, till we had interrupted. We understood. And were amused, mostly, unless we had made an extra effort to go and see him.

I am a bit like that if my children arrive with their blessed dogs just as I am settling down with a drink and the *Evening Standard*. Or if I am just about to go upstairs to watch the football, having waited for it to start all day, fixing my work and household jobs round it. Now they have mucked it up.

Caitlin and Jake each have a dog. I don't care for dogs or cats. They seem to spend so much time shouting at them, taking them to the vet, arranging for friends to look after them when they are away. We never allowed them a dog or a cat when they were young. Children are enough of a responsibility and a worry.

I do have one pet, a tortoise, now almost fifty years old, who lives in our garden. When we first bought her – and you can't buy them now, they are endangered – the pet shop in Parkway, Camden Town said we had to put her in a wooden box with straw when she got sleepy in the autumn. She would then sleep there all winter, protected from rats. That worked for two years, then, on the third year, come the late autumn, we could not find her. Had she been eaten? Died? The children were distraught. Lo and behold, come the spring she waddled out across the lawn from some hiding place against the garden wall. Every year since she has done the same thing – put herself to sleep somewhere. We don't ask where. We respect her privacy.

We don't feed her or water her. Never taken her to the vet or spent a penny on her. She looks after herself totally. Oh, if only children were like that.

For our own amusement, when she first wakes up in the spring, covered with soil, we let the grandchildren wash her and oil her shell. With best virgin oil of course – Margaret insisted. Then we might give her a strawberry or cucumber. Just to amuse us. Sometimes she eats them, sometimes she doesn't. She isn't bothered. Tickling the top of her nose, she quite likes that, but needs coaxing.

One spring, many years ago, when I was giving the lawn its first cut with my hover mower, I went over a bump which I did not remember being there the year before. It was dopey Tortee. For some reason she had put herself to sleep in the middle of the lawn, not against the wall as normal. I had taken a thin slice off the top of her shell. The children were in tears, convinced I had killed her. I refused to take her to the vet, saying the point of the shell was to protect her, which it had. She recovered okay, but you can still see a slight thinness on top of her shell when she gets her first oiling of the year.

I don't let her into the house, although she is desperate to come in – bangs her shell angrily on the back step, trying to barge in. She did get in once and hid behind a couch. Later we discovered she had done a sneaky shit, which we didn't find for ages.

We have a polished wooden floor in the kitchen, which is the big attraction for her. I once wrote a story for *Jackanory*, the BBC children's show, about a tortoise who thinks the house contains a skating rink. She sneaks in, slides around, meets the family and slides out again.

We always call her a her. We did sex her when we first bought her, having been told to look underneath. If they are concave they are female; convex, male. I think I have that right. We have always called her Tortee. Not very imaginative.

We all love her dearly, and so do visitors. When my fifteen Japanese visitors were having their tea in the garden, Tortee emerged from some bush and set off on her slow but stately progress across the lawn. The visitors were entranced. They rushed for their cameras, forgetting about the Beatles.

Tortee will outlive us all, I am sure. Unless she gets stolen. There have been tortoise burglars operating in our area recently. Because you can't buy them any more from pet shops, there is a black market in stolen ones.

She has witnessed so many changes in the garden in the past fifty years – the garage going up, the arrival of the summer house, the arbours, the fruit trees. I wonder if she is aware that Margaret, the other person who lived here all these years, has gone?

Most afternoons, after my snack lunch, I have my siesta, then go into the garden, say hi to Tortee if she is around, then go through the garage and down the mews. I am usually out for around two hours. I go swimming three times a week in Kentish Town pool, or the Hampstead ponds in the summer. Or I walk across the Heath, perhaps take a bus somewhere, such as Kenwood or Hampstead, and walk back. Halfway through my outing I always stop for coffee, always at a place where I can read the papers. I like to read at least three newspapers every day. I love newspapers. I would be lost without them.

On my return home, if I have a crisis on, or what I call a crisis,

I will do another two hours' work before settling down with the *Evening Standard* and a drink. In the evenings, I watch football on the TV. Never watch any other TV. Fortunately these days football is on practically all the year round.

I am in bed, just as I always was when Margaret was alive, at five to ten prompt. I put on Radio 4 for *The World Tonight* and curl up under the blankets. I give it five minutes for the headlines, then switch off, another day over, thinking what bliss to be in bed, even if I am on my own . . .

* * *

About thirty-five years ago, when all the children were still at home, we were having some building work done, due to subsidence. A huge hole was dug in the kitchen and concrete poured in. Before the concrete went in, I placed a time capsule in the bottom of the hole. Inside a tin box I put that day's paper, some coins and other bits and pieces. I also enclosed a list and plan of how the house was organised, what each room was used for, who was living there, our children's names, what we were all doing with our lives and who was at home on that particular day.

I did this because I would like to have known what was happening in this house every year since 1860 when it was built. I long to know about the different families who have lived here and the different uses for the house.

I am sure some future occupant will be fascinated, should their builders dig up that tin box. But who will the occupants be?

I have this fantasy that one of our three children will one day be living here with their family. Doesn't matter which, though I suppose Jake has the best claim, as he was literally born in the house – in a downstairs back room, formerly an outside coal cellar, then a spare bedroom, now our kitchen.

I will leave everything to them, whatever it is I have to leave. I have no trusts or tax avoidance schemes, apart from having to live another, let me see, five years now, to cover the gift to them of the Broadstairs cottage. It is then up to them to work out how to divvy up any left over spoils, after they have settled inheritance tax.

I feel blessed to have all my three children and their families living relatively near to me, all now in north London. For twelve years Caitlin, our oldest and tallest, which is how she often describes herself, lived in Botswana and we missed her so much. For the past few years, she had a little house off the Holloway Road – soon moving to Crouch End. She lives there with her partner Nigel and her eighteen-year-old daughter Ruby.

Flora lives off Green Lanes, on the so-called Harringay Ladder. Her husband is called Richard and their daughters are Amarisse and Sienna, aged ten and nine. She is the furthest away. Jake is the nearest. He lives in Tufnell Park with his wife Rosa and daughter Amelia, now aged nineteen, who has just started at university.

They pop in all the time, invite me for meals and parties. Jake, being the nearest, has got lumbered with driving me once a month to Morrisons for my big shop, now that I don't have a car. He doesn't like Morrisons any more than Margaret did, but she was a snob. She would only buy food from Waitrose or Marks & Spencer. I know Morrisons, can find my way around, and I love their Beaujolais. I don't think I could manage a new supermarket now, no more than I could manage a new woman living with me in my house. Though occasional visits might be nice. How would I find my way round a new supermarket, or a new woman for that matter, know where things were?

People who don't have children, either by choice or because it did not happen, often say they don't miss children, they have lots of nephews and nieces and godchildren instead. They enjoy having total freedom to indulge themselves. I am sure they mean it, that it is true for them. My life, however, would be far, far less rich without my children and grandchildren.

When they were young, and at the local primary school just two streets away and then the local comprehensives, they were a passport to the neighbourhood, an introduction to other local parents and children. Walking them up to school when they were very young I got to know everyone in the playground.

As they grow up, children keep you in touch with modern life, and modern rubbish popular music and silly slang and stupid clothes and haircuts. And of course they do have their uses, explaining how mobiles and laptops work.

My two older grandchildren are about to go to university. I am so looking forward to finding out where they go and hearing about what happens to them. It will be a new experience for them, as well as for me.

I sometimes look at each of my four granddaughters and can't really see me or Margaret in them, no more than I could see us in my own three children. Caitlin, so people often said, is most like me. She has very dark hair, which I had when younger. Flora and Jake are basically Anglo-Saxon, in that they had very fair hair when young, as Margaret did. Their hair has darkened with age.

All my four grandchildren have got mixed blood somewhere inside them –from Botswana, South Africa, Cameroon, France and Ireland. Unlike me and Margaret. Our families were all from the same stock and type, going back for ever, mostly living in the same place. But this modern life, especially modern

London life, does add extra and unusual interest and produces attractive, interesting-looking children.

All three of our children did fine at school, have common sense and many talents. But I suppose we all tend to think that about our own children. We are just amazed they grew up, more or less.

Margaret was always good at art and so are both Flora and Caitlin. Flora was a good actress at school, as was Margaret. It is nice that one of the three, Caitlin, has turned out a writer and has had ten books published. I can rubbish agents and publishers with her, whereas I can't talk barristering with Jake. Flora was in TV as a producer for ten years and is now a designer.

One of the nicest things is that they seem to like each other, are best friends, always in each other's houses, involved in each other's lives and parties and holidays, always helping each other.

I grew away from my brother and sisters, as Margaret did from her siblings. We each moved away from Carlisle at the age of eighteen, going to university and never returning, eventually settling and working in London. We lost contact in some ways, at least day-to-day contact and day-to-day closeness. We followed totally different careers from our own families, forming new circles and friendships. Our three children are all Londoners, living near to each other, which helps.

We used to imagine, when they were still at school and sometimes driving us mad, that once they got to eighteen that would be it. They would be grown up, off our hands, up and away, and we wouldn't have to worry about them any more. Pure fantasy, as all parents find out. As long as you are alive and they are alive, you are the parents and they are the children. At every age and stage, you will still worry about them.

Reading Margaret's diaries, which she kept all her life, she was constantly worrying about them, one at a time, sometimes all three – their health, their relationships, their work, their children. I don't think I ever worried about them the way Margaret did, at least in her diaries. Yet on the surface, she appeared calm and relaxed. When they went abroad, on holiday or for work, she made a great point of telling them there was no need to say they had arrived, no need to ring us up, though of course that would be nice. After a hospital appointment or job interview or other important event she would instruct them that they did not have to immediately tell us what happened. Just in their own time. She deliberately avoided putting the sort of parental pressure on them that her parents had put on her, requiring her to ring or write all the time. But of course in reality, in her diaries, she was like most mothers, permanently concerned about the well-being of her children. They always say that you are only as happy as your least happy child. A cliché, but true.

I worry that I will be a burden to them in the future, still living in this house on my own, becoming less mobile, less active, less self-reliant. I am not like Margaret. She was resolutely independent, hating being beholden to anyone, hated asking for or receiving favours. I think she saw it as a weakness, to borrow anything or ask for assistance. I have got no shame or embarrassment. I have no problem asking for help. I like to think people will like to help me.

Whenever we got lost somewhere she would refuse to ask people for directions. I always do. I love asking people things, even when I don't need to. Even when I know roughly where I am, I will ask a local to help me. Margaret would get annoyed with me for bothering them. I like the social contact. To hear people speak, their accent, see how they will react, how helpful they will be or not.

If there was a crowd ahead, some gathering or incident, she would turn round or cross to the other side of the road, not wanting to know, not wanting to be involved. I will break into a gallop, if I can, if my legs are up to it, rushing to find out what on earth is happening, my nose twitching.

I like to be involved, know what is going on, talk to people. Yet my boredom threshold is low. Once I have drawn all the information I can from someone, asked them personal questions about their lives, I want to move on, by which time they think I am their new best friend. I am using them, really, to get information, to feed my nosy nature, but mainly for my own interest and amusement.

So I won't mind asking my children or any friends or neighbours for help, to drive me somewhere, or make food for me, but at the same time I am trying to remain independent for as long as I can. Inevitably I will need more help, need others to take things over. Just not yet.

BEST THINGS IN LIFE THAT ARE FREE

- Having a good night's sleep.
- Going for a walk.
- Sunbathing.
- Swimming in the sea.
- Children laughing.

- Grandchildren arriving.
- Grandchildren going.
- Kissing.
- Cuddling.
- Another good night's sleep.

WORRIES IN OLD AGE

- Being alone.
- Having no money.
- Falling ill.
- Falling.
- Fading memory.
- No friends.
- Failing to find your specs.
- Failing to find the bathroom.
- Failing.

THINGS WE HAVE LEARNED IN OLD AGE

- Memory plays tricks, usually for the better.
- It was always sunny then.
- It won't happen. Well it hasn't so far, if you are still here.
- Summer will see it out.
- Every new year, every new day, is a bonus.

- Politicians are in it for themselves.
- Don't believe a word of it, we have heard it all before – tell that to the Marines.
- A problem shared means they are going to ask you about it, all the blooming time.
- When someone starts a sentence with 'I am not being...', they are.
- Modern popular music is rubbish. They don't make it like the old days.
- Everything always comes back. There is nothing really new.
- All social media is even more rubbish.
- In fifty years' time, the world will look back and say this was a golden age. Make the most of it.

12

BEING EIGHTY (I.E. BEING OLD)

It's a right old laugh being old, loads of fun, loads of advantages. I am enjoying it so much I wish I had done it earlier.

You just have to think of the alternative, the next stage. Not worth contemplating really, so we'll move on.

The perks we enjoy are well known – the young are always going on about it. Oldies tend to own their own house, own savings, grab all the disabled parking spaces, get a free TV licence, bus pass, winter fuel allowance. We clog up the winter cruises, get called sir and madam all the time. God, we are so lucky.

When I think of the teenage agonies, I am so glad I am not back there. Okay, I did not sleep with anyone, as probably I would have done today, but the perennial teenage agonies are still with us, with us all really, at most ages, even in old age. Oh you know, the usual things most humans tend to worry about, not just teenagers – having spots, no girlfriends, no boyfriends, no friends, nowhere to go on a Saturday, sitting at home, looking out of the window, convinced everyone out there is having a good time but you, contemplating your miserable self, contemplating the future, wishing you were anywhere but here, wishing you were anyone but yourself, wondering what to do in life, wondering if you will ever find anything that you are remotely good at, have a talent for, oh it's not fair, or if you will ever find anyone who will be interested enough in you and you in them to call it love.

I was lucky, finding a love that lasted sixty years. But I didn't know that at fifteen.

In middle age there are the extra burdens of the young and the old to worry about. As with teenage years, you think it will never end; this is it, lumbered for ever. Just as you think as a teenager that exams will go on for ever. But we got through all that, didn't we, those of us now old and still kicking?

When is old? When I was a child, anyone grown up was old, they all looked the same age, give or take a few grey mops.

I felt old at forty, or at least properly grown up. My wife gave a surprise dinner party for me on my fortieth birthday. She invited all the guests, secretly, without telling me, people she assumed were and would always be my friends – getting one wrong, as I have never seen him since. She ordered the wines as well, all without consulting me. I was well surprised and pleased. For my fiftieth, on 7 January 1986, that was going on Concorde to Barbados. Having had forty-nine birthdays in the freezing-cold UK, especially the early ones in Carlisle, I had promised myself that at fifty I would wake up somewhere warm, as a reward for getting there, for making fifty.

I can't remember doing anything special for my sixtieth or my seventieth birthdays. But my eightieth. Wow, what a beezer. I actually went on to have three eightieth birthday parties, spreading them out, in different places, inviting different people. Getting to eighty did seem special and amazing and unbelievable. Well done, me.

When I was younger I used to get upset when older people assumed I was part of their generation, including me in their wild generalisations about generations, referring to 'we' and 'us', moaning about the awful things that they, the youth of today, were doing, assuming I would agree with it all, being of roughly the same age. Excuse me, speak for yourself, you are at least ten years older than me.

But age gaps disappear with age. Flora, our youngest, was always the baby, born eight years after Caitlin, and for decades she remained the baby, left behind when Caitlin was out doing awful teenage things, or left at home playing Scrabble with me, poor soul, while Caitlin was bustling round the world. Now they seem to me to be the same age, at the same stage in life, and are excellent friends, sisters and equals.

Now I do it myself. I lasso people a decade or so younger than me into my so-called generation. Anyone over sixty-seven I assume to be the same age as me – well, roughly, okay, the same vintage, give or take a few decades – and therefore to have similar views and experiences. Which is presumptuous, but I now think it is roughly true, more or less. After all, the post-war years went on for so long. The 1950s felt as if they lasted for about twenty years. It was so boring, little really changed.

There is a camaraderie about being old. On buses I communicate with total strangers, if they look roughly my age. We exchange looks and eyebrow-raising when some awful young person is shouting into their mobile phone, or being stroppy with the driver, or eating awful smelly food, or swearing like a trooper. We oldies are still surprised by all the public swearing that goes on, even if we do it ourselves at home, under our breath, being well brought up, fearing we might get told off.

When it's a young woman doing all the effing and blinding, that does seem particularly shocking.

I like to talk to other oldies, of all types and classes, without, I hope, appearing to be wanting something from them, about to ask for money. If they are women, I know they won't think I am trying to chat them up, not at my age – come on. Do I not look safe and harmless at eighty-two? I work on the principle that we are all in this together, we folks who have seen life. Even when I go abroad, and can't speak the language, I smile at people who look my age, raise my eyebrows at the modern world.

Individually, most old people don't think they are old. It is other people, our contemporaries, folks we were at school or college with, who are. Goodness, don't they look old, we think, unlike we who have remained the same. I have not aged, not in my innocent, blinded mind, until I look in the mirror and think, *Oh no, who is that imposter? Some old geezer is staring out at me, looking frightened and mad and sad and lined and, oh my God, I recognise him, it is me . . .*

We have always had few mirrors in our house, for reasons I can't remember, probably because Margaret was without vanity or self-obsession. And she never used make-up so did not need them. It is an advantage now, hardly ever seeing myself as others see me. It is only when I shave that I see reality. Otherwise I can remain in blissful ignorance. Looking out through your eyes at the world seems very much like it always has been – so you con yourself into thinking that the world looking back at you sees very much what it has always seen.

You think you have fooled them, smiling and whistling under all difficulties, being jaunty and bright and agile, till some kind soul of about fifty takes pity on you and offers you their seat when surely they can see you don't need it, being jaunty and agile. *Oh no*, you think, *the game is up, my disguise did not work. Must go back to that jar we all keep at the door when we go out.* The truth is, I am the age I am. Everyone can see it.

You can't erase the wrinkles or the bags under the eyes, but you can try and walk properly, not slouch or shuffle. As someone who has always slouched and shuffled, even when I was in my twenties, this is hard. I do try to remember, if I see someone I know approaching down the street, especially if they're female, to pull my shoulders back, head up. My mother always told me to do that, and in turn Margaret, but I totally ignored it. Now I do try, when I remember, as I don't want folks passing on by and thinking, *Goodness, old Hunt looks old*.

And of course remember to smile. Smiling hides a million wrinkles. It must scare the pants off many people when I suddenly smile broadly at them for no apparent reason. *Who is this weirdo?* In repose, though, or when you are caught with your mind miles away, not realising you are being observed, we all look pretty awful. Especially if we have our mouths open.

When asked, 'How are you?', the temptation is to say, 'Tottering', or 'Far from perfect', 'Not too terrible ... just managing ...' or 'How long have you got?'

It is vital not to moan or groan though, complain about the world, or complain about your health. No one wants to hear your problems.

I always reply, 'Much better after a bottle of Beaujolais, thank you for asking.'

It is also important not to let ourselves appear old by saying things that old people say, such as, 'In my day ...' or 'I remember when this was all ...'

When getting out of an easy chair I now find myself going,

206

'One, two, three . . .' Not really sure why. I suppose it is because it is often a struggle to get up, after sitting down, so I brace myself, as if about to enter a race – One, two, three, go!

I suspect saying 'One, two, three . . .' when getting up, which often we don't realise we are saying, is inherited from generation to generation. I can vaguely remember my mother saying it, and her mother before her. When you get old, there is a danger of acquiring the habits you have always associated with being old. Like burglars saying 'It's a fair cop' when apprehended, because that's what they have seen burglars on TV saying.

Sighing for no reason – that is a real turn-off. Fortunately I never do that. One woman of my age I know does it all the time. I point it out and she is always totally unaware that she has been doing it. 'It gives such a bad impression, pet,' I tell her, 'do try to desist. People will think you are old and/or wandering.'

My bad habit is whistling to myself. It is always the same pointless, tuneless tune, which I don't realise I am doing. I am not sure if this is a sign of age, but it seems to have increased in recent years.

Loss of memory, that is probably about the most common sign of age. You are unable to remember what you did last year, last week, or yesterday, or what you have agreed to do tomorrow, yet scenes and events and people from fifty years ago are clear in your mind.

Forgetting what you are doing or about to do is also common. I often walk into the kitchen or the bedroom, unable to remember what it was I was going to do. Opening the fridge, then standing there, thinking, *Hmm, now why I have opened the fridge? Okay then, I'll have a glass of wine, even though it is a bit early. Can't waste having opened the fridge door, can I?*

Often I get up to do something, going down the hall, wondering where I am going, and I pass the downstairs lavatory. I think, *Hmm, might as well have a wee, now I'm here.*

My normal memory is fine, as good as it ever was, unless I am preoccupied with other things and not paying attention. I don't forget engagements, people, promises, work, appointments, or to answer emails, make calls. I always know exactly what my self-appointed list of jobs for that day is. And I always get them done, even if I cheat. Sometimes I add things to the list I have already done the day before, just for the satisfaction of writing them down then ticking them straight off. As if anyone knows or cares.

I saw an interview recently with Tom Stoppard, who is my age, and he was quoted as saying that he was conscious of a loss of energy and that his memory 'isn't what it was'. Mine was always bad for things like phone numbers, and still is, out of laziness really, but that doesn't worry me. I know I have always been like that.

One strange thing about memory in age is that you can suddenly remember things you didn't know you had remembered. When I am lying in my bath on a Sunday morning, when there is some religious programme on Radio 4 which I am too lazy to lean forward and switch off, I always turn it up if they start singing hymns. I am always nicely surprised that I know so many of the hymns – all the words and the tunes – and sing along with them. All those years of being forced to go to church with my mother have not been wasted.

Poems come back to me which I learned at school and did not realise I had learned. This is a common phenomenon. Old people who are wandering can't remember yesterday but remember stuff they learned at school. When Dorothy

Wordsworth, William's beloved sister, was sitting by the fireside almost gaga, she would suddenly come out with poems she had learned as a girl, recite them for hours, much to the astonishment of her family, who assumed she was totally gone.

Pop songs from the past have the same effect. I often find Guy Mitchell's 'She Wears Red Feathers' coming into my head – an awful, banal, pathetic, stupid song I hated at the time and hate even more now when it starts bugging me. My mother could always sing Scottish folk songs, even when she was well in the grip of Alzheimer's. Which was charming, except she would insist we all joined in. 'Does anyone know any songs? It's very quiet in here. Does anyone know any poetry? It's very quiet in here . . .'

When I find myself plodding through the telling of a long story and can't remember where I am going, what I was going to say next, that does not worry me. I just laugh at myself, then change the subject, till it comes back to me. I have always been like that, getting lost in my own speech. My mind has always worked quicker than my tongue, so why should I worry now?

I know I am still on the ball, oh yes, mentally, unlike my poor old mum. How else would I still be able to work on so many columns and books and articles, all at the same time, going from one to another, balancing the deadlines, never being late with copy or a manuscript? This might suddenly end tomorrow, of course, after all this boasting, and is bound to change in the years ahead.

I put the mental and physical ability needed to sit down every day and write something, even when I feel like shit, down to the fact that this is what I have always done. As with all things in life, physical and mental, if you don't keep doing it, don't keep in practice, you lose the power and ability to do it. Then eventually you lose the will and the capability.

Numbers and dates are often an awful hurdle for oldies. They ruin otherwise perfectly good stories and sagas by stopping and correcting themselves. 'It was a Tuesday afternoon – no, I tell a lie, Wednesday, because I had been to Marks, which I do every Wednesday, and it was the end of July – no, can't have been, we were on a cruise all July, must have been June – hold on, Aunty Ethel died in June and we spent most of the time going to her care home in Finchley, or was it in Barnet … no, correction, Lytham St Annes, it was Aunt Agnes who died last year, not Ethel, silly me, where was I …'

Just get on with the bloody story.

I tend to bash on when telling a story, avoiding dates and places if I can, or making them up if the story needs a few facts to make it sound genuine.

But I frequently these days realise I have the time span wrong. With age, time seems often to be concertinaed. When I start on about my new knee, and find myself saying, 'When I had my new knee done five years ago', I can hear those words forming in my head, yet I know I will get it wrong. I should have said ten years ago.

This also happens when talking about places I have visited or things I have done: 'When I went to Bequia for the first time ten years ago …' Or, 'When I wrote *The Glory Game* twenty years ago …' The chances are both these figures are a lie. It is usually twice as long ago. I suppose it is because with age life seems to speed up, the weeks and years just flash by. You are living faster in the present because you know you don't have long to live. Something you say you did last week will turn out to be have been a month ago. Or you never did it. You just thought you did.

Modern slang is best avoided. I hate people of my age who say things are cool or hot. Strange how these two words mean the opposite of each other, yet have come to mean the same. I tend to say groovy or fab in emails. Ironically, of course. Those at least are the clichés we used back in the 1960s, when the world was young.

What to call a female friend is difficult. Is she a girlfriend, despite being seventy-five? Or is she just an old chum? Are you and she an item? Or just good friends? We never used the phrase 'dating' when I was young, that was considered too American, but courting now sounds so archaic and clumsy, which it was. Courting could take for ever and lead nowhere. 'Stepping out' – that has a nice ring to it. I think I will say 'stepping out', if I am ever stepping out.

You must make it clear when using old and dated slang that you are sending yourself up. Being self-aware is vital in old age, to be able to look at yourself, hear yourself, see yourself. Which brings us to clothes.

God, clothes can be a nightmare for men and women of a certain age, if you happen to have always cared about clothes in your younger days. Unlike me.

There was a short stage in my life, in the 1960s and '70s, while I was mixing with pop people, then editing the women's pages of the *Sunday Times*, when I was quite smart. I could pass for trendy, especially with my sideburns. People often said, 'Do you know you look like George Best?' To which I would reply, 'He looks like me.'

Since then I have not bothered with clothes. I wear them, otherwise I would get arrested, but I rarely buy anything. Not even from charity shops. Have you seen the prices in charity shops? But shoes are a bugger, as my feet are swollen. I have tried to wear Kumfy Kare shoes, or whatever they are called – those completely unstylish, clumpy, lumpy shoes for the really old, as advertised in the *Radio Times* – but they are not cheap.

Oldies tend to dress beige – beige anorak, beige trousers, beige hat, beige shoes, beige hair, beige complexion. It's as if they are trying to disappear, not draw attention to themselves.

Tracksuit bottoms and fleeces, that's what so many old people wear today. Said to be really cosy. I am saving up to buy some. Many oldies love jeans and trainers, which I swore ten years ago I would never wear again. People over sixty just don't have the figure or the posture for jeans and trainers. It's mutton thinking it's a spring chicken.

I prefer it when elderly gents wear what traditionally elderly gents have always worn, which is a good-quality tweed jacket, however battered and ancient. And I like women in long tweed skirts. On the bus the other day I complimented an old biddy who was getting off the bus on her tweed skirt, worn right down to her ankles. She stared at me for a moment, about to call the police, then smiled nicely, realising it was a compliment.

I do have a tweed jacket, and lots of old pullovers and cardigans, but they have so many stains and dirt marks that I am sometimes ashamed to wear them.

I have got messier with age, spilling my food all over myself. I make it worse by having most of my meals, when I am on my own, lying down on the couch. I spread a tea towel over my chest but it is never enough. I wish someone would create some well-cut, well-designed amusing bibs for the elderly. I would wear them for every meal. Probably in bed as well – be handy when I started dribbling.

From May to October each year, until I am too old and unfit

to get out of the house, or out of bed, I am determined to continue wearing sandals and shorts. My wife hated me in shorts, shuddered at the very sight, used to say I looked like Colin Welland in some TV play in which he played an adult dressed as a schoolboy. I find shorts so comfortable and, honestly, I don't feel the cold on my leggies.

My sandals are Birkenstocks, which I love, though they are not cheap. I can make one pair last a whole year, despite wearing them almost every day for six months. I love the summer or being on winter hols in the West Indies when I don't have to wear socks and long trousers. I hate getting dressed and undressed when I go swimming at Kentish Town baths. In the winter, with proper shoes and socks and long trousers, it takes for ever and I moan like hell.

Technology is a real test for the elderly. The only time in my life I ever shout and scream or am bad-tempered is when my computer plays up, usually because I have touched the wrong key and made things appear on the screen which I can't delete. I am having to pay a techie £40 an hour to set up my new laptop for me, to replace the one that was stolen. With age, the thought of even trying to read instructions is beyond me.

One of the many advantages of having children and grandchildren is that they are in tune with all this rubbish, I mean all the wonderful technological inventions, so whenever they call, even the young ones, I get them to look at my mobile and ask them to delete all the stupid settings I have somehow accumulated and the apps I never asked for and iTunes, whatever that is, which has appeared from nowhere. Grandchildren do have their uses.

Women of my age, and much earlier – in their fifties – often say they have become invisible. By this I presume they mean they don't get wolf-whistled at any more by workmen, strangers don't chat them up in bars, invite them for a drink, compliment them on how they look, which of course men should not do anyway these days. They feel they don't exist any more, as women, as sexual beings.

I don't think that happens in quite the same way with men. Obviously at our age, women are not eyeing us up any more as possible mates, if they ever were. When I was young and attractive (which is what I think now when I look at photos of myself aged thirty, though I did not think that at the time), I was never aware of being visible. I never assumed for one moment that some girl might be taking sneaky side glances. In those days, anyway, men had to do the chasing. Women had to look prim and proper, appear not interested, not available, not bothered. But of course they were, and were just as self-conscious as they are now, aware of their looks, clothes, hair and appearance. But now they can be as bold and upfront as the men, which is good. I don't think this has quite happened yet with the elderly. We do have our old standards. But I live in hope.

Famous people, or celebs as we have to call them today, are always visible. Often over the years when I have been with someone famous, such as the Beatles, or Wayne Rooney, or Gazza, I have felt sorry for them. They get pestered all the time. Total strangers are so rude and pushy and demanding. They get no privacy or peace, even when they are having a meal or clearly out with relations or friends. Fans think they own them, deserve a slice, or at least a selfie. John Lennon quickly used to tell them to fuck off. Paul was normally polite and charming and courteous.

I thought then how I would hate to be famous. And I still

would. Much better to be a watcher than to be watched. Now with great age, and having written loads of stuff, and lived round here for so long, I do get vaguely recognised now and again, about once a month, tops. In Lakeland, walkers will sometimes stop and stare and say they have read one of my Lakeland books. Or on Hampstead Heath a stranger will say he liked my last column. I never ask which column, as they usually get it wrong, can't remember, or confuse me with someone else in a paper I have never written for. I always reply the same way: 'How kind. I thought you looked cultured and educated and well read.' They smile, then I walk on quickly, whistling to myself.

With age, you do get more respect, whether you are recognised or not. Not as much, so we are led to believe, as in the ancient, more gentlemanly, respectful days of yore, or in some cultures where the elderly are always revered and honoured.

But I have noticed since I became eighty that people don't just give up their seat for you, they also vaguely look out for you, help you along the way, don't push and shove you the way they do normal mortals.

I make the most of this, always looking around to ask people on planes to help me lift my bag up onto the rack, or help me carry it up the steps. How kind, you are wonderful, thank you *soooo* much.

I like to think that my grandchildren treat me with a certain amount of respect – when not mocking or teasing me for being slow, stupid, making a mess on my clothes, dropping things, losing things or farting. My own children have known me too long to be openly respectful, so I try not to lay down the law, refrain from saying, 'This is what you do, if I were you I would do it this way . . .' They appear to ignore me or groan when I do, but months later they are often quoting me, having taken some advice – if only to blame me when it all goes wrong.

My children have heard my stories a million times, about air raids during the war, rationing, not knowing what a banana was, being at Wembley for the 1966 World Cup final, being in Abbey Road during the recording of *Sergeant Pepper*. But the grandchildren, poor suckers, I can still impress with some of my memories – the first time round, anyway.

In your eighties, you are bound to have so many memories, good and bad. Too many people you once knew have gone. Memories are a rich source of thought and contemplation, of pleasure and satisfaction, when on our counterpane we lie.

When I read the obituaries in the newspaper, the first thing I look at is the date of birth to see if they were older than me. Then I turn to the birthdays – folks whose birthday it is on that actual day – to find out how old they are.

I play this silly game with myself. Having spent so many years interviewing and meeting well-known people, I have to spot at least one person whom I have personally met in my life. My definition of 'having met' is a bit elastic. It still counts as meeting someone if I was only ever in the same room as them, or saw them on stage, in the street or on the football pitch. In the flesh, of course, that gains me extra points. Each morning I am nervous before I read the birthdays, fingers crossed, hoping I will know someone. If I do, I see it as a good sign – the day will go well. I can now jump up and get on with my life. What's left of it.

Let me see now, today is, as I write, 7 July 2018. In the *Guardian* birthdays, Zoe Heller, writer, is fifty-three, Lady (Glenys Kinnock) is seventy-four, Ringo Starr is seventy-eight.

I have met all of them. Three in one day. It's going to be a really good day ... I will just look in *The Times* and see how many birthday boys and girls I have met along the way ...

Oh, there's so much fun to be had when you are old, if you put your mind to it and don't moan and groan. Keep staggering on – there are so many pleasures and pastimes still to be enjoyed. But of course you have to fight back, keep your pecker up, don't let it get you down.

There is a neat remark in Jennifer Egan's prizewinning novel, *A Visit from the Goon Squad*, which is about age and the passing of time: 'Time's a goon, right? You gonna let that goon push you around?'

But one thing, alas, is likely to push you around. It is hard to cope with as the chances are it will be out of your hands, however sensibly and wisely and carefully and actively you have lived your life. Health is a bugger.

WHAT I LIKE ABOUT BEING OLD

- I am alive.
- I have been young.
- Free bus pass.
- Endless respect from your children, oh yes, calling you 'sir', 'your worship', especially after you've lent them some money ...
- All the memories.

WHAT I DON'T LIKE ABOUT BEING OLD

- Looking old.
- Fear of falling.
- Not being able to run up Skiddaw.
- Having the desire but not the capability.
- Worrying about aches and pains and what they might mean.

SIGNS OF OLD AGE

- Feeling stiff.
- Saying 'One, two, three…' when you get up out of a chair.
- Saying 'In my day…'
- Hair in the nose and the ears, but not on the head.
- Forgetting whatever it is you have forgotten.
- Choosing clothes purely for comfort not fashion.
- An afternoon nap.
- Struggling with all modern technology.
- Avoiding heavy lifting.
- Complaining about the rubbish on TV/pop music/ modern fashions.
- Preferring Radio 4 to Radio 1.
- Gasping for a cup of tea.
- Taking a keen interest in the garden.
- Giving your opinion, whether asked or not.

- Saying 'The nights are drawing in'.
- Driving in the slow lane. Avoiding reversing if possible. Giving up the car.

OLDIES ARE THE HAPPIEST, OH YES

- Pensioners are happier, have a greater sense of self-worth and are less anxious than any other age group, according to a well-being survey from the Office of National Statistics of 2018.
- Twenty per cent of those aged sixteen to thirty-four show signs of depression, anxiety, and mental ill-health compared with only 12 per cent of those aged sixty-five to seventy-five and 15 per cent over seventy-five.
- Unhappiness and dissatisfaction is at its peak in the late thirties and forties.
- Stress starts to drop after the age of fifty.
- From sixty-five to seventy-five is the best time. Older people are relatively happy with their income level, less competitive, live for today, willing to help others.
- Many tend to have their own home, which helps, their own parents are dead, their children are off their hands – so they hope.
- We are mostly happy when we are young because we are full of optimism – which might prove unrealistic.
- We are mostly happy when we are old because we live in the present – and we don't waste time on optimism.

13

HEALTH

When I used to moan about my tummy, complaining I was overweight, wondering how on earth I could get rid of all those extra pounds, Margaret would roll her eyes. 'I have told you a hundred times. The solution in your case is very simple. Stop drinking as much. You will lose weight at once.'

I am now up to at least a bottle of wine every day, drinking two glasses at lunch and three in the evening. Small ones, of course. I like to drink little but often.

I only drink wine – a glass of white to begin with, at present either Pinot Grigio or Sauvignon Blanc, whatever is on special offer at Morrisons, and then red, which is always Beaujolais. I never drink beer or spirits. White wine in fact I don't look upon as alcoholic. Just a nicer sort of water. I never drink water at all. I look upon it as a waste of stomach space.

After Margaret's cancer returned in 2007, and she was on awful drugs, she lost her taste for wine, so I made up for it, drinking for her, which is why my intake increased over the years. And my weight.

We always weighed ourselves at Christmas, when we listed the highlights of that year and predictions for the year ahead.

Two years ago I was 12 stone 4, which is too heavy for someone who is only 5ft 9.

Since she died in 2016 something strange has happened. I am now down to 11 stone. I have lost over a stone in weight. Yet if anything I am drinking even more.

Is it grieving, loss and mourning? I don't think so. Is it being on my own, cooking for myself and eating less? I don't think I am really eating much less, except for potatoes. I never miss meals. And when I go out, which is at least once a week, I stuff myself, and always on meat.

My theory for the weight loss is that it is mainly the ageing process. I have noticed that people do get smaller and thinner with age, so now I am in my eighties it is probably happening to me.

I did get worried, though, when the weight loss seemed to be sudden and dramatic, so when I was recently at the GP I asked her about it. She sent me for loads of blood tests. When I rang the surgery about them, they said nothing urgent needed to be done; I should just discuss the results with the doctor next time I was there. I propose therefore to do nowt. I have enough to worry about, thank you very much. Losing weight is the least of my current health worries.

* * *

I was a sickly child. I had the most appalling asthma, which was not helped by both my parents smoking – and doing so over my cot, so my grandmother maintained. But in those days the dangers of smoking were not recognised.

I had weeks off school, endless tests and medications and potions, none of which really worked, and for years I was excused from games. Eventually, in my twenties, my asthma lifted, or I grew out of it.

Recently it has come back in a mild form. Now and again, in the winter, on a misty night, or when I can't sleep, I begin to feel a bit wheezy. I half think the wheeze is self-induced or imaginary, but I convince myself a quick puff of my inhaler will get me off to sleep – what harm can it do?

I open the drawer beside my bed, scratch around for an inhaler and check the sell-by date, as I tend to keep all my old inhalers, even when empty. A quick puff always does get me back to sleep. This only happens about six or seven nights a year but it is reassuring to know a Ventolin inhaler is still there, a comfort and cure. Correction. They are now something called Salamol, which sounds like a children's game. I wish I had had these inhalers as a child. They didn't come in till I was grown up.

After my childhood asthma subsided, I had a brilliant few decades of health, with no illness or disease until I was approaching sixty, no real problems, accidents or broken bones. My only problems were self-induced – and all to do with playing football.

I played football till I was fifty, in a dads' team on Hampstead Heath, every Sunday morning, picking two teams, charging up and down, shouting and screaming at each other. Gosh, it was fun. I still miss it.

What happened was that I remained fit enough till I was fifty to play football but not fit enough to recover from playing football. I would come home injured, aching and sore, then spend a whole week putting on heat pads, rubbing on embrocations, till the aches decreased – just in time for the next game. Then I would go through the whole process again.

During this time I had two cartilage operations, so it was daft to have carried on. I later paid the price for playing for so long and buggering up my knees, having to have a knee replacement. That reduced my Lakeland walking. I could not climb to the top of the fells any more, or even manage rough terrain, though I could toddle round a lake on the flat for two hours. For ten years or so, I was quite happy with that.

But from the age of sixty I began to be racked with the most awful arthritis – both sorts. It ruined my life and my sleep for the next ten years. All Margaret's diaries for that period are filled with my constant moans, especially in Lakeland, where on some days I was unable to walk anywhere. My ankles and knees and elbows got swollen, and huge, knobbly unsightly things appeared. My joints would get hot and swell up in the night and I would be screaming, dragging myself up and staggering round the house, looking for a knife to cut off the offending joint – anything would be better that suffering it.

I acquired two rheumatology consultants, one in Carlisle and one in London, droning on to each for six months, then giving them a break when we changed house. I went through the usual process most arthritis sufferers have to go through. I would be given a steroid injection when things were unbearable. GPs don't like doing it and don't do it very well, not always managing to inject the right spot. And of course you are warned not to have too many in one year.

Then I got on to proper drugs, starting with sulfasalazine. That worked for while, did seem to improve things, but after three years or so the goodness decreased. I moved on to something stronger, methotrexate, which they use to treat cancer, so it is much more powerful. It necessitated regular blood tests to check that my liver or any other organs were not being damaged. Eventually, that drug stopped working as well. The pain and swelling and unsightly bursas all came back. What next? Was this it? Would I now be doomed to suffer for ever?

I can vaguely remember in my childhood being taken to visit elderly relations and seeing them totally crippled with arthritis – slumped in a wheelchair, or lying on a couch by the coal fire, their limbs contorted and their faces and bodies inflated and bloated, having been given some form of early steroids. Poor things. I wanted to hide my eyes.

I met one such sufferer about ten years ago, Peter Wainwright, the son of Alfred Wainwright, the great Lakeland walker and writer. I was doing Wainwright's biography and this was his only child. They had never really got on and Peter had lived most of his life abroad in the Gulf working for oil companies. He had now retired on health grounds and was living back in Lakeland. He was grotesque. Totally crippled with arthritis. I thought such conditions had disappeared since my childhood. I wondered if I would end up like poor Peter, now that all my current treatments were failing.

My consultant at the Royal Free, Huw Beynon, said he had one treatment he could try, but it did not work for everyone and was very expensive, costing several thousand a year. There was a tight budget for such drugs and he would have to make a case, saying that in his opinion I might well respond. So he put me on Humira. That is the trade name. Officially it is a drug called adalimumab.

I had to inject it into my tummy with a little syringe every two weeks. That was one reason I never really worried when I was overweight and had a belly. Having a little belly makes it easier to inject. You hardly feel it going in. It must be agony injecting into a flat bony stomach, however fit and attractive it makes you look.

The effects were always immediate and miraculous. The syringes get delivered to my door in a refrigerated van every month. They were even driven to Loweswater when we lived up there. I don't pay a penny. Isn't the NHS marvellous?

I do know of people for whom it has done no good, and also people for whom it has done some good but because they have other problems, such as cancer, needing other treatments, they have had to give it up. Humira is so strong that it can have a negative effect on other medications.

But I am still on it after ten years and count my blessings all the time. My ankles and elbows and wrists are now normal. I don't wake up in the night screaming with pain. Injecting myself into my tum with a little syringe just once every two weeks is a doddle. I dread the day that the effectiveness of Humira might start lessening.

I now go around boasting that I take no pills. Yes, at my great age, I don't swallow pills or potions or anything else. Would you believe it? Amazing.

Most of my contemporaries carry around pills of some sort and have enough supplies by their bedsides to open a pharmacy. I was put on statins at one time, but gave them up after a few weeks – my cholesterol was only marginally over the limit, so despite the doctor advising me to take them, I decided it was a nonsense. I believe the medical profession has been brainwashed by the statin manufacturers. I also don't take blood-pressure pills – my blood pressure is good. Mostly.

I am of course being economical with the truth – or lying, as we sometimes call it – when I say 'I take no pills.' It is technically true. My little Humira syringes are not pills. I don't swallow anything. I inject. The syringes have got smaller and neater since I started on them. The only drag is that if I am away on a trip or a holiday of two weeks or more, I have to take one with me for my fortnightly injection. That means wrapping them in ice and putting them in a fridge the moment I arrive in my hotel, as they have always to be kept at a low temperature.

I often take the injection two days early at home before I go, or two days later when I get back, to save me carting the drugs around the word. So far I have had no ill effects.

I did have a different worry a year ago when I got an awful rash on my back and my groin. I eventually went to see a dermatologist. They seemed to think it was eczema, which could be connected with the asthma I had as a child, and it could possibly have been a side effect of the Humira, so I should stop the Humira. No chance, I said. And I refused to do so. I look upon it as my miracle drug and I am not going to willingly give it up.

Eventually they found some creams that worked, and it has all disappeared. So all is well now with my skin. It is as lovely and smooth and baby-like as it ever was. More or less. In the dark with the light behind me.

* * *

My hair, when I look in the mirror, is still black. When people such as my grandchildren say I have grey hair I say, 'Don't be daft, what are you on about?' They must be colour-blind.

There is not much of it these days, either grey or black. It began to go about twenty years ago when I was in my sixties. It was the first warm day of spring and I was sitting outside, leaning against the glass door that leads into the garden. I leaned back and thought, hmm, that's funny, it feels as if ice cubes have been pressed against the back of my head. I stood up, examined the back of my head and discovered a bald patch, which I swear had not been there the previous year. That was why I could feel the cold of the windowpane.

The bald patch that day was about the size of a sixpence. What's a sixpence, Humper? It is now the size of a plate. Normally I don't see the back of my head, except when my hair is being cut. It is also thinning at the sides and on top, despite some artful brushing. I fear I might be brushing it into a Bobby Charlton comb-over. At least he saw sense in the end and cut it all short. Eventually I will probably have it all shaved. A neater, tidier look than having a few stray strands. Am I bothered? Not really. No bloke likes losing his hair, but my self-image is still surprisingly positive. I did have thick black hair most of my life and never thought about it, never valued it, never thought how lucky I was. I don't remember when young ever shampooing it. We did not have shampoos in our house, or a shower. Hot water was a big treat, and could only be created once a week when the immersion was solemnly put on.

I am, though, worried about going deaf. This has been happening for three years, starting when Margaret was still alive. I used to say she was mumbling, or tell her not to talk to me from two rooms away – how was I supposed to hear her? At first it was just a certain word I had not caught and would ask her to repeat it. She would repeat everything she had just said, shouting it out in annoyance. I would shout back that I was not deaf, woman. There was just one word she had mumbled, her fault, speak more clearly.

Then I began to notice when listening to football on the TV that I was putting the sound higher and higher. While talking on the telephone I was telling people to speak up. I knew if I asked Margaret what I should do she would say go to the doctor, at once. So I didn't ask her. I just kept telling her not to mumble.

Being on my own this is one thing I miss – having someone

to discuss boring things with, from should I get a hair cut, do you think this patch on my skin is worrying, to should I sell this car, buy that seaside house, go on that trip, agree to do that book. I would ask Margaret her advice and she would say, 'It is up to you to decide.' If she did give me her opinion, nine out of ten times I would ignore it. She would then say, 'I knew you would just do what you wanted to do all along. You always do. I don't know why I bother.'

I eventually did go and get my ears tested. I was told I was going deaf – not seriously, but definitely, and it would get worse. I was given a hearing aid, on the national health, which I wore for a day. Coming home, it made the traffic noise deafening, as if there had been an explosion. Sitting at home with it on, all I could hear was loud buzzing and heavy crackling. So I gave up.

It's not vanity, not really. I just hate carrying anything on my person. I have never worn a watch or any jewellery, nor have I carried bags or wallets. I relied on Margaret when we were out together to carry things for me.

I suppose I will have to wear some sort of hearing aid eventually, but I think the deterioration is quite slow and not really serious yet. So I tell myself.

Now I am on my own, no one is talking to me from another room. And I can have the football on as loud as I want. No one need be disturbed by it.

Talking on the phone – that *is* annoying. I have bought a new phone which is supposed to help the hard of hearing, but it doesn't seem to do much good. I put the volume up, and the crackling goes up. Whenever I do a radio interview, on the phone from home, I just keep shouting, hoping I am guessing what the question is, or the subject, till they cut me off.

Going out on social occasions, if it is one to one I sit opposite the other person, and it is fine. On a table of four or six or more, I can't hear what is being said. Most frustrating is being in a car as the passenger in the front seat. The driver talks to you but they are facing the front, talking to the front window or the road, so I can't hear what they are saying. I nod and smile and say yes or no but mostly I am guessing, assuming they are rambling on anyway, stuff I don't need to take in. Which is rude, I know.

When I ask the family and close friends if they have noticed me becoming deafer in the past year they all say yes. I smile and groan, say well spotted, then 'Oh God, yes, I know, I know, you are right, but I ain't doing nuffink, not yet.'

I tell myself I don't feel my life so far is being seriously impaired by my current state of deafness. I know this is self-deception, and silly, but that is how I intend to continue for the moment. The hearing aids I tried did no good, just amplified the things I did not want amplified, such as the rustling of my newspaper. I hated having them in my ears, even for just that one day. Right, I am not talking about it anymore. I have more important things to worry about.

I made a vow many years ago never to discuss or mention my health with people younger than myself. They don't want to know. You are old, what do you expect at your age? But with my contemporaries, we always get on to health in some form over lunch, though I do find it pretty boring. Everyone over the age of eighty has something wrong with them. If you meet someone you have not seen for ages and say, 'How is the back?' they will not stop for the next half-hour. So I don't ask them.

* * *

I did have a bit of a do the Christmas before last, which worried me at the time, for at least half a day. At Valerie Grove's party I had a slight dizzy turn.

I drove there, so was not drinking, but while standing up talking, my left arm went all pins and needles. It then started spreading along the whole of my left arm and shoulder and then, weirdly, into my jaw and lips. Never knew you could get pins and needles in your lips.

I sat down and told Val, who said, 'Oh lord, don't say I will have to dial 999.'

I said I was okay, just needed to sit down. I sat thinking, *Oh God, I will never be able to drive home, I will have to leave my car*, then, *When will I pick it up?*. But after half an hour the dizziness began to fade. In an hour, it had all gone. I ate all the meal, which was delicious as ever, cooked by Val's husband Trevor, but I did not drink, just in case, and drove home, no bother.

At home, I remembered a similar incident a few years earlier when I felt dizzy at Faro airport. Oh God, then it came back to me, there was a more serious episode at Flora's wedding ten years ago at Nice.

I had recently had my knee replaced, was just out of hospital and still on heavy-duty painkillers. I drank all the way through the wedding, which I should not have done. But I felt fine, went back with Margaret to our hotel, had a swim and went to bed and slept.

Next morning all the wedding guests assembled on a beach near Nice. I had a long swim, on my own, then came back and was ordering drinks and lunch for everyone, when I passed out. Apparently, so I was told later, I started frothing at the mouth. I woke up to find I was in an ambulance, hurtling along the coast road. I spent two days at Cannes General Hospital in a horrible ward surrounded by moaning, yelling youths who had been involved in some cycling race accident.

Back home I had endless tests. They decided I had probably had some sort of fit or stroke and was also probably an alcoholic. I should not have confessed how many mojito cocktails I had drunk over a six-hour period. And even stupider, drinking while on tramadol. In the small print it did say that a possible side effect was seizures – made worse, of course, by drinking alcohol. All my own fault. It is always reassuring if you can decide or persuade yourself you know what caused something.

I lost my driving licence for a year – that was the worst part of it. But nothing like it has happened again.

But after my pins and needles at Valerie's party, I remembered those two previous incidents and thought I had better get myself checked out. I rang 111, the NHS emergency number, as it was the weekend. A few hours later I saw an emergency doctor at a local hospital.

He did not think it was a stroke, because there were no other symptoms, such as chest pains, speech problems or slurring. The emergency doc who was testing me was huge and overweight – and he slurred. I wasn't sure if it was drink or his use of English, but I thought he had a blooming cheek, asking me if I ever slurred.

I did have a check-up afterwards, an ECG and all that, and was pronounced fine. Nothing like that has occurred since. So I have wiped all such incidents and possible future incidents from my mind, as I always do. I wiped from my mind that Margaret had had a double mastectomy for breast cancer. That seemed to work for forty years.

* * *

I count my blessings all the time that my awful arthritis has now gone, touch wood. I feel fit and healthy for someone of my age, rushing around doing too much, walking for two hours every day, swimming three times a week. I take no pills – or have I already said that? Then ah ha, I should not have boasted. I have recently acquired a new problem, well two problems, which I fear are my own fault.

Last summer I did such a lot of gardening, being full-time in London now, cutting and pruning, buying the summer house and the arbours. To install the two arbours I had to clear the ground and lay a base, with concrete slabs followed by some cementing. I spent three hours one day in the blazing sun, stripped to the waist, digging, bending, moving the slabs, mixing the concrete. Oh God, how stupid, someone of eighty-one doing all that heavy lifting. I did not feel any pains at the time, apart from being totally knackered.

Next day my back felt hellish, but I had already arranged to go to Broadstairs with the family. The weather was fab and I swam three times in one day in the sea, going up and down some very long steps each time to the beach. I think that was what finally ruined my back. Those steps.

I was in agony for six weeks, taking painkillers, slapping on those useless heat pads, before I finally gave in and saw the doctor. I was sent for an MRI scan in a car park in Green Lanes, very near Flora's house. I had supper afterwards with her and the girls.

The upshot was that I had done something to my back. It was not a tumour, but something was wrong with the lower lumber discs, partly wear and tear caused by age. A canal of some sort had gone thin and was causing all the problems. I might need surgery to correct it, but surgery in that part of the lower spine is dangerous, and not to be recommended unless absolutely necessary. In the meantime they would give me an epidural, the sort they give to women in childbirth when they are screaming in agony.

I had it done, in a bed in hospital at the Royal Free. It only took a couple of hours and it has, so far, eased the pain in that particular part of my back.

Alas, I then begun to have other pains, in the same lower region, but at the front, in my groin area. For a few weeks I felt a sort of tingling in my right testicle and I thought, *Oh no, am I getting what old men get, whatever that is?*

One day in the bath I happened to feel my groin and I found a lump, just under the surface, which I had never noticed before. Not painful, not prominent, but there all the same, where there had never been a lump before.

With no Margaret to discuss it with, or to get to feel it, lucky her, to make sure I was not imagining it, I decided I should be sensible. So I got an emergency appointment at my GP's, the sort where you only have ten minutes and can only discuss one ailment. The doctor was a young woman who looked about thirteen, fresh out of Cambridge. I don't suppose she had felt many elderly males in any sensitive position but she quickly announced it was a hernia. She would send me to see a consultant at the Royal Free. I might then need an operation for a mesh, but there would be a three-month wait before I would be seen.

I did not ask what she meant by a mesh. As it was an emergency appointment, I thought it might be classed as a second topic. I wondered if it would be like the chicken wire that I used in the garden in Loweswater to keep out the rabbits. Or perhaps a plastic mesh, the sort they wrap bundles of lemons in at supermarkets.

I kept feeling it every day, convinced it was getting bigger. I could not bear to wait three months for a hospital appointment, as I had so much work on, so I decided to break all my principles and go private.

I got the partner at my GP practice to recommend someone and he suggested a professor. I rang his secretary and she rang back with an appointment the next day. Awful really what you can achieve when you pay money.

The consulting rooms were up in a lift in a posh block with smart furniture and smart nurses. There was a long corridor like a top-class hotel, with black leather chairs outside various rooms where you had to sit and wait. The names on each suite seemed to be a professor. Top docs hire these rooms by the hour, shove their name up and have wealthy Arabs lining up.

I had Googled my professor and he appeared amazingly well qualified, had been a prof at the Royal Free and the chairman of various boards.

I had chatted up his secretary when she rang me with my appointment, which was at 6.30. I said I hoped I would be back in time for the football. She asked who I followed. When I told her, she said, 'Oh the prof is a mad West Ham fan.'

So I took with me five West Ham programmes from the early 1970s, thinking that would be his period. Which it was. I explained I had a present for him and made him close his eyes and hold out his hand. (Margaret would have been appalled if I'd told her about it, as I would have done, blow by blow.)

He did not look like a medical professor, whatever they look like, for he had long, grey hair, 1970s style. But he was awfully clean and tall, impressive and confident, witty and amused.

I told him my story, how a week earlier I had felt this lump, how the young Cambridge grad GP had said a mesh might be called for.

He examined me and said there was a lump but it was small, low down on the groin. 'I'll look at the crown jewels while I am at it,' he said, moving his hand lower down to check my bollocks. 'Yes, all fine and in order.'

He said I had a direct inguinal hernia. I could look it up if I liked. I said, 'No chance, I hate looking things up on the internet – I would prefer it if you tell me now.' *Well*, I thought, *I am paying.*

He explained the difference between hernias in young men – which are genetic, the defects are there at birth and need surgery as they can be dodgy – and in old age, which are different, with different causes and needing different treatments. He thought I did not need surgery, not yet. It was a low-risk hernia. 'As a surgeon, I always advise patients to avoid surgery.'

If it does flare up and cause pain, he said, I should lie down, massage it, try to push it back. If that does not work, go to A & E.

'You will find the sudden agony is likely to happen in the middle of the night, on a Saturday or Sunday, so good luck with A & E . . .'

He said I should avoid heavy lifting or sudden jerking movements, but otherwise carry on as normal and come back to see him in six months.

As I was leaving, I asked if there was anything else, er, I should avoid doing such as, er, certain physical activities, stuff I should not engage in now that I have a hernia in my groin.

'It is a myth,' he said, 'that a groin hernia is connected with sex in any way, either as a cause or a reason to avoid it.

Unless, of course, you are diving from a chandelier, which I personally would not advise anyway . . .'

HEALTH AND EFFICIENCY

- If you are not in pain, consider yourself to be winning.
- When meeting some old friend you have not seen for a long time, ask them how their back is. They won't stop talking for half an hour. When they pause, it is your turn to bore them.
- Never discuss your ailments with anyone much younger than yourself. They don't want to know. You are old, what else do you expect?
- There isn't a pill for old age.
- The best painkiller of all is regular doses of wine. Doctors recommend Beaujolais. Thank you, Dr Davies.

THE MOST IMPORTANT THINGS
IN LIFE WHEN YOU ARE OLD

- Activity – for the brain and for the body.
- Something to look forward to.
- Getting into bed at last.
- A good night's sleep.
- A regular bowel movement.
- Remember – these are the good days.
- Growing old is a pain in the arse but growing old alone is a pain in the soul.
- A companion.

TOP SONGS AMONGST
DEMENTIA PATIENTS

If you do have to go into a home, it won't be all that bad. Think of the excellent songs you will be able to join in and sing, such as the top ten faves ...

- 'Bring Me Sunshine' – Morecambe and Wise
- 'It's a Long Way to Tipperary'
- 'You Are My Sunshine'
- 'We'll Meet Again' – Vera Lynn
- 'Oh, What a Beautiful Mornin'' – Gordon McRae
- 'The White Cliffs of Dover' – Vera Lynn
- 'Que Sera, Sera' – Doris Day
- 'Over the Rainbow' – Judy Garland
- 'Singin' in the Rain' – Gene Kelly
- 'My Way' – Frank Sinatra

14

COMPANIONS

About a year after Margaret died, friends started asking if I would get married again. I said no chance. Nor do I want to live with anybody.

Which was true. I had my routines, what I did at what time and how, and didn't want to change them or share them. Nor did I want to move, to set up house with anyone else. I love my own house and own things and own life too much.

I had got into the rhythm of cooking for myself, such as it was, provisioning and clearing up, after a fashion. I almost always remember the dustmen come on Tuesday and that all the rubbish has to be put in three separate bins – for paper, food and non-recyclable stuff. To confuse matters, the garden waste is collected on a Saturday. That is hard to remember. But I think I have now mastered it.

Oh, and milk gets delivered on Monday, Wednesday and Friday. If I forget and leave it out all day it either gets stolen or goes off. Powder has to be bought for the washing machine and the dishwasher needs, er, now what does it need, apart from tablets? Oh yes, rinse aid and salt.

Having mastered so many amazingly complicated and

technical processes, which I had never had to do before, why would I want to change my life and throw away all these new-found skills? Such as they are. Why waste all that learning by having a stranger moving into the house and wanting to do things their way?

Answer – it does get a bit lonely on your own.

I tried to analyse it. On the whole I was not lonely in the house. Obviously I missed someone to share all the trivia and idle chat and banal observations thrown up by the day, but I was fortunate in having my children popping in all the time and so many good neighbours. I was rarely lonely for long, in the sense of more than one whole day going by without seeing or talking to someone.

Most of all I had work, for which I felt and still feel enormously pleased and grateful. And with accepting more work all the time, plus offers and invitations to events, meals and parties, I could easily have been out and about or busy and occupied all the time. Why would I want or need to share any of my fun-filled life with anyone else?

Margaret and I often used to discuss the things that matter most in life, especially if she was fretting about one of the children, whether they were happy or not.

What makes people happy? The usual things get trotted out by everyone when this sort of topic comes up. Money, for example. You are not going to be all that happy if you have no money and worry every day about surviving. A house or a roof over your head? That is pretty vital. Good health? Not much fun without good health. Bad health can cloud everything.

Having agreed how essential these three elements are, what about work? Surely we all need some sort of action or activity to keep the body and mind alert and in working order.

Social intercourse, mingling and meeting and interacting with other members of the human race – that is also pretty useful. Few people can get through life totally on their own, all the time, every day. You do need some sort of stimulation.

And love? Does not love make the world go round? All you need is love. When John Lennon sang that song he was aware that there was a hidden minor meaning. On the surface it suggests love is everything, but it can also refer to someone for whom love is lacking, that is what you are missing, love is not there, you might have everything – except love. So John told me, long after he had written that song, but it might have been hindsight, polishing up his memories.

Of all those things, Margaret believed that a happy, loving relationship was the most important single thing in life. I used to argue, partly to be contrary, that work was the most important thing. Having a good fulfilling career could keep you going when love and marriage and relationships fell apart or were proving difficult, making you miserable and unhappy. Work is all you need. Tra la.

I do get such satisfaction out of work. I can lose myself in it. A bad mood, which I rarely have, or a headache, or pains and aches, can all disappear when I sit down and start writing. Time passes, I don't know where I am. If it has been vaguely successful, and I have written something, I come out refreshed, cleansed, feeling I deserve a good drink, a good meal, some enjoyment, cos I have earned it. The day has not been pointless. Life has had a purpose. I have done some work. Huzzah. Open the bottle. Bring on the dancing girls.

Margaret was right, of course. Most people would agree that love, not work, is the single thing that matters most in life. And I was so fortunate to have had a long, loving, happy relationship for sixty years. I should not be greedy. I clearly could not expect it to be replaced or duplicated – that would be impossible.

On the other hand, doing things, going out, having a meal, attending an event, going somewhere new, trying something new, is always more pleasurable if you have someone to share it with, someone sympathetic, in tune and compatible with you, to laugh and joke and gossip and bitch, observe and comment, then recall and remember. Someone to share normal, ordinary human life, and of course normal human pleasures, the sort most of us enjoy, and many of us need, or tell ourselves we need, to make us happy, make us fulfilled, while we are still on the planet and have most of our faculties.

As the year went on, I did begin to think that yes, a companion, a chum, that might be nice. And of course I was thinking of a lady chum. I am male. I am human. I am attracted to women. I would like one to be able to join me when I feel most lonely – which usually happens on holiday. Or in bed.

People often say that men don't have men friends the way women have women friends, whom they carry with them through life. Men drop their friends by the wayside, and even their own family, when they get married, and they rarely get replaced.

I do have five regular male chums, had them for years, each of whom I meet up with by arrangement once a year. Even though we might meet by chance during the year, we always set an annual lunch date, just the two of us, to chew over and share what has happened during the year – with our wives, children, house, money, work and health. Personal stuff gets revealed, man to man, but is never passed on.

One of my regular lunch-date male chums lives in Cumbria;

another, who is German, lives in the West Indies. The rest are roughly around London. All of them I have known for many years. Some I only see once a year, when we have our annual. Others I bump into regularly, but we still have our *petit à deux*.

There used to be six, but one of them, Michael Bateman, a fellow journalist, whom I had known since the 1950s, has now died. I do miss his chat and interest and knowledge of my life – and my knowledge of his.

I also have lots of women chums whom I lunch with. Many of them tend to be much younger than me, in their forties and fifties, the ages of my children. This is because they are people I work with, or have worked with in the past, in newspapers and magazines, publishing and broadcasting. Several are or have been my bosses, in that they run the section I am working on or are involved with editing my books, so I like to keep in with them.

They tend to be married, with a loving husband and young children, so I see myself as a sort of father figure, knowing roughly how they feel at the age they are now, with their family, with their job, for I have been there and understand what they are going through. I love them dearly and I feel they love me. In the general sense of the word.

But they are not the sort of people, or of the right age and stage in life, nor do we have the sort of relationship for me to invite them to go with me on a jaunt, to a party, far less a holiday, however short. But it would be nice to have someone to do these sorts of things with.

So I began to wonder what sort of female chum, in a fantasy world, I would like to come into my life, to do things with. You have to start thinking somewhere, once you start thinking like this.

I began to tell friends, when they asked me such questions, about the sort of person I would ideally like, who I might be looking for. Firstly age: between sixty-five and seventy-five I would have thought – old, but not quite as old as me. Or is that being ageist, wanting a slightly younger woman? I doubt if any woman or man of that age considers themselves young any more. Anyone younger would be about the ages of my own daughters, which would be a bit creepy and gross, apart from being unrealistic.

Married or attached women often tend to be younger than their male partners. Margaret was two years younger than me, so perhaps someone ten to fifteen years younger might be a bit ambitious? But socially acceptable, just.

I would want them to have been married, and be either widowed or divorced, it wouldn't matter. And ideally have their own family, their own house, their own interests and concerns, their own activities and pastimes.

Thinking about it, I think I want them to be like me, in my sort of situation, at the same sort of stage as me, looking for someone to do things with, an occasional companion, not someone to move in with and live with.

Obviously I want them to be lively, cheerful, outgoing, sociable, open to new experiences, not a moaner, not a depressive. Everyone says they want that.

And attractive? Best not go into that. Attraction is in the eye of the beholder. How can you describe what people should look like in a list of fantasy wants? Life and human attraction does not work that way. You get attracted to people for reasons you often can't understand, which surprise you and delight you. Or so you hope.

When I was reeling off the list of things my fantasy

companion should have to anyone who began to ask, I added 'own teeth'. They must have their own teeth. This was a joke, or at least a euphemism, indicating that this fantasy person should still be fit, still interested in companionship, especially male companionship.

I never for one moment thought of advertising, of going online, meeting a total stranger. My daughter Caitlin did this, after her marriage in Africa had collapsed and she had been living for some time in England as a single mother. She went on a dating site – and it worked well. Over twelve years later she and Nigel are still happy and together.

It is the modern way, easy and efficient, and seems to work, so many say, but it felt unseemly at the age of eighty-one to advertise for a woman friend. I know that elderly people do it these days and it can work out well. I know someone who fairly late in middle age acquired a young Thai bride, and they are very happy, with a lovely child.

But I felt somehow it would and should be unnecessary. Surely I did not have to resort to advertising? I reckoned there must be enough people I have met in my sixty years of working and travelling and meeting people, in lots of places, in different circles, people I vaguely already know, or friends of people I know, who will be in the same position as me and might be interested to meet up, if just for chats.

I did not want to start a relationship with a total stranger, starting from scratch, with absolutely no connection, no past or history in common. I wanted my new friend or friends to be people I already had some passing relationship or connection with, or at least, friends in common.

In the months after Margaret died I got lots of letters from old friends and contacts I had not met or even thought about for years. They wrote with their condolences. Some suggested lunch, sometime, if I was free. Being polite, being kind, being caring, perhaps taking pity on me, so I presumed.

Quite a few told me of their own circumstances, how their husband had died of cancer, or had a heart attack, so they understood how I must feel. Even if I felt they were just being sociable, I wrote back, saying how kind, but at the moment I had so many things still to do, what with probate and selling Loweswater, perhaps lunch later in the year, that might be nice. Then mostly I forgot about them, lost their letters.

But after about a year, when I started telling friends I quite fancied a female companion for outings, the result was that several people started inviting me to meals or parties where it turned out there were single women, just by chance invited, har har, in a similar situation to mine.

One occasion was a lunch party organised by an old friend I used to work with at the BBC back in the 1980s when presenting a programme called *Bookshelf* on Radio 4. It was a sort of reunion of people from that period in the department. It was surprising how many of the women I had once worked with had ended up single for one reason or another.

I invited two of them back for lunch, but nothing came of it. They seemed happy and settled and contented enough being single, with their own lives and with their own families.

At another party I thought I was getting on well with a very attractive widow, an actress, whose late husband had been a media person I had always admired, handsome and athletic. She came to lunch, but I never got invited back. I think she was still in mourning. Or didn't fancy me.

I did get an interesting lunch invite from a woman in her mid-fifties, whom I had known many years ago, when I was a close friend of her father. She went on to be a well-known actress and married a multimillionaire. She wrote early doors, after Margaret died, and then again later, insistent I must have lunch with her. She would send her chauffeur. *Hmm*, I thought, *this could be interesting*.

It turned out she wanted me to meet her mother-in-law, a widowed woman of my age. Like me, so my friend said, she was lively and did not show her age and she was sure I would love her. So I agreed to meet her. All three of us had lunch at the Tate Gallery. It was nice, and jolly, but goodness, we had nothing in common. Her life had been and was still so different from mine. She was in fact exactly my age – eighty-one. I hate to say this, but really, when I said I would like to meet someone near my age, I didn't mean it literally. Not that near anyway.

I do in fact have women friends who are indeed my age, and I love them dearly. Jilly Cooper is one – someone I have known for decades and always love having lunch with. But she has made it clear, if not in so many words, that she is no longer interested in what I might be interested in. Her real passion in life appears to be her dogs. 'But I am still interested in love,' she said. 'And if it happens, it happens.'

Another is Joan Bakewell, whom I have known and liked for about forty years. She is now a dame and a lady. She had invited me to her eightieth party two years earlier, proving she was even older than me, but still lovely and lively and attractive with it. She and Jilly were among those old friends I invited to my eightieth at the Groucho.

Joan came for lunch, and we got on fine, as we always did, but I picked up that she too was not looking for a male companion. She preferred to go on holiday with women friends. That part of her life was over. Not interested any more. Thanks for asking.

In fact she did not quite say thanks. And I did not actually propose anything. I like to think I was more subtle, not overtly making any suggestions, just finding out about her life at present, and then telling her about mine.

* * *

When the first year after Margaret's death was up, in February 2017, the *Sunday Times* asked me to write a piece about how the year had gone, how I had coped with being on my own. When Margaret had died, I had written several pieces about our life together. So this was a sort of follow-up.

I wrote about the problems cooking on my own, living on my own, trying to run the house, recounting things we had done together in our long married life. Then at the end I added one small paragraph saying that now I was thinking of looking for a suitable companion to do things with, listing some of the attributes she might have. It was only in passing at the end, not the point of the piece, but the rotten subs made it into a headline, totally out of context.

WIDOWER, FINALLY LETTING GO, OWN TEETH, OWN HOUSE, SEEKS COMPANION

When you write something for a newspaper, unless you are actually in the office and you are some sort of editor, you have no control over how much they will use, what they will cut out, what illustration they will use, the captions or the headlines they will put on. In the case of a paper like the *Daily Mail*, they might also add sentences you never wrote, link bits together that were not meant to go together. At least the *Sunday Times* does not do that, but they don't always let you see the headlines, which tend to be done at the last moment, as they are going to press.

I was so furious about that headline. It gave the wrong impression, made me sound wanton and shameless and desperate. Friends of course said ah ha, I did not know the *Sunday Times* was a dating agency these days.

The result was that in the next three days I got sixty-one proposals. Not overt proposals, such as come and see my etchings. They were almost all from nice, sympathetic, friendly, well-brought-up women, who wrote good understanding letters, but clearly hoping for a reply and to meet up. Many sent photographs, which was thoughtful. As if it really was a dating agency – not that I know anything about them. One was from a woman in Broadstairs, who must somehow have heard we had bought a house down there. She invited me for walks and said that if I ever needed fresh fish, she could provide it. I wrote back and said I was fine for walks and fresh fish, thanks.

I only replied to a few, then gave up. Almost all the letters and emails had gone to the newspaper, so I did not feel too obliged to reply personally. I did not have the time or energy or desire to meet total strangers. Anyway, I would never get any work done if I took up all their offers.

Or have time to have lunch with the women I eventually, if slowly, did really want to meet, to get to know a bit better.

As the weeks went on, a surprising number of women whom I did know, or had met in the past, or met at social occasions, or were friends of friends, contacted me at my home address, or friends suggested I should contact them. After a few letters and emails, several did sound interesting.

I had not realised how fortunate blokes of a certain age are, for the simple reason that there are fewer of us. Men generally die younger than women, leaving women who were younger than their partners with many years still to live. Or these days they divorce quite young, leaving ex-wives to find a new life for themselves. Many reach the stage where they would like a companion again.

It resulted in a most interesting, if exhausting, summer – having lunch with a stream of likely ladies. Well, in my head they sounded likely, in my eighty-year-old, teenage-fantasy head. I mean they seemed nice, sounded likely, but of course I did not know what they would think, or would want, till we had met and caught up, swapped stories and histories.

Some were friends from my past, some of whom I could scarcely remember or recall what they looked like, who had contacted me or had their names passed on by other friends. Some were people I had met at parties or social occasions, or at events such as book festivals, people I had not seen for many years. I suppose in all it came to about ten people. And I found myself getting into the same sort of routine with each of them.

I invited them to have lunch with me, but not at my house. I thought that was not just presumptuous but also a right faff, having to do some proper cooking, which would involve thinking as well as preparing the meal. I might never want to see them again. Or they me.

What I did was invite them to my house at twelve-thirty for a drink. I gave them a glass of cheapo white wine and some smoked salmon sandwiches. That is provisioning, not cooking. It was a good, sunny summer so mostly we sat in the summer house, admiring my now lovely garden, idly chatting and catching up on each other's lives. I always hoped the tortoise would appear, which she mostly did. She proved a good talking point and mostly agreed to selfies. I usually had a couple of soggy strawberries ready, in expectation of Tortee's emergence, which I would give my lady friend to feed to her.

I always told them about the summer house, that half of Margaret ashes are scattered underneath, and how she had said that over her dead body would she want a summer house. I wondered what Margaret would have thought, looking down from on high, to see me with these ladies, being charming and entertaining. I like to think she would have been pleased and amused. And desperate to hear what happened next. If anything.

During those seven years when she became really ill, and I went on my own in January to the West Indies to the hotel where we had always stayed together, she told me to enjoy myself – but to make sure I returned. When she was in the hospice, and I was chuntering on about being lonely at home, she said, 'You will be fine' – with a nice smile.

I felt no guilt about having all these women coming into my garden, and possibly into my life. Goodness knows what the neighbours thought. Or my children. But I did not tell them. I was too embarrassed. They might get the wrong impression. All I was looking for was an occasional chum. Anyway, I am sure they did not want to know. Too uncomfortable for them. I decided to work on the need-to-know principle. And they did not need to know.

After a summer house drink, I took each of my visitors into the house to show them round, a tour of my collections, which include football, the Beatles, suffragettes, books, postcards – oh, loads of different things, which meant I could always find something they would be interested in personally.

I also took them into Margaret's room, showed them where she worked, her fountain pen, her handwritten manuscripts, piled up waiting for the British Library to come and take them away. As most of my lady friends were of a certain age, graduate women types, many had read Margaret's books and a few had met her.

Then we went out for lunch. I took them through the back garden into the mews, across the road, to an amusing bistro on the edge of Hampstead Heath, just five minutes' walk away. I know Tino, the main man at Bistro Laz, and all the waiters and waitresses as I go there most days for morning coffee. I am sure they were amused and intrigued to see me suddenly bringing a string of different women throughout that lovely summer.

I paid for the meal, refusing to divvy it up. It was my suggestion, my invite, my treat, they were my guests. They had trailed all this way across London, or from further away, to please me. It saved me the fag of going into central London. After lunch I saw them to the bus, or the Tube or the Overground. Perhaps a quick peck on the cheek or warm handshake. I never invited them back to my house after that lunch, not on a first date.

If, over the next few weeks, they invited me to have lunch with them, at a place near where they lived, or at their house, and I decided I liked them, then I thought, *Hmm, interesting, something might possibly come of this.*

By the end of that year I had ended up with about six regular lunch friends whom I met up with every month or so for chats, gossip and a catch-up. That list included two younger women, in their fifties, whom I had already known for some time and whom I always keep in touch with anyway. One of them actually stayed with me when she was in London. All above board of course. I do have an empty flat on the top floor – except on Mondays and Tuesdays.

I also stayed with two women at their country homes for the

weekend, all of it innocent. One is married and lives with her husband in a big house in Sussex. The other one had just separated from her husband, a well-known member of the House of Lords, but that too is innocent, going back forty years. She put me in her guest suite, at the far end from her quarters.

I invited two of my new lunching chums, both happily married, to join me at various events. One asked her husband if she could go with me to Edinburgh for a literary event, staying overnight, and he said yes. That amazed me. I assume he thought that, at eighty-one, and of course being a gentleman, I would not suggest or attempt or be capable of anything improper with his wife.

It was such fun, such a distraction, having all these nice women in my life, enjoying a lovely lunch every week with a different woman. It was so unexpected at my age. The year Margaret had died I hardly had time for social occasions, what with all the legal things to do, selling one house, buying another. Now it was all fun.

It reminded me of my youth, my early teenage years, over sixty years ago, before I met Margaret. We did not go out properly till I was nineteen and she was seventeen, as she had rebuffed me.

But until then, in the sixth form and in my first year at Durham, I always seemed to have a girlfriend. I would pick them up at a Saturday-night hop, at a college dance or a dance hall in town, walk them home or to their college, then invite them back next afternoon to have crumpets in my room in Durham Castle. Bit of a snog, bit of a fumble, if I was lucky, but that was all of course. This was the 1950s. Sex had not been invented.

When I became editor of *Palatinate*, the student newspaper, all my staff seemed to be women and I did so enjoy their company. In journalism, the best fun I ever had was being women's editor of the *Sunday Times.* Today I am still surrounded by women, in the sense that I have two daughters and four granddaughters. Most of my media contacts and friends are women. Surely I must know a thing or two about women by now? Fat chance.

I suppose in a way I should use the horrible American term 'dating', which has come in since I last chatted up women, back in the 1950s, when customs and behaviour were rather different from today. It has been strange getting to know these new women friends, and going out on dates, after fifty-five years of being married to the same woman, going everywhere with her, doing everything with her.

As the year went on, I could see some similarities, history repeating itself, or at least me being my old self. I could sense one or two of my new friends becoming slightly irritated with me when I was asking the same questions, not listening properly, not taking things in, such as dates and arrangements and phone numbers. Margaret used to shout at me, refusing to answer the same dopey questions, saying I had to think properly, she was not going to tell me again.

But I also came across new features and personal characteristics – new at least to me – such as vegetarians. While Margaret did not much like meat, she still made it for me, but it turned out that two of my new lady friends were total vegetarians. I had not been aware of this when we first started meeting, but when they invited me back to their places it was all veg. Now, I do like vegetables, but I like them best when they accompany meat. I also like salads, which vegetarians make all the time, but not very well. They go for tough, chewy salads, with very minimal salad dressing. Have you ever eaten raw kale? Ugh.

As for animal lovers, dear God! It was often hard to take when I found I had fallen among animal fans. Or to compete with. So many women seem besotted with their pets, appearing to love them more than humans. Margaret and I never had any animals, apart from the tortoise, and neither of us ever wanted any. But on a couple of occasions I went to stay with women whose lives seemed to revolve round their blessed animals, having to get up at five in the morning to feed their pigs, or go out and exercise their ponies, check their chickens had not been eaten. Then they worried all day about the animals' state of health, fretting if they appeared off colour or showed signs of some skin complaint, fussing about whether they should ring the vet. The vet was always a dear friend, a treasure, and yummy, and clearly they fancied the vet much more than they fancied me.

The ones with domestic animals, dogs and cats, allowed indoors, they were worse. Cats have cat flaps and go their own way, going in and out, minding their own business, apart from bringing dead and smelly birds to you when you are naked in the shower, but dogs are doted upon, the true love hearts of single ladies of a certain age. They always maintain at first that they never let their dog into the house, or at least upstairs, and certainly not into the bedroom. So don't worry, it won't happen. All lies. They are very like those people who boast about how little time it takes them to drive to their country cottage on a Friday evening. They lie to themselves.

While I was visiting one animal-loving friend, her old dog took a fancy to me. In the middle of the night he pushed open the bedroom door, came in staggering and wheezing, then got into bed beside me. I kicked him as hard as I could, forced him out of the bed, hoping the lady of the house did not hear the barks and yelps and the solid thud of his body hitting the floor. He was rather overweight.

On another occasion, having travelled to the back of beyond, by appointment, expecting a possibly romantic evening, or at least a good tuck in and lots to eat, my hostess announced after half an hour that she had to go off to obedience classes.

I wondered for a moment if her ex-husband had put something in their divorce settlement – no money unless she changed her annoying, bolshie ways – but it turned out the obedience classes were for a stray mongrel, Clarence, which she had just adopted and who, poor darling, needed some training, being very nervous and shy. I said I am very shy as well, but she ignored that.

'Don't worry, I won't be long,' she said. 'I am sure there is some footie on the telly for you.'

The obedience classes were 20 miles away. There fortunately *was* football on the telly, which I watched, including extra time and penalties. Nevertheless, I was in bed asleep long before she returned. So much for the romantic weekend.

When I was a lad, we had what we called cock teasers, who would let you dance with them at the hop, close up, real smoochy, even letting you get your knee between their thighs, ooh Ivy, which wasn't all that fun if they wore a petticoat which they had starched to make it stick out under their flared skirt. It was like dancing with a plate-glass window.

You would have the last waltz and they would say yes, you can take me home, and you would get your duffel coat, thinking you were set, only to find she was waiting outside with her best mate, who unaccountably had not managed to pull. You ended up taking both of them all the way home, to parts of the towns with no buses, and a very angry-looking dad at the front gate. It was always your own fault, for misreading the signs, so you vowed never to get caught again.

In some ways life does not change. Even at eighty, courting ladies of seventy, you can still misread the signs, get carried away, think they are really interested in you convinced it is not the free meal, the free holiday, the free flight, the size of your house or all your treasures which has so attracted them but your incredibly fascinating personality. Perhaps even they are attracted by your amazing physical condition, considering your age, and of course your awfully amusing stories about the folks you have met in your long career. That must be why they are totally enthralled, or at least appear keen. So you tell yourself. Okay then, let's say they do appear vaguely interested. How wrong, how stupid, how deluded you can often turn out to be.

Obsessive tidiness, that was another new trait that was hard to get used to. Our house always looked clean, but it wasn't really, just colourful and attractive. There was dust and still is behind everything, peeling wallpaper, damp patches, all the windows need painting. But did we care? Did we heck. Margaret was very tidy and clean in herself, but she was as uninterested as I was in having the whole house painted every year, as some of our neighbours do. We told ourselves we had other more important concerns, such as our work.

So going into a house where the first thing you are told is shoes off, coat off, that was a bit of a shock. I once put my rucksack on a chaise longue, in the hall just behind the front door, and my hostess immediately flew down the hall to pick it up, as if I had brought in a bomb. She put gloves on to pick it up, explaining that as I had been on the train, possibly with poor people, my rucksack could easily have picked up anything.

All weekend I felt scared that I would ruin something, just

by my presence – use a towel that wasn't meant for me, or sit in a chair that was valuable or somehow sacred and not for sitting on. One woman watched me brush my teeth in her bathroom, then bustled me aside and made a huge palaver of washing the sink as if I had the plague. I was scared to breathe, far less sit down anywhere, least of all on her bed in my outdoor clothes. But then I am very untidy. I always leave clothes lying around, the lavatory seat up – or is it down? I can never remember what you are not supposed to do.

When I had a return match, when she came to stay with me, I dreaded her seeing the state of my carpets and curtains, paintwork and sinks. One put on an apron, after we had been having a very nice quiet afternoon rest, and started scrubbing all the floors.

I suppose one of the most difficult sorts of new chums to deal with at this stage in life, when you start getting a glimpse into their lives, if just marginally, are those with strong political views different from your own. There was one lady friend I was very fond of who was very left wing, only read *The Guardian*. I was scared to confess that I wrote travel features for the *Mail on Sunday*, one of my guilty secrets, which I was not aware was so shameful, till then.

We went into her local town and I wanted to go for coffee, but she would not let me enter any chain of any sort, such as a Costa or Pret. We were only allowed to patronise the independents. Have you seen the prices? At least £2.80. And they won't put hot chocolate on top as that is not artisan or organic and ruins the natural, pure flavour, don't you know?

One turned out to be the total opposite – a complete right-winger, which caught me entirely by surprise. She was a graduate from a good university and had seemed so bright and sensible and normal in every other way, till she made some passing remark, half laughing, about 'Mossies'. I thought she meant mosquitos at first. Turned out it was Muslims. She was equally unkeen on gays, blacks, Scots, Irish, Yorkshire people or young children. I thought she must be joking at first – I could hardly believe it. So that did not last long.

These were mainly passing friendships, not meant to last, picking up the pieces from the past, seeing where it might go. When things were clearly not going anywhere, or I did not get invited back, it didn't really worry me. I knew others would probably come along, or ones I had already seen and not heard from recently, who might be busy or occupied with their own family, might suddenly reappear and invite me back.

Things did get a bit complicated for a while in the autumn. By chance certain arrangements got changed, dates had to be rescheduled. I had always tried to space out the entertaining and visits, keep them well apart, for obvious reasons, and not just for the benefit of my own stamina, but during one particular two-week spell I found myself entertaining, or being entertained by, four different lady friends. It reminded me of being freelance. You take on too much work for fear you won't get any more offers, and you end up trying to fit in too many jobs at the same time.

I did not lie to them. From the beginning, I had made it clear that all I was looking for was companionship, people who might be available and willing to have the odd meal, go out, do certain things. They knew I was not looking for someone to marry or to live with, and it was the same situation with them. They were single. I was single. They were happy being single, having a full life with their own family and friends. When we were together, they seemed happy to enjoy what I seemed to enjoy, pleased with the diversion, with a bloke in their lives, a gentleman caller.

Several were content to let the months go past with just the occasional email between us. And then they fell away, getting on with their own lives. Or finding someone else.

During one hectic period, while sending out the same awfully amusing email to all my new friends, recounting whatever I had been doing or where I had been, I worried that I might send it to the wrong person. I would always tell the same stories in my emails, but top and tail them differently, and work out the appropriate number of xxxs at the end.

Once I sent a personal email to Sue, an invite to an overnight event, but it was the wrong Sue. Oh God. I have about four Sues in my life, along with three Beckys – old friends, neighbours and relations, known them for years – not all of whom I was lunching. I feared that they, or even worse their husbands, must have been surprised by my invite, plus comments and descriptions I might have added. The invite did not spell out the overnight arrangements. I was always careful never to make too personal remarks or suggestive comments in emails, leaving things ambiguous. I kept away from any obvious flirting. I have read too many stories of emails coming back to haunt people. If the two friends who had husbands ever came across my emails, I was always careful with the wording, leaving myself the opportunity to say I was just joking – didn't you realise?

This did not happen in the 1950s. It was harder to incriminate yourself if you had two girlfriends. There were no mobiles and most people did not have phones. Unless you were spotted at the town hall, seeing another girl, or holding hands with her on the bus when you were supposed to be at home swotting, you were pretty safe. On the other hand, emails and texts are brilliant for people today who are doing things they should not be doing, booking rooms, saying they are at home when they are on the train, being in places they should not be in.

I was clearly thinking of my own pleasures and convenience in looking for a chum, someone who would suit me. It was the same with the death of Margaret. My whole focus was on me, on losing a wife, forgetting that my three children had lost a mother.

Looking for someone ten years or so younger than me, which did not seem to be a problem, not for me, it rarely struck me how they must feel about my age. This must happen to everyone, men and women, who start courting in old age. No one wants to end up as a carer. That must always loom at the back of the mind of the younger partner. And probably mine as well, sub-consciously, hence my endless boasting about taking no pills.

So where did it all lead? That frantic, hectic, madly social, unexpectedly exciting year? Well, quite a few fell silent. Or I fell silent. I began to think I might not meet the fantasy woman, the one in my mind, in my dreams. I didn't feel guilty, having so many girlfriends, which is what I called them in my mind, despite their ages (and all of them did turn out to be between sixty-five and seventy-five). In my mind, I always used the word auditions, a word I would obviously never have used out loud. It did seem like that though, to me at least.

While not feeling guilty personally, seeing so many women, and having various degrees of platonic friendships with them, I would have been a bit embarrassed if my children had found out. Some of my neighbours raised a few eyebrows, saying they had seen a woman in my back garden, and clearly dying to know what was going on. Male friends asked me more directly if I was having any luck, but I held back from revealing all. It would sound either like boasting or lying, all of it my sad fantasy. Either way I would appear rather pathetic.

Anyway, no one wants to know what a man of my age might get up to. And yet here we are. For anyone under fifty it probably makes their flesh creep. Which is a shame in a way, and a true example of ageism. Why can't normal human beings carry on acting like normal human beings, regardless of their age, as long as they have consenting partners and the energy and don't disturb the horses, pigs, dogs or anyone else – and they still have their own teeth? Most younger people, and many of my own age, would rather not know. So I held back from revealing details. I let them, and you, imagine whatever they and you want to imagine.

And, in the end, tarrah tarrah, hurrah hurrah, oh joy and jubilation, I did meet the woman of my waking dreams. She is a young woman of seventy, so spot on age-wise, with her own house, grandchildren and interests, someone I was first in contact with thirty years ago through work. We used to meet regularly for lunch, just for work reasons, and we always got on well. She was one of the many who wrote to me after Margaret died. She had followed my career, and Margaret's, and asked how I was getting on. I remembered her name, and remembered liking her, but I could not quite remember what she looked like. I put off suggesting meeting her for several months, as I was so busy, then we met up again, on neutral territory, just to catch up. It progressed slowly over this past year.

It took me a while to gain her confidence, as I stupidly confessed to her I had been meeting several woman in the previous few months, all platonic, just looking for a chum. But now I knew she was the one, I was sure of it, and I would see no others.

We now meet each week, either at her house or mine. She

has a full life, looking after her grandchildren, and lots of interests and friends. We get on so well, in every way. She is not a replacement for Margaret, how could she be? She is totally different in almost every way, but she is exactly what I was hoping for, looking for, longing to happen.

We shall see what happens. I await events.

THE SIMPLE PLEASURES IN LIFE WHEN YOU ARE OLD

- A kiss and a cuddle.
- An empty seat on the bus or train.
- Someone to open tins and packages for you.
- Getting a real person at the supermarket checkout.
- Not having to walk up stairs and down long corridors at Tubes, railway stations or airports.
- Someone to carry your bag or lift it onto the rack.
- A companion to do things with, go places with.
- Lunch with someone nice and/or interesting – and awake.
- The first drink of the evening, or possibly afternoon, let's say twelve o'clock.
- Obviously your own family, children and grandchildren. They come first.
- Getting into bed.
- Another kiss and cuddle – well, you can live in hope.

LOVE (AND SEX) IN OLD AGE

- A lady friend/gentleman caller will always take no for an answer, unlike youth or middle age where it can fester, cause resentment, fury and frustrations which can last for years.
- Lying together is an end and a joy in itself.
- Love in the afternoon is never a waste of an afternoon.
- And in the evening, you know there will be no baby crying to be fed, or toddler barging in at the wrong moment demanding a story, a drink or to be taken to the lavatory.
- And during the night, no teenager will crash home drunk and clatter round the house.
- Always of course a remote chance that a husband/ wife/window cleaner might be the one who barges in. In which case under the blankets at once.
- We are not in a hurry, we can take our time, it is not a competition. On the other hand, our time might be up at any moment, so make the most of it. And if so, what a way to go.
- The chances are you have each in your long life seen a naked male/female body before, so why be embarrassed? Yes, you are embarrassed by what has happened to that once wonderfully fit, lean body. But that's what curtains are for. Close them.
- All together now: 'What do we want?'
- 'One last bit of hanky panky!'
- 'And when do we want it?'

- 'Now, just as soon as we have found our spectacles…'
- 'Have a lover at sixty. You don't have to be shoved in a corner doing knitting.' Lesley Manville, actress aged sixty-one
- 'I'm eighty. I've closed shop down there.' Jane Fonda
- 'When people ask me what I miss in old age, I reply, "Tennis. Harold. And high heels. In no particular order."' Lady Antonia Fraser, widow of Harold Pinter
- 'Of course you still feel desire. Does that ever go? To the older woman I would say, don't give it up.' Dame Judi Dench, aged eighty-two
- When asked if he still engaged in sex in old age, Sophocles replied, 'Heaven forbid. I am delighted to have escaped from such a savage and cruel master.'

HAPPINESS

- The smile on my face does not mean my life is perfect. It means I appreciate what I have and what I have been blessed with. I choose to be happy.
- Worry won't stop the bad stuff happening. It just stops you from enjoying the good stuff.
- A good laugh and a long sleep are the best cures for anything.
- I don't have time to worry about who doesn't like me. I am too busy loving the people who love me.
- 'Growing old is a pain in the arse, but growing old together is less of a pain.' Roddy Doyle

- 'Ageing is a fight you can't win, so you either lose with dignity or you end up looking like a circus freak.' Graham Norton
- 'A quiet and modest life brings more joy than a pursuit of success bound with constant unrest.' Albert Einstein, passing on some advice to a messenger boy in lieu of a tip
- 'In human relationships, kindness and lies are worth a thousand truths.' Graham Greene
- 'Those we love don't go away, they walk beside us every day.' Epitaph seen on a seat on Hampstead Heath

15

LAST WORD

I hope this is not my last word, but of course it could be. If I were to go now at eighty-two I would have to consider I had had a good innings, but I would be furious. I want to see my four grandchildren growing up, I want to see Spurs win the Premiership, I don't want to be outlived by the tortoise. More immediately, as I write these words, I want at least a few weeks more, to get to proof stage, see what sort of dopey cover the publisher proposes for this book, smell that delicious smell of the first hardback, and then of course enjoy the rave reviews as it climbs up the bestseller lists, oh yes.

I have not died so far, so why should it happen now? That's what I keep telling myself. No future is perfect, all futures are imperfect. I did do Latin O levels, and was once good on grammar, but now all is forgotten. Who knows what will happen next, but we are all in the same boat, we folks who are still living. No one gets out of here alive.

There is so much to feel grateful for when you reach your eighties. By your eighties, your own parents will have gone, be off your shoulders, out of your daily thoughts and worries, and with a bit of luck your children should have reached some sort of settled life, you hope, though you will still always be thinking about then. Then, if you have grandchildren, that is a new lease of life all round, new pleasures you could not have imagined, and new sorts of worries. You become a star again, a focal point, feel needed, even if it is just for sweets and treats.

I do feel incredibly happy to be alive and well, more or less, though obviously I would have liked my wife to be alive and still living at home with me. I always expected our marriage would last for ever, which it did, till one of us died. I always assumed I would go first, despite her long history of cancer. I always seemed to be the one moaning about there being something wrong with me, an ache or a pain or a spot, or more likely I would do something really stupid like crossing a main road without looking. I have always done that, and still do, just as I used to drive down one-way streets the wrong way or go swimming where it clearly said no swimming.

My children and close friends still think that is how I will go, crossing Highgate Road in the rush hour, unwilling to wait for the lights or a gap in the traffic, setting off blithely as usual, convinced I am indestructible, or that surely they will stop in time?

When was I happiest? People often get asked that, or ask themselves, especially when they get into their eighties, as if all happiness must be in the past, gone for ever. I always say *now*. And I mean it. I am happy. I am happy to have had my past and I am happy looking forward to tomorrow.

You have so much to remember at this age, to live off in quiet moments. I think of Margaret all the time. I will always have her, inside my memory box. But if God offered to transport me back to any age or stage in my past, I would say no. Done that, been there. I like it here. I like it now.

When for thirty years we had our Lakeland home we used to say it was like living twice – an urban life and a country life, all in the same lifespan. Getting to eighty you have in a sense lived twice if not thrice, having experienced being young, then middle-aged, and now you are experiencing being old. All part of the tapestry, the human narrative.

Two years ago, on my eightieth birthday, I wanted to get to eighty-four, which today is a reasonable lifespan for a man. My ambition now is to get to ninety-four. It's been surprising in recent years how many people have got to ninety-four. When I check the obits in the newspapers, I always start with how old they were, then where they were born and went to school or college. I skip all the middle stuff about their achievements, and skim to the end, hoping they will give a clue to how the person dies.

How will I go? Apart from copping it while crossing a road, though surely I will get more sensible and less fearless with age. My wife would have said alcohol poisoning, but that was just to scare me. I have drunk a bottle of wine every day for so long that I can't believe it will harm me now. And I do have regular blood tests to check my liver.

A heart attack or a stroke? I did have those minor scares, but for some illogical reason it never worried me. I don't now expect to get MS like my father and there are no signs of dementia, which ruined my mother's last ten years. My asthma has never really returned. I am clearly going deaf, and eventually I will have to wear those dratted NHS ear things I was given, but it won't be the end of the world. The end of the world in my case will be, well, I don't know what, caused by something or other I hadn't thought of.

I wonder if you can bet on how and when you will die? The

betting industry has gone mad in recent years, offering bets on every conceivable topic – some of them pretty ghoulish, such as who will be the next manager to get the sack. Which is similar to dying. There are folks who have had bets on exactly which day the queen will die.

I like to think I will die happy, with no regrets – well, nothing I can remember or that would be worth mentioning if I could. John Betjeman, when asked what he regretted when he was dying, said he wished he had had more sex. At some stages in my life I have thought that, but now, no, I don't think that will be the case.

I am so happy to have a companion to do occasional things with, share things with. And I am ecstatically happy still to be in work – perhaps my best bit of luck of all, though I know that will soon recede.

Looking back at my days in proper, office-based work as a journalist, I had the best of times, back in the days of hot metal and rolling print. Long lunches, big expenses, big staff, going out interviewing people, at home and abroad, taking as long as I liked. Now they are crammed into horrible open-plan factories, never go out, never have lunch, crouching over their computers all day, hardly ever doing real stories, hardly ever meeting real people, scared of the sack or redundancy, and most of them badly paid, unable ever to buy their own place. Newspapers are on the wain. Publishing is not what it was, now the conglomerates and the suits have taken over. I was so lucky, doing what I did, and doing it at that time.

But generally I still believe almost everything has got better. There is nothing like the poverty of the 1930s or the dreary days of rationing and belt tightening when I was growing up in the 1940s and '50s. We are healthier, we live longer, and the

National Health Service, despite all its current problems, is still one of the wonders and blessings of our age. I would probably be in a wheelchair with arthritis but for the NHS.

I often think of my mother doing the washing in an out-house, heating water in a big copper tub, washing the clothes by hand, rubbing them on a washboard, ringing them out, then hanging them out and praying it would not rain or the clouds of noxious black smoke and dust from the railway and factories would not make them filthy again. Domestically, lives have been transformed.

When people of my generation, and younger, run down today, rubbish modern youth, hate all politicians, suspect all our leaders, despise the so-called elite, hate the loony left, fear the fascist right, despair of Brexit, will it ever end, what a mess, democracy no longer works, I refuse to join in with the moaning. I maintain that nothing has really changed about our so-called leaders and betters. They have always been more or less the same, only we did not know so much about it. Now we know. Know too much, if anything – no wonder we are all so cynical. I am not cynical about modern life. I am ever hopeful and optimistic about the human race. It is the only one we have got. You have to believe things are getting better, otherwise what is the point? I know more and more people who say life is meaningless, there is no point. The point is now. Living now, that's the point. See it out. You won't get a second go. Just try not to upset the horses.

As you get older, many things mean less. Money for example. I can't afford any more time or energy to think about making money. Time is too short.

My only worry now, as I write and as I lie awake in the middle of the night, is that I will end up crippled, that something awful will happen to my back, or my hernia will explode. So far, so good.

Then I think back to the various stages in my life, such as during my arthritis years, when I was sure that was it, that I was knackered, there was no help for me now. I used to worry about what I would do if my hands were totally useless and could not type. Could I dictate? I only ever know what I want to write when I start writing.

If my back does go, I won't be able to walk or move properly, let alone sit at my machine. Oh God, that will be awful. Then I think, *Good job I installed that downstairs shower. Good job I have my children nearby. Good job I have the money to pay for care. Good job I now have a companion who appears fond of me and will come and make me chicken soup with barley. Might even do lamb and roast potatoes. Lucky old me, happy old me,* I keep telling myself. *How do I love this life,* I ask myself, *let me count the ways.* Then I fall asleep, counting the ways in which I am so lucky.

Margaret was a worrier, always imagining the most awful things, could see and touch them, which she maintained helped her in the end. When they did happen, she was prepared. So she believed.

I don't really worry, or get depressed, or not for long – half an hour perhaps. It is usually to do with this stupid computer playing up, trying to buy or book something on the internet. That really does make me scream and shout and swear in fury. For about ten minutes, anyway.

But if I become crippled and housebound or bedridden, in constant pain and agony, I don't know how I would cope. My cheerful-chappie character might prove a mirage.

I would never willingly end my life, which Margaret always said she would, sending regular donations to Dignitas. In the end, she did not have the strength to leave the house and go to Switzerland. I am staying here in this house, whatever happens. I plan to finish myself off with an enormous amount of Beaujolais.

Let's hope I can manage to make it to bed first.

There's an old joke about the old woman who says to the old man, 'Come upstairs and make love.'

And he replies, 'I am not sure I can do both, pet.'

That will doubtless happen to me, but not this week, or next month, I hope.

I have got rather carried away with my love, my girlfriend, my companion and chum, booking up events for up to six months ahead, places we will go, holidays we have booked, plane tickets bought. What if we fall out – or fall ill? Am I being presumptuous or premature and tempting fate?

I found her just in time. She told me last week that before we met up again, when she was still aged sixty-nine and a half, she had decided that, at the age of seventy, she would get a dog. That would be her companion from now on. When we meet up, at least once every week, I go around saying woof woof.

At my age, I feel I can't mess around, so I want to see her as often as I can. I have too little time left to waste time.

I had a drink yesterday with an old friend and neighbour, Alan Budd, who used to be the chief economic advisor at the Treasury. He said that economic studies indicate people in their seventies underestimate how long they have to live – in other words, they fear they will pop off soon, so they start worrying about spending too much, saving hard in case they will be a burden and end up with a long and expensive and awful ailment.

In fact, most of the seventy-year-olds today do reach their

eighties, and then they overestimate – thinking, *Hurrah, got this far, got ages to live yet.*

And, of course, they have got this wrong. We folks entering our eighties have to realise we will be lucky to reach eighty-four.

In fact, only a quarter of people in their eighties end up suffering a long and expensive illness, which is why people who die in their eighties leave more than they intended to, luckily for the Treasury.

I never really quite believe or understand these economic surveys, but I intend to take two morals from what I think my friend told me and intend to follow them from now on.

Live, live, live.

Spend, spend, spend.

Thank you. You've been a lovely audience. G'nite.

APPENDIX

Eighty-Two Reasons
I am Cheerful at Eighty-Two

1. I am here.

2. I have been young, but the young have not been old, so I am the winner.

3. The happiest, most contented people are aged over sixty-five, so recent surveys say. I don't believe surveys, recent or otherwise. At eighty-two I've seen them all, seen them contradict each other. But this one I do believe. Drinks all round.

4. And there are so many of us, we eighty-plus people, growing all the time, almost a million of us, which is such a good sign. The queen has got to ninety-two, still doing handstands in the grounds at Buckingham Palace. Okay, I made that bit up, but standing for hours shaking hands with boring people getting medals, for I have seen her doing so. Well done. An inspiration to all us oldies.

5. One of them in 2014 was me. What a fun day that was. My wife refused to come, but my children came and loved it. We feared it might be Princess Anne but we got the queen herself. I got three articles out of it.

6. Obviously in my long-legged life I have had my ups and downs. I blame my new knee – it has left me with a funny walk, but I can still walk.

7. My childhood asthma, which blighted my young life, has long gone.

8. I do have arthritis, but the drug I inject into my tummy every two weeks, on a Tuesday, has worked miracles. Not sure how it came to be Tuesday. But it does give a point to the day.

9. To make the injection easy, I have to keep my belly plump. The doctor recommends Beaujolais. Skinny people, oh I do feel sorry for them.

10. I am only just over 11 stone. I lost a stone in a year but I am not looking for it. I don't want it back, thanks.

11. I have lost 2 inches in height. On my first passport it said I was 5ft 11. What a fib. You were able to write in your own height in those days, so most men added an inch or two. I am in fact 5ft 9. As I always have been.

12. My father died aged fifty-three in 1958. He had MS and was bedridden for years. My mother got no help, no benefits, no

care. Goodness knows how she coped. Every year since I turned fifty-three I have considered a bonus.

13. My mother died at seventy-eight, so I have eventually beaten her. She had a hellish last ten years with Alzheimer's. I rang her once, at home in Carlisle, when she could only have been a young woman of sixty. 'Hi, Mum, it's me, Hunter.' 'Oh, Hunter doesn't live here any more,' she said, and hung up. That's when I knew she was beginning to wander.

14. I try never to talk about my own health, not to people younger than me. They don't want to know. You're old, they think, so what do you expect? But with my own generation, we take turns to chunter on, get out our pills and count them, showing off.

15. I always boast that I don't actually take any pills. I decided statins were a con, all the GPs have been brainwashed, and as for supplementary howsyourfathers, oil of evening dandelions, it's all a nonsense.

16. Thank God for the NHS, one of the most wonderful things to have happened in my lifetime. All those generations before us had to pay or suffer.

17. Free education. Another amazing development in my life. I was just so lucky, being born in 1936, in time to benefit from of all those post-war social revolutions, such as the 1944 Education Act.

18. My wife and I grew up in council houses, where no one had ever been to university, and we got every penny of our university education paid. I even got my train fare every time I travelled from Carlisle to Durham. When my wife left Oxford she still had £100 left over from her grant. Which I helped her spend.

19. The NHS is still free, hurrah, but free university education for all has collapsed, boo. Still, another reason for we oldies to look back, smile and feel smug.

20. We bought our London house in 1963 for £5,000. Today it is worth, oh I dunno, almost £3 million. I really should not go on about it all the time. It does make young couples sick, so sorry. Did I mention I paid £5k? It was actually on the market for £5,500 but I got them down by £500!

21. My wife – God, bit late mentioning her, but obviously the best thing that ever happened to me in my life. The cleverest person I ever met, not just intellectually but knowing what people will do and think and feel. She always gave such strong, sensible advice – which, of course, I often ignored.

22. My dear children. I have three, all living near us.

23. One did live in Africa for ten years, which was a right drag. Nothing wrong with Africa, but it took us three days every time to get there. I used to say – in my head, as I was not to say it out loud to her – oh, if only she had married a West Indian, the flights to Barbados are all excellent, plus the hotels and beaches are fab.

24. I have four granddaughters, two teenagers and two younger ones, nine and ten, all equally wonderful. And what they say is true – as a grandparent you have all the fun with none of the responsibility. You can spoil them, indulge them, give them sweets and money, let them run riot, get them overexcited till the noise and commotion is appalling, then just when your head is splitting and you regret winding them up, you can chuck them out. Phew.

25. My blood is pure Scottish, going back generations, though the legend in the family is that we had a Welsh ancestor – hence my surname – who changed sides at Waterloo. No, not joined the French, but moved from a Welsh regiment to a Scottish one.

26. My wife's blood was pure English, pure Cumbrian, mostly on the Borders, going back centuries. The Forsters even appear in Walter Scott's 'Young Lockinvar' – 'The Forsters, the Fenwicks, they rode and they ran.' I have asked my dear Cumbrian friend Melvyn Bragg if his family gets a mention in any poetry. Not a sausage.

27. And yet all our four grandchildren, through their grand-parents, have mixed blood – from Botswana, South Africa, Cameroon, France, Italy and Ireland plus England and Scotland. This is a sign and evidence of the wonderful mixed times in which we are all lucky to live.

28. I was brought up at a time and in a place where we saw no foreigners, no immigrants, no black faces, no Muslims and not even any Catholics. We were not aware of the existence

HAPPY OLD ME

of gay or transgender people. This is just a fact, not a matter
of rejoicing. But it has meant life since then has been one
of long discovery, constantly opening my eyes about the
delights of diversity.

29. During that ancient time, and in that place, we were free
to play in the empty streets all day, or roam the fields,
even during the war. Strange how people of my generation, even those brought up in urban areas, all remember
playing in fields. Oh, we were happy and carefree then.
We tell ourselves.

30. And also thin and healthy, fact, thanks to wartime rations
and no sweets. If only people at the time had told us how
lucky we were. I went to bed dreaming of choc ices, Smiths
crisps and Mars Bars.

31. War time. In theory, that was not a cheerful time, but for
most children, it was just normal, how life was.

32. There was no bombing in Carlisle, though we did have
blackouts and gas masks. For a spell I was sent to relations
in Glasgow and can remember sleeping in a shelter and
watching the night sky with explosions, flashes and bar-
rage balloons. I wonder why I was sent there when Carlisle
was so safe?

33. Since 1945, we have not been involved in any world war. So
far. Our parents' generation had to go through two. How
lucky was that.

34. In 1960, when I joined the staff of the *Sunday Times*, I would drive home from work in the winter time and not be able to find my way. The London smog was so thick, and yellow, horrible and chokey, killing thousands every winter. All gone, thanks to the Clean Air Act. Amazing what governments can do, when they really want to.

35. England's World Cup win. I was there at Wembley in 1966, and still have the ticket to prove it. Do you think England will ever win the World Cup again in my lifetime? Okay, that is not long. Then in the lifetime of my grandchildren? Fat chance.

36. England getting to the World Cup semi-final in 2018. So that was news. And Harry Kane did win the Golden Boot.

37. Football is better. I have nothing against all the foreign players, or managers, or their whopping salaries. It's capitalism at its most stark. The speed, the technique, the skill, the fitness have greatly improved since I was a lad.

38. And the pitches. They were a quagmire every winter. Now look at them, at least in the Prem. The pitches are like snooker tables.

39. I don't watch TV, except for the football, and we now have live games almost every night of the week. The technology is wonderful, showing every angle, every haircut. I often think to myself, when I get really old, I will drink Beaujolais and watch football all day long. It cheers me up, just thinking about it.

40. Modern technology. Emails are marvellous, and I do like being able to send copy instantly without having to type, print and post, which I did for decades, but when my computer plays up, oh lordy, do I scream and shout. It always seems worse than when your pen ran out of ink or your pencil broke.

41. Mobile phones. I do have one, but rarely use it, and never take it out. I don't want to be connected. There's too much connection in this world.

42. I am still working at eighty-two, but then with the sort of job I have had all my life, shifting words, there is no age limit. You just stagger on, hoping to get away with it, repeating this sort of stuff for example ...

43. By still working at this age, all my bosses are miles younger. In fact the women editors who boss me around, in publishing houses or newspapers, look about thirteen. Some of them, alas, are a bit slow to reply to my emails. I always want to know my stuff has got there, and of course it would be nice to hear it is absolutely wonderful. Some, alas, never reply at all, or give no reaction, the rotters. With the benefit of age and experience, I comfort myself by thinking, *Hmm, very soon they too will be freelance, working from home, then they will realise what it is like, and how we like to be treated.*

44. I have gone through life accumulating, never knowingly throwing stuff out, and acquired about twenty different collections. They have given me such pleasure and will do

in the future. When there is no football on the telly, I will sit and play with them. Or give them away. Or sell them at auction, probably at a loss, proving how stupid I was.

45. My wife was working on a book about women who changed the lives of other women, so for her birthday one year I gave her the autographs of the three Pankhursts. 'Why would I want that? I have no interest in autographs.' Blow you, I thought, I will keep them myself. So I started a suffragette collection. It is now huge and includes anti-suffragette comic postcards and pro-suffragette comic postcards. I was able to help my older daughter Caitlin, who is an author, with some material for her book about Holloway Prison – real letters from Holloway, on headed notepaper, by suffragettes. So my collection was not wasted. Wish my wife was here so I could tell her.

46. When I left the *Sunday Times* staff in about 1980, and was clearing my desk, I found I had letters from three prime ministers – Attlee, Macmillan and Wilson. I know, I said to myself, I will try to collect autographs or letters by every prime minister, back to Walpole in the 1770s. Which I did. Only took me ten years.

47. I also collect Number Ones, the very first editions, of newspapers and magazines. They include *Punch* (1841), *Tatler* (1901), *Daily Mail* (1896), *Daily Mirror* (1903), *Hotspur* (1933), *Picture Post* (1938), *Woman's Own* (1937), *Private Eye* (1961), *Oz* (1967), *The Independent* (1986). Guess which is the most valuable? *Private Eye*, by far (around £4,000), because only 500 copies of the first edition were printed.

48. My football collection is probably the biggest – I have thousands of programmes, magazines, books, postcards, annuals and souvenirs.

49. Followed by the Beatles. My best stuff is no longer at home but in the British Library, handed over to the nation – the original handwritten lyrics of some nine of their songs, which I got for free, from them or picked up from the floor of Abbey Road.

50. Because I have so many different collections of rubbish, I mean treasures, when I haunted the second-hand shops, collector's fairs and car boots, I was always able to find something to buy. Even though very often I got home and found I already had it.

51. Right, that's enough about my collections. I can see faces going glazed. But honestly, you would not believe the pleasure they have given me in life – and how my own little face lights up when I meet a fellow collector.

52. When I was sitting in the Abbey Road studio in 1967 during the making of *Sergeant Pepper*, I used to think to myself that if John and Paul have a spat, things start going wrong, and they turn on me and tell me to get out, I will at least be able to tell myself, *I was there, I witnessed them creating music. Even if the book never comes out and no one ever knows.*

53. Same with the *Glory Game*, a book I did in 1972, about a year in the life with Tottenham Hotspur. I can hardly believe now the access I got – at training, in the dressing

room during and after games. When the cups were flying, and Bill Nicholson was shouting at Martin Chivers, I would crouch in a corner, hoping he would not see me and order me out. I still think today how lucky I was to be able to experience two of my passions, football and the Beatles, from the inside. Not many fans can say that.

54. My interests in life might be trivial, but I like to think my interest in all my interests is seriously trivial.

55. My log fire. I did say the Clean Air Act had stopped us all having coal fires, but in the winter, in my room, I quietly light a log fire. Takes me back to my childhood, when an open fire was all we had for heating and cooking. The grandchildren love it. What are logs made of, Humper?

56. The garden. I am rubbish at gardening, do the absolute minimum, but this does not stop me taking enormous pleasure in spring, watching my flowers, my fruit trees, my grass, my weeds bursting quietly into life.

57. And our tortoise, quietly emerging. Tortoises are always quiet, apart from sexually coupling, but our poor soul has lived in our garden alone for fifty years. Seems ever so happy. We never feed or water her, or even put her to bed. She does it all by herself. Oh, if only children were as easy to look after.

58. The West Indies, which began as a treat for my fiftieth birthday in January 1986. I have been back to the Caribbean

every year since. I like the fact that when it rains, most showers last about ten seconds.

59. Did I mention we went that first time on Concorde? In fact, I went on Concorde three times. Because of the time difference, you could leave London and be in Barbados before you had left London. Which meant you could have a second breakfast. I boast about Concorde now to my grandchildren and they say, 'You what? Never heard of it.'

60. I have been to thirty-two different islands but I have decided my favourite is Bequia. It's near Mustique, but Mustique, though it has nice beaches, is a manicured garden suburb. Bequia is real, living, with people doing normal work, the West Indies as it used to be.

61. Sleeping. Goodness, I love it. During that first hol in the Caribbean I got into the habit of having a siesta after lunch. Kept it up ever since. Even when I don't need it. I always get under the blankets, close the curtains, and snooze for at least thirty minutes. Oh, rapture.

62. The Lake District. I think I love it even more than the West Indies, though landscapes should never be in competition. In that small Cumbrian compass, you have all the wonders of nature, from lush pastures, lakes and valleys to craggy mountains.

63. For thirty years we had a holiday home at Loweswater, with three lakes within walking distance – Crummock Water, Buttermere and Loweswater, three pearls on a string.

64. We normally stayed there from May to October, without coming back to London, working and living there. It meant we have had each year an urban and a rural life. After my wife died in 2016, I sold it. Could not bear to live there alone. But we had thirty wonderful years there, half of every year.

65. But now the family has a holiday home by the seaside at Broadstairs, which I am allowed to use now and again. And take a friend. A new landscape, a new outlook, a new sort of life. Don't we all want that in our eighties?

66. Radio 4. I do love the *Today* programme, despite shouting at *Thought for the Day* or when Jim Naughtie's questions used to go on longer than the programme. It's the daily background to intelligent British life.

67. Muesli at breakfast. We have always made our own, out of oats and flakes and stuff, and then pile on all sorts of fruit – bananas, raspberries, strawberries, blueberries. I do so look forward to it every morning when I first open my piggy eyes.

68. Blackcurrants. Nearly forgot them. My all-time favourite berries. I grew them for thirty years at our Lakeland house. The only trouble is their season is far too short. Yet I do like seasons, which is something you don't get in the West

Indies. When you get tulips in the autumn, or football on the telly in July, there always seems something wrong and wonky.

69. Bargains. You would not believe the simple pleasure I have in finding a 5p coin in the gutter. Or on the bus. Or getting two packets of raspberries for £1 from a street stall. I am such a cheapskate. I am willing to lash out hundreds on a posh holiday, or give thousands to a charity like Marie Curie, but saving a few pennies on a bargain buy, wow, I am in a lather of excitement.

70. Swimming. I played football till I was fifty, and nothing has really taken its place, but I do like swimming and go three times a week. The only drag is getting undressed and dressed again.

71. So it is great when I can wear shorts, which I try to do all summer, though my wife always moaned, said I looked awful, a sight, I should not wear them, not at my age. Do I care? Do I heckers.

72. And sandals. I love Birkenstocks, expensive though they are. They fit so well, are so comfy, I can walk for miles in them.

73. Newspapers. Oh, I do love them. What would I do without them? It was so worrying about ten years ago when the clever clogs started saying that print was dead, the internet would take over, everyone would read online, you'll see. But print is fighting back. I read two daily papers every

day, plus the evening paper, the *Sunday Times*, plus loads of magazines, such as the *New Statesmen*, *Private Eye*, *The Oldie*, *Cumbria Life*. The quality of my life would be sadly dimmed without newsprint.

74. Drinking. I drink every day, at lunch and supper. The idea of a dry January, or a dry week, or even a dry half-day, appals me. How could I cope? I never drink beer or whisky, just wine. A white wine before supper, when I am reading the paper, then two glasses of Beaujolais with the meal. I never drink between meals, or after meals. In fact I often wonder how I get through so much. But I do have one rule. I limit myself to no more than a litre a day. Come on, I am eighty-two. Can't do me much harm at this age.

75. When I turned eighty, I found myself telling people my age, which I never did when younger, dragging it into the conversation. Do you know how old I am? Well just shurrup, I was talking first. I remember when, no, don't interrupt, I am eighty. Pass that bottle, I can drink as much as I like, don't you know how old I am?

76. Having reached my eighties, I am not fussed about whether Heathrow or Gatwick will be expanded, or whether Crossrail, whatever that is, will ever be finished, or whether Brexit will finally click into place. I won't be here. Global warming, though, I would like that to come soon. I have bought all these shorts and need to wear them before it's too late.

77. You have so many memories when you are eighty, which you are willing to share, whether people ask for them or not. And you can flam them up, improve them, as the chances are other people were not even alive.

78. In the 1980s, when our children were still at school, they started coming home saying they were doing a history project – on the 1960s. You what? The '60s have not finished yet, what's going on? So always remember – we are part of history.

79. The war. Goodness, I am now on the second sharing of my war memories. I am now telling my grandchildren my old stories, which get better with age.

80. I have already excavated almost everything that has ever happened to me, however piddling, in books and articles. The memory span of the average reader is five years, so you can recycle everything in due course. With age of course, I can't remember what I have written earlier in this book, or last week, or even just five minutes ago. Or what I have just said. That is what is supposed to happen in old age but it never bothers me. Even when young, I would start sentences and get lost, forgetting names, dates, places. When it happens now, I smile, tell myself I was always like this, and bash on.

81. Which is what I am going to do. If I don't make ninety, I will be spitting. We all have to have aims and targets in life.

82. Late luck – having recently found a companion, a woman friend, to do things with, go places, have meals, holidays, and who will be with me for the rest of my life, however long or short it lasts.

Er, that's it. Now I'm going for my siesta ...

25. Your self control
26. Your trust in people.
27. You're lovable optimism
28. Your humility.
29. Your appetite 30. Nose.
40. You never say sorry
41. The bumps on your shoulder
42. You are bashful in the funniest way.
43. You don't have any opinions
44. You were once a Casanova
45. You love your mother.
46. You're so un-snobbish
47. You can be jealous
48. You don't plan.
49. You're infuriating.
50. You can be pathetic.
51. You have glorious lips.
52. You can always make love
53. You can love so gently
54. You can love so fiercely
55. You can love so cruelly
56. You can love so hatefully
57. You can love so happily
58. Y.C.L. so ecstatically
59. You always humour me.
60. You think you always humour me.
61. You look so sensual dancing.
62. You attract other women
63. You know it!

64. You have correct values in life
65. You're not brilliant.
66. You never say enough
67. You talk too much.
68. You don't hate anyone.
69. You complain so much.
70. You apologise for complaining
71. You look adorable in pyjamas
72. You are mischievous (!) 73. You
like children. 74. You think you are
cunning. 75. Your attitude to senile
76. Bloody Palahniuk. 77. You're so
easily swayed 78. You're tender.
79. You're so dependent. 80. Your hair
secrets. 81. You don't sleep with your
mouth open. 82. You don't think I am
clever. 83. Shaving. 84. Swimming
85. In shorts. 86. When you're
protective 87. Feet. 88. Ears
89. Attitude to your face.
90. In working mens clothes
91. You're starving 92. You
can cry. 93. You never cry
94. Ties. 95. Pullover
96. No pride. 97.
Thumb. 98. Neck
99. Don't smoke
100. Thin.
101. Cheeks!